Seduced by the Light

SEDUCED BY THE LIGHT

The Mina Miller Edison Story

ALEXANDRA RIMER

Essex, Connecticut

An imprint of Globe Pequot, the trade division of
The Rowman & Littlefield Publishing Group, Inc.
4501 Forbes Blvd., Ste. 200
Lanham, MD 20706
www.rowman.com

Distributed by NATIONAL BOOK NETWORK

British Library Cataloguing in Publication Information available

Library of Congress Cataloging-in-Publication Data

Names: Rimer, Alexandra, 1970- author.
Title: Seduced by the light : the Mina Miller Edison story / Alexandra
  Rimer.
Description: Essex, Connecticut : Lyons Press, 2023. | Includes
  bibliographical references and index.
Identifiers: LCCN 2022042913 (print) | LCCN 2022042914 (ebook) | ISBN
  9781493069415 (cloth) | ISBN 9781493073733 (epub)
Subjects: LCSH: Edison, Mina Miller, 1865-1947. | Edison, Mina Miller,
  1865-1947—Marriage. | Edison, Thomas A. (Thomas Alva),
  1847-1931—Family. | West Orange (N.J.)—Biography.
Classification: LCC F139.E35 R56 2023 (print) | LCC F139.E35 (ebook) |
  DDC 974.9/042092 [B]—dc23/eng/20220906
LC record available at https://lccn.loc.gov/2022042913
LC ebook record available at https://lccn.loc.gov/2022042914

∞™ The paper used in this publication meets the minimum requirements of American National
Standard for Information Sciences—Permanence of Paper for Printed Library Materials, ANSI/
NISO Z39.48-1992.

For the strong women in my life who have taught me to be resilient—
my maternal grandmother, Lilly;
my mother, Carole Rimer;
and
my daughter, Dalya

Contents

PREFACE

AS A GRADUATE STUDENT ALMOST TWENTY YEARS AGO, I BEGAN WORK-ing at the Thomas Edison Papers at Rutgers University. At that time, I knew as much as the average American knew about Thomas Alva Edison, his phonograph, and his incandescent electric light inventions. However, I was not entirely aware that he amassed a record of 1,093 patents cover-ing innovations and improvements in a wide range of fields, including telecommunications, electric power, sound recording, motion pictures, primary and storage batteries, and mining and cement technology. In addition, there were more than five million pages of documents that chronicled his extraordinary life and achievements.

I became part of a team to produce a selective ten-volume book edi-tion of transcribed and annotated documents. The scholarly volumes provide an overview of Edison's life and career and significant resources for understanding technological development and the emergence of new industries in the late nineteenth and early twentieth centuries and allowed each editor to develop expertise.

Everyone on the staff developed a subspecialty. It helped divide up the research. As a social historian, I was committed to understanding the lives of ordinary people who have faced particular challenges. My field intersects with the study of families, childhood, gender, race, labor, reli-gion, crime, poverty, health, and disability.

I initially thought the Edison Papers would be a short stop on my career path to other archives with more intriguing family letters, scrap-books, and events. Yet, I knew nothing about Edison's family at that time. I did not even know his son became the governor of New Jersey. But why would I? I am a New Yorker and never fully felt at home in the "Garden State."

To my satisfying surprise, the story of the Edison family was not a boring tale with a paternal figure at the helm, trailed by mindless devo-tees. Instead, it was a sweeping saga of dreams, titanic struggles, dark passions, drugs, suicide, and forbidden love. I learned that Thomas Edison was known as one of the world's greatest and most financially successful inventors. However, Edison's success in science and business did not translate into success in marriage or family. Very few people in America know Thomas Edison was a dreadful father and an appalling husband.

His first wife, Mary, died young, leaving three young children in his care. Edison had no desire to care for them properly. After Mary's death, colleagues informed him that he needed a wife to care for his children. An assortment of women paraded in front of him. Finally, he decided on Mina Miller, barely twenty years old and nineteen years his junior. A toxic mixture of Mina's naivete and Edison's sophistication made for a hasty match.

Unfortunately, once Mina realized her fate, she could not extricate herself from the union, and her destiny was sealed. She would now have to tap into every morsel of emotional energy to give the public a cheerful face.

Mina's life became a series of struggles that she had to endure daily. Too religious to gravitate to morphine or alcohol as a palliative, Mina attempted to divert her isolation and depression by thrusting herself into the lives of her children, her large family, and charity work. But it was to no avail. As a result, Mina remained depressed and lonely throughout her life.

Mina Miller Edison made her life's work protecting the Edison name. Covering up numerous family scandals and Edison's own shortcomings as a husband and father became her full-time occupation.

Mina's story is of a woman born into privilege in the Gilded Age who was forced to sacrifice love and happiness on the altar of progress for the public image of Edison. The six children, well-aware of their mothers' sacrifice, would not always pray to the same altar. Each one, in his or her own way, struggled and battled with Edison. Some of the family battles were won; others were lost. However, all the battles were left with numerous casualties and even death.

Mina's love humanized Edison, but it dehumanized her. *Seduced by the Light*, the first and only biography of Mina Miller Edison, tells the story of an increasingly desperate wife swallowed by her husband's long shadow.

I

Secrets and Courtships

Miss Abby H. Johnson's Home and Day School for Young Ladies, found on 18 Newbury Street in Boston, catered to the daughters of wealthy industrialists. The stately brick building was situated only a short block away from the western edge of Boston's famed Public Garden. The young ladies who attended her school could be seen on Sunday afternoons after they returned from church, strolling along the winding paths in tasteful hats and dresses trimmed with European lace. Mina Miller of Akron, Ohio, had the good fortune of being one of those young ladies.

Mina's parents, Lewis and Mary Valinda Miller, were discerning when choosing a school for their daughter. Miss Johnson's school filled all their criteria. The student body consisted of several young women from Beacon Hill. The picturesque neighborhood had steep cobblestone streets and tree-lined blocks. These ladies were the exact young women with whom the Millers wanted Mina to mix and mingle. The local girls lived in the nearby opulent homes inhabited by Boston Brahmins. The Millers lived in their own opulent home as well, in Akron, Ohio. Their dearest friends were the Studebakers, Firestones, and other heads of the burgeoning industry. Sending Mina to Boston for school would expand their circle of high society in the northeast and ensure she would spend the rest of her life amongst them.[1]

Miss Johnson was one of the top educators of young women in the United States. Highly regarded among her peers, she drew leading historians from Harvard to teach there. In addition to Mina's set curriculum, her parents arranged that she study piano privately with a distinguished professor from the New England Conservatory of Music.[2]

Mina was the seventh of Lewis and Mary Valinda's eleven children. Her father was the co-founder and superintendent of Aultman, Miller & Co., a successful farming equipment manufacturer. He had invented the Buckeye Mower and Reaper and had a sizeable number of patents in his name. He also co-founded the prestigious Chautauqua Institution in upstate New York, a summer educational community that explores social, religious, and political issues.[3]

The Millers' growing wealth and status in Akron allowed for a lavish lifestyle. In their mansion on twenty-five acres overlooking downtown Akron, the Millers entertained prominent politicians, businessmen, and religious leaders from throughout the United States. With her social circle came invitations to parties, museums, and theatres. The expectations for all the Miller children were extremely high, and any deviating from the strict social conventions of the time was not tolerated. Maintaining the family's reputation was of the highest priority. On Mina's thirteenth birthday, she was counseled by her older sister Jennie that soon, she would be a young lady and a leader in society. She must learn as much as she can to be fully prepared for her future. Mina heeded her sister's advice. By the time she was enrolled at Miss Johnson's finishing school, her comings and goings were closely covered by the society pages of the Ohio newspapers. The family enjoyed the attention; it confirmed that the Millers were an essential part of Akron society. A widespread custom for young adults of that era was the requisite trip abroad to expand their cultural horizons. Mina took a four-month trip to Europe in the summer of 1884 with her brother Lewis and sisters Jane, Mame, and Grace.[4]

Upon returning home, Mina was reluctant to return to Miss Johnson's school in the fall. Mina did not have the bubbly personality of the other young girls at school. She was shy and reserved. Her behavior was rooted in her religious Methodist upbringing. Many girls were shrewd and sophisticated and enjoyed playing pranks on the teachers and other girls. Mina's reticent nature caused her to be teased. She often experienced bouts of self-doubt.

Moreover, she tended to be overweight and frequently compared herself to slender young girls in her social circles. Many girls were unpleasant and snobby, and Mina was on the receiving end of specific nastiness. Expressing distress about her school, Mina wrote home, "I am so tired of it here, it seems as though I am making myself more and more disliked. Perhaps it is myself. I know I'm 'dumpy' but some how I cannot shake it off." Mina's mother constantly reassured her about her positive character traits, such as her kindhearted nature and concern for others; if she would look deep into herself and recognize them, she could have a more upbeat outlook on life. Mina tried to believe she had the inner qualities her mother spoke of, hoping it would bolster her spirits during the school year. Her mother's constant and nearly daily encouragement convinced Mina she should return to Boston in the fall of 1884.[5]

Mina's other comfort was her longtime suitor, George Vincent of Plainfield, Illinois, studying nearby at Yale. He was set to graduate that June, which coincided with the end of her schooling and their future together. Mina's mother encouraged her to spend time with George to lift her spirits. The Millers approved of how George comported himself in public. He was a frequent visitor to their home, and they observed his good breeding. Mina's mother urged her to watch, learn, and take pride in how comfortably George interacted with others.[6]

Mina had known George for ten years. He was the only child of Methodist Reverend John Heyl Vincent, the charismatic preacher who co-founded the Chautauqua Institute with her father. As children, they spent summers together, running and playing on the bucolic Chautauqua campgrounds while their fathers focused on Institute business. Before Chautauqua's prominence, only a handful of families attended the summer camp meetings. The early Methodist meetings were held outdoors for several days, with attendees setting up tents around the pulpit and listening to sermons. The couple, only a year and a half apart in age, shared similar interests. They were both devout Methodists who shared a love of scripture, the outdoors, and poetry. George was enchanted with Mina's clear olive skin, distinct brown eyes, and long, flowing black hair.[7]

When whispers of their desire to be engaged reached both sets of parents, the joy was genuine. The Millers were so taken with the Vincents they named Mina's younger brother John after the Reverend. Mina's beau, George, was tall and quite attractive, with blond hair and light eyes. His passion for learning, tolerance of others, and strong religious conviction mirrored that of the Miller family, and George believed in his heart that Mina was his soul mate. While at Yale, he wrote his mother that his first inclination was to hop on the next train to Boston and visit her when he received letters from Mina. George was never that impetuous. He knew he needed to remain at Yale and attend to his studies. His motivation for sharing those thoughts was to convey how much he loved Mina to his mother.

While at school, the young couple intentionally did not inform friends or siblings about their plans to marry. Mina's mother was so pleased with the match that she simply could not conceal her happiness. She wrote to Mina, "I can safely say yes, you have done right." Mina would be the first of her eleven children to get married. Though significantly older than Mina and gainfully employed at the father's business, her older brothers had been unable to settle down with suitable mates. Although Mina's mother promised to keep the engagement a secret, she let it slip out to Mina's older sister Jennie. This was a calculated decision by Mina's mother. She not only trusted Jennie with important decisions regarding the family, but Jennie also behaved more maturely and sensibly than the other siblings, even her older brothers. In her following letter to Boston, Mina's mother said that she trusted Mina would not have an "objection of dear sister Jennie knowing [about George] . . . when your Pa read it to me, I could not refuse her letting her read it too." She assured Mina that Jennie would not tell anyone about it.[8]

Mary, known to the family as Mame, was Mina's closest younger sister both in age and manner. She was counting the days until Mina returned home from school. Mina's mother used every opportunity to foster the sisterly bond and told Mina that Mame got so lonesome without her that she had to sleep with her mother. Worried about Mame's condition, Mina's mother also revealed the engagement news to her. Mame was predisposed to anxiety and nervousness, and Mina's absence left a void in her life.[9]

When Mina learned that her mother had disclosed the news of the engagement to her sisters, it yielded unexpected results. Mina was livid that her secret had been revealed. Her response was quite unusual as she was known for her placid personality and rarely showed anger to anyone. The Miller children were not raised to raise their voices or express rage, even in a letter. Mina's anger stemmed from the doubts that she shared with her mother about her future with George. The last thing she wanted was for her sisters to start getting excited about a wedding for which she was not ready. Mary Valinda tried to explain her actions: "Dear Mina, you know Dear Mame thinks a great deal of you and loves you … we often talk about you … it was hard for me not to say something." Mina's mother believed it was best for her to be honest with Mame and prepare her for the impending loss she would feel. It would soften the shock if she knew that Mina loved someone else and would not be living with them much longer. Hoping to lessen Mina's ire, her mother assured her that Mame would not reveal this to anyone.[10]

Mina, unable to remain angry, recognized it was not Mame's fault that her engagement was no longer a secret to her family. Mame and Mina had a solid sisterly bond; their mutual support was stronger than any argument. Mame looked up to and tried to emulate Mina, a conscientious student, a dutiful daughter, and a loving sister. Endeavoring to smooth things over with Mina, Mary Valinda told her that many women at church commented that Mame looked and acted like Mina. Mary Valinda's effort to flatter her daughter left Mina in better spirits about their quarrel. Being away at school gave Mina time to reflect and remind herself of her connection with her sister as a confidant and someone with whom she could share her anxieties and disappointments.

Jennie, Mina's older sister by ten years (there were four brothers born between them), could not have been more different. Known to be overbearing, bossy, and critical of others, Jennie always knew how everyone else should behave. Ever the taskmaster, if Mina was not studying, Jennie insisted she practice piano and, after that, practice her needlework. While entertaining anyone at home, Jennie watched that they would behave gracefully in front of her guests. Also, Jennie believed in tough love and criticized Mina's behavior and appearance when she judged it necessary. Furthermore, she felt Mina should be vigilant about being neat and clean, keeping her hair in order, and having a spotless collar and cuffs. Clearly, Mina could not please Jennie no matter what she did.[11]

Perhaps Jennie was domineering because that was her nature, but she was also plagued by a family tragedy that had transpired years earlier—the death of their older sister Eva, the Millers' firstborn. Eva was beautiful, intelligent, and vivacious. She always had a bevy of friends looking to her for advice. A firstborn golden child, the family was devastated and shocked when she died unexpectedly after contracting pneumonia. Not even a well-heated home with plenty of servants and access to the best doctors in Ohio kept the illness at bay. At Eva's death, Jennie, fourteen years old, took her loss the hardest. The other siblings were too young (or not yet born) to be affected by the loss. Over time it became an unwritten rule to allow Jennie a very wide berth when she spiraled into one of her lectures on what was most appropriate. While traveling in Europe with her sisters, Mina confided in her mother that Jennie seemed quite anxious, and she thought her sisters had learned to appreciate her more than they had in the past. Mina had also shared her disdain for Jennie with other members of the family. Now she had the opportunity to see Jennie's vulnerable side, which lessened Mina's irritation with her remarks.[12]

During the time George and Mina were courting and finishing school, Jennie was thirty years old and still unmarried, but not without a suitor. Richard Pratt Marvin, an attorney and the son of a congressman from Ohio, had been vying for Jennie's hand in marriage for some time. He was a respectable match in the eyes of the Miller family, who adored him and encouraged him to visit often. But Jennie, with her emotional baggage, continually pushed him away. She ignored her parents' advice to marry Richard and instead chose to be her father's companion on business trips. Jennie was psychologically paralyzed when it came to thinking about her future. Mary Valinda confided in Mina that "Mr. Marvin and Jennie have gone to the greenhouse, and they are going to take a ride. I do hope that they will get contented with each other. Please remember I do not want you or any of the rest to do as Jennie." Richard, apparently lovestruck, was not to be deterred. He continued his pursuit for years on end with no concrete marriage plans in sight. Jennie's inability to make definitive plans were the subject of relentless conversation in the Miller family.[13]

Jennie's reluctance to marry Richard seems to have been rooted in an unfortunate affection for her father's business partner, George's father,

Rev. Vincent. Although married to George's mother for more than twenty years, the Reverend could not hide his fondness for Jennie, who was twenty-three years his junior. He wrote several letters to Mina inquiring about Jennie's travel plans and his attempts to meet her. "When does Jennie sail?" Eager to know her whereabouts, he asked a second time that same week, "Did Jennie come to New York? Your father said she would be there the week after he was in Washington, but I did not see her. I tried to find her, but I could not." At the end of the month, he wrote, "Tell Jennie I'm afraid I cannot meet her on Friday next. . . . Tell her to call [me in New York]." Later that summer, he wrote Mina, "be a good girl, meet me at Chautauqua in August & we will have a talk about Jennie, and I will try to tell you then what I can not tell you now."[14]

Jennie traveled to Europe with the Vincents without informing Richard of her plans. According to Richard, the Reverend was deeply in love with Jennie. Jennie wrote home to Mina how much pleasure she had when traveling with him. She anticipated they would sail on the Rhine together. Richard, unnerved by the situation, could not keep his opinions to himself and, still carrying his unresolved anger, shared his displeasure with his niece.

The Millers did not want to alter the relationship between the two families. The Reverend drew huge crowds to Chautauqua and secured its future prominence. Jennie was far from the only woman who was enamored with Rev. Vincent. Ida Tarbell, a writer, investigative journalist, and lecturer, was one of the leading muckrakers of the Progressive Era. She worked at Chautauqua in its early years, and her autobiography, *All in a Day's Work*, describes how his commanding presence and penetrating eyes affected countless women at the Chautauqua campground. "The immediacy of their response was in a degree accounted for by their devotion to Dr. Vincent. I suppose most of the women who frequented Chautauqua were more or less in love with him." The women in his audiences "would have preferred to die rather than reveal their secret passion." Tarbell further added, "All those repressed sexual feelings were peaking and ready to explode in the name of Methodism. He made each woman feel as though their individual part will change the direction of their salvation."[15]

Mina wished that Jennie had married Richard years ago. She, too, thought he was a kind and patient gentleman and was the perfect match for her strong-willed sister. But unfortunately, Jennie, caught up in her feelings toward the Rev. Vincent and her indecisiveness regarding Richard, refused to accept any advice, especially from her younger sister Mina.

Avoiding conflict, Mina turned her thoughts to George. He visited Mina in Boston and often read poetry in the sitting room for hours. She, in turn, traveled to New Haven to see George at Yale. Thrilled that Mina returned his affection, he wrote to his mother that he anticipated they would soon be married. George courted Mina with gusto and delight. During the two years she studied in Boston, the couple spent as much time together as their schedules allowed. Mina spent Thanksgiving with George's family or visited her in Akron during the winter break. During summers in Chautauqua, Rev. Vincent was always pleased by the couple's incessant flirting. He assured his wife, who missed their only son when he was away with the Millers, that George was so happy and "manly" while in Akron. Wanting to ensure that the Millers understood his determination to marry Mina, George even visited them in Akron while Mina was away at school.[16]

As Mina's school year continued, her chronic self-doubt returned and shifted into a depression that began to engulf her. Regardless of recent cheerful moments with George, Mina was incapable of stemming the tides of her depression. Finally, confident that George would pull Mina out of her funk, Mary Valinda suggested that Mina spend the upcoming school break with the Vincents at their home in Illinois. When news of the plan reached the Reverend, he offered to escort Mina to their home rather than having her travel alone. The Vincents thoroughly enjoyed Mina's visit and observed the young couple's mutual affection. At the same time, Mina, rarely truly trusting her instincts, inquired of her mother how often she should write to George when they were apart, wondering if once a week was too often.[17]

Mina still could not evade her constant depressive state. Finally, Mina's kindhearted friend, Louise Igoe, who lived in Indianapolis, introduced Mina to her friend Lillian, another Indianapolis native who had since moved to Boston and lived at the Hotel Huntington only a few blocks from Mina's school. Louise was sure that a friendship would grow between the two women and help pull Mina out of her despondency. A few years older than Mina, Lillian was married to Ezra Gilliland, the head of American Bell Telephone's experimental shop in Boston.[18]

Years before obtaining the position in Boston, Ezra traveled to many locales educating himself as much as he could learn about telephone and telegraph manufacturing. Early in his career, while working in Cincinnati, he met a fellow young telegrapher named Thomas Edison. Realizing their meager salaries barely covered rent and other expenses, they became roommates. Despite Edison's uncouth manners and frayed clothing, Ezra liked him. Ezra and Edison shared a similar sense of humor and enjoyment of Shakespeare, which was regularly performed at the local theatre. Ezra and Edison would practice their telegraphy and transmit parts of plays during their leisure. Ezra would transmit them, and Edison would copy them. Edison was becoming an expert receiver for his clear, rapid handwriting. Although Ezra's and Edison's friendship solidified in those early years, other telegrapher operators did not tolerate Edison's brashness, introversion, and fondness for practical jokes and often avoided him.

Edison's professional aspirations relocated him to Newark to advance his career in telegraphy and other inventions. The two men continued to correspond, sharing ideas about each other's innovations. Gilliland learned of Edison's recent accomplishments and moved to Newark to work with him. At that time, Edison was manufacturing the electric pen, a handheld needle battery-operated and powered by a small motor. The invention enabled office workers to make copies of written documents. Many years later, the electric pen was adapted for another entirely different purpose and used as the first electric tattoo needle.[19]

Tired of the city, Edison eventually moved to New Jersey and opened his laboratory in Menlo Park, in what was considered the country at the time. Ezra moved to Boston to pursue his own career. Backdrops to both of their careers were recent marriages. Edison now had three children; Ezra did not have any. Two decades after they were spirited roommates in Cincinnati, their friendship was as strong as ever; his association with Gilliland and his wife, Lillian, would set in motion several chains of events that would reshape Edison's life.

Edison's first wife died of a possible morphine overdose in August 1884. The doctor in attendance reported that she died of congestion of the brain, a general diagnosis based on symptoms that could result from several more specific causes of death. Contemporary medical authorities recognized "congestion of the brain" as a physical symptom of fatal morphine overdose. Some obituaries reported that she had been using the opiate in the course of treatment for chronic nervousness since 1878. Marion, their daughter, in her oral history remembered that her "Mother was not very happy in Menlo Park, as my father neglected her for his work . . . he would often skip meals and very often not come home until early morning, or not at all." Two years before her death in 1882, her doctor wrote in her file of her recurrent "uterine troubles" and suggested travel as a way to calm her nervous system. None of the extant documents suggests a mounting crisis. Whatever was the true cause of her death, Edison was left with three young children to bring up on his own.[20]

After her death, he traveled to the Philadelphia Exhibition. He left the older boys with his mother-in-law and allowed Marion to accompany him. At the exhibition, he reconnected with his friend Gilliland. Their fortuitous meeting resulted in Edison spending a considerable time working with Gilliland on a system for rail telegraphy in Boston, which was considered the country's oldest and most sophisticated telegraph community.

Only two things provided solace for Edison: fishing and hunting in Florida. He knew that his friend Ezra enjoyed the same pastime and invited him along. Ezra readily agreed to join him. Despite Edison's children's need to be with their father during the difficult time after the loss of their mother, he left two younger sons with his late wife's relatives in Menlo Park

Accompanied by Edison's daughter Marion and Gilliland's wife, they set out on a circuitous journey to Gilliland's Michigan hometown, then to Chicago, and lastly to New Orleans, where an industrial exposition was taking place. Then they headed to Jacksonville before turning west again across central Florida to the Gulf Coast. After the enjoyable trip, Edison dropped Marion in New York, where she returned to school.

As Louise had hoped, Mina instantly liked Lillian, and their friendship lifted her spirits. Mina was awed by her new friend's impeccable taste in clothes and that she knew the absolute best places to buy fabric for dresses and hats. Lillian was sophisticated, having traveled the world, and she set out to help Mina navigate Boston society. Mina wrote home praising her newfound friend and hoping to strengthen the friendship. Appearances were vital to the Millers, and Mary Valinda was thrilled that her daughter had a sunnier disposition.[21]

Lillian decided to host a dinner party to introduce Mina to her friends on the evening of Sunday, January 25th, 1885. For Mina, the dinner was a respite from tasteless school food. Lillian rounded out the guest list by inviting her husband's colleagues. A seasoned hostess, she made sure that Mina would not be left unattended. Mina was shown off to the guests by Lillian as a just-blossomed rose fresh from her garden. Though the Gillilands and their friends were considerably older than Mina, she was in her element, as her parents frequently hosted her father's colleagues in the Miller home. Mina was asked to play piano for the guests during the party, and she readily complied. She was frequently asked to play piano at home and was studying piano at school. In an interview many years later, Mina recalled she never gave that evening a second thought; aside from Lillian, she thought she would never see these people again.[22]

One of the other guests at the party was the world-famous Thomas Edison. Unbeknownst to Mina, he was examining her while she played piano. Mina was unaffected by his presence. Countless prominent men were invited to the Miller home, and his celebrity did not faze her. Although Edison accepted an invitation from the Rev. Vincent to speak at Chautauqua in 1878, when Mina was just thirteen years old, he never showed up to display his newly invented phonograph.[23]

It was precisely Mina's blasé response that triggered Edison's interest. He found her reaction to his fame refreshing. He hated people fawning over him. Years later, Edison described how he saw Mina for the first time as Ezra Gilliland approached with "a beautiful girl whose bearing had the composure of the uncrowned Victoria at the moment she received the announcement of her accession to the throne." On further reflection about her piano playing, Edison said, "I could not help in being interested immediately in anyone who would play and sing without hesitation when they did it as bad as that."[24]

However, no record exists that Edison made any lasting impression on Mina that evening. Had she been privy to Edison's mocking comments, she would have been alerted to a side of him that she would have to shoulder for the rest of her life.

Lillian and Mina became closer friends, which led to yet another invitation to spend a week in July at her beach house, Woodside Villa, on the shore of Boston Harbor in Winthrop, Massachusetts. Lillian also invited their mutual friend, Louise. Mina eagerly looked forward to spending time with her girlfriends. She also understood the invitation as a gracious gesture that would allow her a well-deserved rest after a long school year. Even more so, Mina relished spending time with Louise, who was intelligent and witty. Louise's letters to Mina were replete with compliments she needed when feeling depressed. Mina loved Louise like an older sister.

Mina's parents, anxious to get her home at the end of the term, were reluctant to allow her to accept the invitation. Mina assured them that she would be back in Akron after a week's stay at the seaside. Furthermore, before her visit to Winthrop, Mina would accompany George's parents to attend his graduation from Yale and see the Harvard-Yale boat race. Her spirits were high as she looked forward to the thrilling social scene and to seeing George.[25]

Lillian knew Edison and his obstinate personality well enough to know she had to intervene when finding him a suitable wife. Since his first wife died, Edison's two young sons, nine-year-old Tom Jr. and seven-year-old William, were handed off from family member to family member while Edison was in his lab or traveling for business. Meanwhile, his oldest child, twelve-year-old Marion, who seemed to have more spunk than the younger two, accompanied Edison everywhere, from Delmonico's to laboratories. Yet, regardless of the environment, she craved her father's love and attention and did not protest.[26]

All three children needed stability in the wake of their mother's death. Someone had to fill that void for these children, but Edison was not going to reinvent himself and become a warm, loving, attentive father, nor would he ever. He was busy, of course, but also simply uninterested in their daily needs. So, Lillian took it upon herself to introduce him to young ladies who could fill the shoes as the new Mrs. Edison. It would not be an easy task. Edison never went out and, therefore, was not going to meet someone on his own. So, she started inviting young ladies from the Midwest to parade in front of Edison during those steamy, hot summer days at the seashore. For nine days, Edison kept a journal commenting on his leisure and his impression of the young ladies who visited Winthrop while he was there.

Despite Mina's relationship with George, Lillian saw her as a promising candidate to be the future Mrs. Thomas Edison. Months later, Jennie blamed Lillian for interfering in Mina's love life. Mina could never stand firm and tell Lillian she intended to marry George Vincent. On the other hand, George thought deeply about Mina daily. He was aware of Mina's comings and goings, including her excursion to the Boston seaside. "You asked for a few words, and here they are," George wrote his parents. "I love you and Mother dearly if I do not write you as much as I do, [it is because I write] to a certain young lady." George had no reason to think Mina's trip might jeopardize their future together. "I am well, happy in anticipation of my visit in Akron, and very well contented with my present lot." George also knew Louise well and would never think she could be complicit in Mina finding another love interest. Louise knew of his deep love for Mina.[27]

Louise was something of a permanent fixture around the Millers' Akron home and the summer lake house in Chautauqua. Louise's connection to the Millers went back ten years, when she was first introduced as a friend of Jennie's. Mina's family thought very highly of Louise, especially Mina's older brother Robert, who had been courting her for close to a year. She was a master storyteller who kept the family riveted with her tales. Likewise, she had an active, playful side. The first time Jennie introduced Louise to the Millers, she described her as a refined young lady. That night Louise said she was "drawn into a pillow fight in the spacious hall." The fight was initiated by Mina's father, Lewis Miller. Louise thought this must be how the family lived in the Miller home and started hitting others with her pillows with great enthusiasm. Robert, Mina's older brother, known to be quite impish, saw that Louise's playful traits were similar to his own, and he was smitten with her.[28]

George might have believed that Mina's spending time with her more mature friend Louise would advance his cause. It was no secret that Louise was on her way to marrying Robert. Mina would be exposed to "girl talk" about courtship and marriage, and it would put her into the right frame of mind to take the natural next step with George toward a public engagement and marriage.

Edison also spent time at the Gillilands' cottage earlier in the summer to discuss plans for their joint acquisition. He and Ezra bought a tract of land in the wilds of Fort Myers, Florida; it was practically a jungle. They purchased two fabricated houses from Maine and shipped them down to Florida. It is not surprising that Edison would pick such an undeveloped spot for his future work. He loved roughing it, and the opportunities for hunting and fishing all appealed to Edison. In addition, there were no existing pipes in the area that were needed for indoor plumbing or running water. It was perfect for a man who reveled in scoffing at the luxuries of life.[29]

Though Mina was raised to be modest and reserved, she let down her guard as the days progressed and became more comfortable speaking with the other guests. By the second or third day in the Gillilands' cottage, Mina and Edison became better acquainted. He entertained the company with his humorous stories about his climb to fame. Edison lacked formal education, something he had in common with Mina's beloved father. Additionally, both men were inventors with patents to their names. Both were extremely knowledgeable in the world's ways and gave off an air of confidence.

Edison had purchased a recently published book titled *How Success Is Won*, which contained biographical sketches of Rev. Vincent, Lewis Miller, and Edison. The book interested both Edison and Mina. Edison learned of her father's achievements, and Mina recognized the similarities she had noted between Edison and her father.[30]

George, on the other hand, was starting his life. He had an education yet lacked the experience of a man like Edison. A twenty-year-old could not compete with one of the most famous men in the United States. Without George even aware of it, Mina was slowly slipping from his grasp. Doubts about her future with George were growing. Finally, around July 6th, Mina returned to Akron, happy to see her family for the first time since Christmas. She arrived just in time for her twentieth birthday.[31]

Meanwhile, Edison left the cottage at Winthrop to go to New York to give testimony in a lawsuit regarding one of his patents. He planned to return to Winthrop the next week to meet more young women. This time he would bring his daughter, Marion, who had been staying in the house in Menlo Park.

Lillian wanted to make the next week even more lively for her guests and suggested purchasing a diary to keep while staying at her house. The guests were asked to write about their daily activities and observations at her cottage, then take turns reading their entries out loud to the others. This activity was a common parlor game and a form of amusement at that time.[32]

Edison, very much taken by Mina, used his diary entries to tell his host and other female guests about his romantic interest in her. Marion, who deeply cared for her father, at once understood, "my Father was in love with the Ohio girl, Mina Miller, whom he previously met." Marion preferred Mina's friend Louise who was still a guest in Winthrop "because she was a blonde like my Mother more than any other reason." Louise, however, was romantically involved with Robert, Mina's older brother. Unlike Mina or Jennie, Louise was self-assured in her decision-making and entirely set on marrying Robert.[33]

Edison's diary is the only known place where he deliberately wrote thoughts of a personal nature that were intended to be read aloud for the amusement of guests. Edison knew of the closeness between Louise and Mina and was certain that his comments would wind their way back to Akron via Mina's brother. After observing Louise reading Robert's letters, Edison wrote in his diary, "Miss Igoe was involved in a correspondence with a brother of Miss Mina who resides at Canton Ohio relating to the Mower & reaper firm of Aultman & Miller . . . A post office courtship is a novelty to me, so I have resolved to follow up this matter for the experience which I will obtain— This may come handy should My head ever become the dupe of my heart."[34]

As he continued the diary, Edison expressed his thoughts about Mina in colorful language. In one entry, he described her appearance thus:

"Took Mina as a basis, tried to improve her beauty by discarding and adding certain features borrowed from Daisy (who was another young lady visiting at Winthrop) and Mamma G (Lillian Gilliland). a sort of Raphaelized beauty, went to bed worked my imagination for a supply of maidens, only saw Mina Daisy & Mamma." In another entry, Edison provided a witty account intended to flatter the young, naïve Mina: "Saw a lady who looked like Mina—got thinking about Mina and came near being run over by a street car— If Mina interferes much more, I will have to take out an accident policy . . . constantly talking about Mina who . . . [we] use a sort of yardstick measuring perfection makes Dot [Marion] jealous." This last entry was a prophecy; Mina and Marion were about to enter an extremely contentious relationship that lasted for decades.[35]

Edison's interest in Mina was expressed through his diary, and his letters to her lifted her spirits in a way nothing had ever done before, including the attention of George Vincent. It was clear to Mina that one of the most famous men in the world was commenting favorably on her beauty in a public and dramatic way.

Edison also wrote about his views on art, religion, literature, and even marriage in his diary, which he described as "bucketsful of misery." Mina surely would have winced at Edison's comment on religion when he told the guests that his "conscience seems to be oblivious of Sunday—it must be encrusted with a sort of irreligious tartar."[36]

Edison's public interest in Mina signaled to Lillian that she had accomplished her task of finding him a new wife. He chose Mina over the other young ladies. Edison wanted to spend more time with Mina, whom he referred to in his diary as the "Maid of Chautauqua."[37]

He asked Mina to join him, the Gillilands, and his daughter, Marion, on a trip to the White Mountains in New Hampshire in his letters to her. Mina's parents initially did not consent to this arrangement because they were quite religious and felt it improper. Their refusal prompted Edison to meet her family in Chautauqua. Edison forced himself to feign enjoyment in a social setting. He needed to persuade her parents to allow Mina to join him and his guests in the White Mountains. According to Mina, Edison made the trip sound so attractive that her parents acquiesced. While Edison was in Chautauqua, he created a chart of the characteristics and traits of people he had recently met and already knew. He had a long-standing interest in phrenology, the study of the conformation of the skull as indicative of mental faculties and traits of character, and he had recently purchased Johann Lavater's book *The Science of Physiognomy*. The topics of his chart included education level to the size of one's nose (Figure 1).[38]

At that same time, George, unaware Edison was coming to visit, was heading up to Chautauqua to spend time with his beloved Mina. George wrote to his mother that he was so excited to see Mina after what seemed to him a long time apart. It was the first time in their lives that neither was in school, and they could begin to make concrete plans about their future. In a tongue-in-cheek way, he apologized to his father for not writing him as often as he might have wished because he had been preoccupied with writing to Mina.

Edison arrived at Chautauqua on August 10th and remained through August 18th. He, Mina, the Gillilands, Louise (her joining the party may have been a condition of allowing Mina to go), and Marion headed to Alexandria Bay, New York, where they stayed at the Thousand Island House, a summer resort on the St. Lawrence River. The town, which was promoted as a young Venice being "romantic and highly picturesque," was becoming increasingly popular with American tourists.[39]

The group then traveled to Montreal, where they stayed briefly at the Windsor Hotel, before going to the Maplewood Hotel in Bethlehem, New Hampshire, on August 23rd. The large hotel, known for its architecture and beauty, was surrounded by hills and had access to pure spring water. They stayed there until the last day of August. One night at the hotel, after spending the day on top of Mount Washington, Edison began teaching Mina all the characters of the Morse Code. Mina, eager to please Edison, had memorized them all by the next morning.

At the same time, George arrived by train in Akron, hoping to be there when Mina returned from her trip. Mina's father picked him up at the train station and gave him a tour of his sprawling Buckeye Mower and Reaper Works. George was uneasy about Mina again taking leave to gallivant with Edison and his crew. George wrote home that he intended to write to Mina "fifteen times as much" as he had in the past.[40]

But it was too late. The following day, in the presence of his daughter, Marion, Edison proposed to Mina in Morse Code. Recalling that event years later, Marion claimed, "Mina responded to her father's question by merely blushing and nodding yes." In that instant, without an audible word passed between the couple, and after only knowing Thomas Edison personally for approximately one month, Mina Miller decided to entirely alter the path of her life, discard George Vincent, and marry one of the most famous men in the world.[41]

2

Cost of Consent

Upon returning to Akron the first week of September, Mina was overflowing with excitement. She had captured the heart of the most prominent man in the United States. The years of self-doubt melted away, and now she held her head high among the other young ladies in society. Yet, nothing would rob her of the initial happiness of sharing her big news with close friends and family.

With absolute indifference, Mina relegated George's needs to a back burner. Unaware that Mina had plans to marry Edison, he continued to write her often. George was oblivious that his entire life trajectory had been altered in a matter of a few weeks. George Vincent was not destined to be the first son-in-law to the famed Lewis Miller. Mina knew he would be devastated but avoided confronting him. It would not be until September 16th, almost two weeks later, that George would hear the news firsthand. Unaware of the distress it would trigger, the local society pages reported a visit of Mina's suitor, George Vincent, to the Miller mansion.[1]

Mina's parents had mixed feelings about Edison's proposal, however. Lewis, a self-made millionaire, saw Edison as a younger version of himself—an inventor who also valued knowledge and a desire to expand one's intellectual horizons. Countless people knew of the vast accomplishments of Edison, and Lewis had enjoyed hearing his daughter's new suitor share personal anecdotes about his rise to fame. They shared a vision about the future of business and were both determined to make a difference in society. Edison once wrote of Miller, "He was one of the kindest and most lovable men I ever knew, and spent his life trying to make it possible for all of mankind to reach the higher planes of living."[2]

Born only seventeen years after Lewis, Edison's age and accomplishments engendered a bond more like a younger brother than a prospective son-in-law. He, too, had been born in Ohio and had several siblings. Edison was the youngest of seven children. His mother, Nancy, had been a schoolteacher; his father, Samuel, had been a Canadian political agitator expelled from his country. When Edison was seven years old, the family moved to Port Huron, Michigan, and his father became a carpenter and had varied other business interests, and had the ability to earn respectable wages to support his family.

Three of Edison's older siblings died before he was born. His mother had buried his six-year-old sister and two three-year-old siblings. When Edison was born, his three surviving siblings were significantly older than he. Marion was eighteen; William Pitt was sixteen; and Harriet Anne was fourteen. By Edison's second birthday, Marion had married and moved out of the house. Between his eighth and ninth birthday, Harriet and William were also married. As a Baptist minister's daughter, Edison's mother was a religious woman and accepted her blessings and tragedies as God's will. She was a resilient woman and redirected any sadness into happily bringing up Thomas.[3]

Nancy Edison spent her days providing her young son with unlimited attention and care. Edison was primarily taught at home by his mother, who emphasized the value of self-education through reading from his father's library. When he was twelve years old, he told his mother, "Ma, I'm a bushel of wheat. I weigh just sixty pounds." His mother realized her child understood aspects of the world differently than others. She needed to raise Edison in a different way than her previous children. He and his mother would pass the days reading and conversing together. Realizing his aptitude, she introduced him to Hume's *History of England* and Gibbon's *Decline and Fall of the Roman Empire*. She also had him read digests of general knowledge, including biology, literature, geography, and other sciences. Edison read quickly, and his memory of details had extraordinary precision. Edison's book of particular interest was his father's copy of Thomas Paine's *The Age of Reason*. Much of the content and language was over Edison's head when he first encountered it. Later in life, Edison would hold up Paine as the epitome of an enlightened freethinker and contrast Paine's *Age of Reason* with the ideas of the Church that "my mother forced me to attend."[4]

When asked about his success, Edison admitted, "My mother was the making of me; she was true, so sure of me, I felt that I had someone to live for, someone I must not disappoint." When Edison turned fifteen, he longed to discover the world beyond his own home and left his mother's side to work as a newsboy selling newspapers, magazines, and candy on the Grand Trunk Railroad line between Detroit and his home in Port Huron. The Civil War was raging, and the *Detroit Free Press* reported the battle of Shiloh. Edison talked the editor into giving him extra copies on credit. He then had the headlines telegraphed ahead to the trains' scheduled stops. The demand for the papers was so great that he steadily increased the price at each station, making a handsome profit. Edison learned a valuable lesson about the power of good marketing.[5]

Like Lewis Miller, he had the drive to create something out of nothing—he transformed part of a baggage car into a moving laboratory for his chemical experiments. While working on the train, he learned to send and receive telegraph messages from the workers at the various train stations. Finally, at only fifteen years old, he had learned enough telegraphy to find employment as an operator in a local office. Edison enthusiastically used the rest of his teenage years traveling throughout the Midwest and the South as an itinerant telegrapher. He traveled through Cincinnati, Fort Wayne, Indianapolis, Memphis, and Louisville. He read extensively, studied, experimented with telegraph technology, and acquainted himself with electrical science, essentially giving himself electrical training.[6]

By the age of twenty-two, Edison moved to Boston when a friend found him a position in the main office of Western Union and Franklin Telegraph. There he discovered that the city was also a center of telegraph manufacturing. Ambitious and capable young men flocked to Boston to absorb all they could about this growing technology. Western Union hired Edison to work at night to receive press reports from New York. Established entrepreneurs invested in local machine shops and permitted eager young inventors to try their new ideas. The arrangement was perfect for Edison, who could use the daytime hours to visit machine shops.

Telegraphy had permeated every industry. Municipal offices, financial institutions, and other businesses were all sending telegraphs. By 1870, the businesses of Boston sent over nine million telegraphs annually. This figure grew larger each year, leading companies to chase new technology to edge the competition. Soon there were specialized telegraph systems for fire and police call systems, private line telegraphs between offices and private residences, and reporting services that allowed financial and commodity price information. These inventions transformed communication in the United States. Edison's prior work, combined with his thirst for more knowledge—focused his mind on improving telegraph machinery.

Edison signed an agreement with two businessmen from Boston who helped him patent his first viable idea, an improved printing telegraph later known as the stock ticker. At the time, they provided brokers with up-to-date prices from the gold and stock exchanges. It essentially printed telegraphed stock prices to bankers and investors from a central office. There were existing stock tickers at the time; however, Edison's invention was more streamlined—it used one wire instead of three. In addition, it reduced the cost of the system on which it was used by significantly reducing the number of cables and batteries. The financial success of the invention allowed Edison to leave Western Union for more challenging work.[7]

He moved to New York the following year and worked as an independent inventor for other telegraph companies. In addition, he built his own manufacturing shops in Newark, New Jersey, and hired experimental machinists to assist in his inventive work with the money he made. As a result, Edison acquired a reputation as an exceptionally talented inventor. In addition to stock tickers, his work included fire alarms and methods of sending simultaneous messages on one wire. From 1869 to 1875, Edison was so productive he submitted 110 patents to the United States Patent Office.

Before his thirtieth birthday, Edison had created his research laboratory in Menlo Park, New Jersey, which included a machine shop and laboratory. Edison worked under contract with Western Union on acoustic telegraphy, which telegraphed messages over a single wire using different audio frequencies. Publicity about Alexander Graham Bell's new telephone, which had emerged from Bell's own acoustic telegraph experiments, turned Edison's attention to this new technology. Bell's telephone used a metal diaphragm and a magnet wrapped in wire to transmit speech. The human voice caused the diaphragm to vibrate, creating a current in the wire. The current re-created the vibration on the receiving end, enabling the person to hear what was said. The signal, however, was not strong. Edison rose to the occasion and invented a better transmitter in which a carbon button varied the current's resistance to reproduce the speech sound wave more accurately. This principle would be used in telephones for the next century.

While working on the telephone and experimenting with different forms of diaphragms to store speech, Edison even surprised himself by discovering a method of recording sound. The first experiment that led him to conceive the phonograph used a telephone diaphragm with a needle to record on waxed paper. Within a few months, he had developed a machine that recorded and played back sound on tinfoil. Edison's new phonograph was little more than an exhibition curiosity that astounded listeners. But it made Edison famous as he became known as the Wizard of Menlo Park. Although the invention needed extensive development before it became commercially successful, Edison instead spent the next three years developing a complete incandescent electric lighting system. In 1881, he left Menlo Park to establish factories and offices in New York City. Over the next five years, he manufactured, improved, and installed his electrical system around the world.[8]

In 1885, when Mina introduced her renowned admirer to her father, Lewis had the opportunity to hear Edison's life story face-to-face; he was overjoyed with Edison's mind and stamina. His life's triumphs were far ahead of George Vincent's, and Lewis easily changed gears and fully embraced Mina's new suitor. Mina observed that her father and Edison had maternal figures in their lives who had shaped them into the men they became. Moreover, she had internalized the Victorian mores that her mother followed. Mary Valinda did all in her power to support her husband by running the household, which allowed her husband to achieve his well-earned professional reputation. Mina wanted to do just that, following in her mother's footsteps as Edison's wife and aid him in his continued success.

With the acceptance of Edison as a new son-in-law came three children from his previous marriage. Lewis, the product of a blended family himself, looked back fondly on his childhood with half-siblings. He genuinely expected that Mina would rise to the occasion and love Edison's three children from his first marriage as though they were her very own.[9]

———

Lewis saw many similarities between himself and Edison. Born in Greentown, Ohio, Lewis was the third of three sons of John and Elizabeth Miller. They lived in a log cabin on a farm across from her brother and wife. Unfortunately, Lewis's mother died a few months after he was born. Nevertheless, the warmhearted and solicitous aunt and uncle took in baby Lewis and nursed him, caring for him along with their own baby until Lewis's father remarried and was able to care for his son with his new wife.

Lewis's stepmother, Elizabeth Aultman, a young widow, added her two children to Lewis's family. The newly blended family numbered five children, with Lewis as the youngest. Six more siblings would eventually be born, and the Millers also adopted three children from a destitute clergyman. Unfortunately, only four of the clan would live into adulthood. Lewis quickly learned that living in a blended family often included adopting children and coping with death. But love and contentment are the essential components that make up a happy family.

Strict religious observance permeated all aspects of the Miller home. Elizabeth's love for all the children was as unwavering as her faith. Lewis's father was loving and patient with all his children, while his mother kept a meticulous household. She cherished all the children as though she had borne them herself. Each morning, Lewis's father read from a German Bible, followed by an offering of prayer. The children all worked on the farm and attended a subscription school part-time because there was no local public school. Lewis was a serious student and spent all his leisure time reading. A subscription school differed from a public school in that parents paid the teacher according to how many days the child attended. This education model was well-suited for rural areas and pre-industrial life. He and his siblings were often required to do farm labor during extended periods in those years. The subscription schools were only open during the winter months, when the agricultural season was dormant.[10]

By the time he was sixteen years old, Lewis himself had become a part-time subscription schoolteacher during the winter months. Lewis was particularly curious about the psychology of teaching. He was deeply interested in identifying how to study and the best way to impart knowledge to others. He learned that teaching was a nuanced activity that did not involve rote memorization or teaching all the same methods. Moreover, teaching was a skill that could only truly be mastered through the love of a subject. He believed it had to be diligently practiced and constantly needed innovation and ingenuity. Lewis was born with the desire to learn. He studied or taught school every winter until adulthood, reading every book he could get his hands on. Both parents expected that he would become a teacher when Lewis had an opportunity to leave the family farm.

In 1849, at age nineteen, Lewis realized that his meager teaching salary was never going to provide him with the means to support a wife and family and that he had to expand his horizons beyond the classroom. He moved in with his sister and her husband. Lewis's stepbrother Cornelius lived in the same town as well. Cornelius worked in a machine shop owned by his father-in-law. Lewis, known for his work ethic on and off the farm, was hired as a junior mechanic for fixing farm-cultivating instruments. Cornelius's father-in-law and his business partners in the machine shop made it a habit to keep abreast of their competition. They were interested in the newest technology regarding reaping machines and farming equipment. They read all they could in the trade magazines about other inventions and attempted to make improved reapers themselves. With Cornelius's help, they built the first reaper made in their shop in Greentown, Ohio.[11]

Cornelius and Lewis were close growing up, only two years apart in age. Lewis was eager to learn and ambitious. He paid attention to

Cornelius's work, and his discussion with other family members about how their new harvesters would change how farming would be done. Finally, Cornelius was asked by his brother-in-law, who was also in the farming business, to begin manufacturing and selling the new harvesters. Cognizant of Lewis's intelligence and ambition, Cornelius invited him to travel westward to Illinois. Yearning to learn the latest technology, Lewis accepted the invitation.

Lewis, Cornelius, and their extended family all journeyed by covered wagon to Plainfield, Illinois, over four hundred miles away from their home in Greentown, Ohio. The trip took days, which gave Lewis ample time to read and think about the next phase of his life's adventure.

Unexpectedly, the journey to Illinois also led Lewis to the love of his life, Mina's mother. Lewis saw resilience in Mary Valinda that would be the foundation of strength he desired in a wife. She also wanted a large family and expressed that she would be proud to support his larger aspirations.[12]

Mary Valinda was also the product of a blended family and experienced the loss of siblings at a young age. Ten years before her birth, her father, Hugh Alexander, had previously been married. That woman died, leaving six children, the eldest of whom died before reaching adulthood. Hugh fell in love again and married Cynthia Manville Alexander. She gave birth to twin girls. They were christened Mary Valinda and Martha Arminda. Mary Valinda was born so tiny and appeared so fragile that her parents did not change her baby clothing for fear they might break her limbs. She remained in the same bunting for the first four days of her life. Although she appeared much stronger at birth, Martha Arminda would die at the age of three. Mary Valinda was left without her twin sister—the first of several tragedies that would test her resilience. Five other children from that marriage also died in infancy. Grief and loss were frequent visitors in the Alexander home.[13]

When Mary Valinda was diagnosed with rheumatism at age eleven, her parents worried about losing another child. They followed the standard medical prescription of the time and confined Mary Valinda to her bed for the next few years. Because she was unable to attend school with her peers, Mary Valinda never learned to write well and wrote phonetically in her correspondence as an adult.

Although she missed out on her early primary schooling, Mary Valinda was still afforded the luxuries of being the daughter of well-to-do parents. Her father had made a fortune selling land in the heart of Chicago before moving to Illinois. A successful farmer in Plainfield, he purchased a large estate with two massive fireplaces, a great luxury at that time. Despite the numerous deaths in her family, Mary Valinda's mother, much like Lewis's mother, made sure that she and her surviving siblings grew up in a happy home. At the age of nineteen, Mary Valinda returned to school several grades behind her peers.[14]

After finally returning to school, Mary Valinda encountered Lewis Miller, who had recently relocated to Illinois with several extended family members to establish themselves in the farming equipment business. Lewis spent most of his free time with Mary Valinda and quickly became attached to her. It was no secret that her parents supported the match, admiring both his love of education and his business acumen.

A year later, Lewis was her steady beau. But by the end of the harvest season of 1850, Cornelius's family was aware of his knowledge of the industry, and he was asked by his father-in-law to return to Greentown; he convinced Lewis to leave Illinois and return home to Ohio.

Because of their short courtship, Lewis wished to be noble, and he told Mary Valinda to follow her heart if she found a better suitor. After he left, they continued their courtship through a constant exchange of love letters sent between the two young sweethearts, regularly considering their future life together.

Cornelius was to buy one-third interest in his manufacturing shop. Lewis had also gained more responsibility in the machine shop and returned with him. When they returned to Greentown, Ohio, Cornelius sold him a sixth of his interest in the shop. Lewis was overjoyed. His hard work had paid off, and he was rewarded by becoming a partner. Cornelius did the same with other family members.[15]

In December 1850, Mary Valinda wrote Lewis, "[I] formed some new acquaintances since you left, but I still feel that I can spend my days most pleasantly with you. I have spoken with Mother about our plan, and she is willing . . . Father will not raise any objection." Lewis was delighted that the family still welcomed him. He confessed that he almost concluded that another suitor had stepped into his place because he had not heard from her for so long. He wrote to her that he was not interested in making a connection with any other young ladies: "You are my choice among all the Fair Sex." The couple finally decided that May might be a suitable time for their wedding.[16]

On February 21, 1852, Lewis wrote to the Alexanders formally asking for their daughter's hand in marriage. Acknowledging their long courtship, he stated that "[I] formed an attachment with your respected daughter that cannot easily be removed." In the spring of 1853, Mary Valinda and Lewis married at the Alexanders' stately home. Unfortunately, Lewis forgot to get his pants sewn amidst all the excitement of travel. Proving what a fitting match Mary Valinda and Lewis were, she gathered some of her friends together on the morning of the wedding and ensured that his pants would be ready for the ceremony without a drop of consternation.[17]

Lewis knew that Mary Valinda had grown up accustomed to comfort and elegance. He had to provide surroundings with which she would be pleased. Lewis and Mary Valinda moved to a large home in Canton close to his new business. Within a few years, the happy couple had five children and moved to their second home in Canton to accommodate their growing family. The Millers hired a woman to help with the household. She stayed with them until the children reached adulthood.[18]

The business was also growing quickly. Sales of the mowers and reapers were proving very profitable. However, Lewis was now living in a large home with household help. So, Lewis's role slowly evolved from a mechanic to a designer of the mower and reapers at the plant. Lewis began thinking up and introducing more new models for the harvesters.

As a farmer himself, he knew it was common for a driver to be thrown from the seat of a mower when he hit a hole or a bump. If a driver fell in front of the blade, he could be seriously injured or die. So, Lewis shifted the blade to the side of the machine, so a driver who fell could avoid the blade. Lewis's design innovations led to several patents, and the United States Agricultural Society awarded medals for safety and ingenuity.

By 1857, their Buckeye Mower and Reaper received positive recognition from its competitors. The business was booming, and the partners faced some big business decisions. One of the partners believed he could make more money on his own and sold his share to the others. The company now produced 1,500 mowers and reapers and 150 threshing machines and had outgrown the Canton workshop's capacity.[19]

Although the business was thriving, Lewis felt unfulfilled. He had been spending most of his days attending to the growing business, yet he was unable to nurture the intellectual and religious yearnings he developed as a younger man. As a result, he became an active member of the Methodist Church.

Lewis noticed the children in the congregation did not have a strong connection to the Church's teachings. Although he was raised as a Methodist, he had not believed he had to follow its rigid dogma. Lewis envisioned new ways of disseminating its views. For example, in the late nineteenth century, the Methodist Church forbade any play on the Sabbath. Lewis considered that edict to be incongruent with the innate happiness of childhood. He knew he would have to apply his innovative business skills to engage more children with the Sunday school program. If he could engage the children, he could make them lifelong believers.[20]

He proposed an age-based system, separating the children according to their corresponding classes in school to learn at a level they could understand. Lewis also had to find qualified teachers who could impart the material in a way a child would comprehend. He believed Sunday schools needed dedicated buildings, and he hired an architect to restructure the school. He designed an open, semicircular hall that looked like a rotunda. It was to be built several stories high to produce excellent acoustics in the main hall. The rotunda then opened up into many classrooms and lecture halls. Doors to the many classrooms could be left open, allowing all classes to hear a single lecturer simultaneously. The Sunday school in Akron included poetry, drama, and science in the coursework. Lewis persuaded many local school instructors to join his new Sunday school faculty. One of his favorite teachers in Canton was Helen McKinley, who had a brother named William, a young lawyer in town. The McKinleys were frequent visitors at the Millers' home and became close friends. William married Ida Saxton, the daughter of Lewis's patent attorney, and went on to have a fruitful political career, eventually becoming the twenty-fifth president of the United States.

The school flourished, and the architectural design was formally known as the Akron Plan. The plan was officially recognized at the National Sunday School Convention and was adopted by Protestant churches throughout the United States. These changes were the first steps for Lewis's grand plans for religious teaching in the Methodist Church.[21]

The Canton shop no longer could meet the high demand for mowers and reapers, and the partners needed to expand the business. So, in 1863, they built a new factory in Akron, and the firm there became known as Aultman, Miller & Co. The Canton and Akron shops produced eight thousand Buckeye machines and five hundred threshing machines by the following year. Both plants were incorporated as one legal entity, with Lewis Miller as the superintendent who managed the daily business matters of both plants. The new Buckeye Mower became the standard device for most farmers in the Midwest, and royalties were now paid to Lewis's company. Throughout Lewis's rise to fame, Mary Valinda was by his side. They were a unified front—partners from the earliest days of their marriage.

The unwavering support Mary Valinda provided her husband was always effortless. When Mina shared the news about Edison with her mother, it prompted a vastly different response from her father's keenness about the union. Edison, a widower, was nineteen years older than Mina and had three children from his previous marriage. Mina's mother was deeply concerned about the sustainability of the proposed union. She believed the couple had nothing in common. Edison was not religious and had no intention of becoming a Methodist. Religion was an essential part of the Miller family life. George Vincent was also a Methodist, and if they married, there was no doubt they would naturally continue to be Methodist. On the other hand, Edison was a heathen and not shy about admitting it. Mary Valinda was not thrilled.

Though Edison was from Ohio, he now lived in the cosmopolitan and less-religious Northeast. That region would become Mina's new home— not what Mary Valinda envisioned for her daughter's future. To make matters worse, the courtship was occurring too rapidly for Mary Valinda, unlike her lengthy courtship with Mina's father. But, seeing her daughter's happiness, she understood she had no choice but to support Mina's wishes and hope for the best.[22]

Despite her lack of formal education, Mary Valinda possessed a keen understanding of interpersonal relationships and was fully aware of the repercussions once Mina ended her courtship with George. The aftereffects could be grim. For the past seventeen years, the Millers and the Vincents had been friends and business partners in building the Chautauqua Institution. The news would devastate the Vincents.

❧

When the Miller and Vincent families met years prior, they immediately bonded over religion and education. They had certain religious expectations for their children to follow. Both Mina and George mirrored their parents' values and ensured their actions were grounded in their faith. Both families watched Mina and George become closer over the years and believed it was a match made in heaven.

Rev. Vincent was a well-known proponent of advancing the Methodist Sunday school education and was the editor of *Sunday School Quarterly*. Rev. Vincent and Lewis deeply cared about training teachers to effectively reach the Sunday school students. Although more part of the elite society than Rev. Vincent, Lewis was not preoccupied with maintaining the moral and social order. Lewis cared about creating a communitarian utopia. He wanted to emphasize the connection between the individual and the community. He believed that a person's social identity and personality are molded by community relationships rather than individualism. Vincent had been working on a parallel track. He organized a Sunday school college that awarded diplomas to students who completed a four-year course of study. Lewis's Akron Plan was essentially creating a space that was an urban counterpart to the existing Methodist Camp Meeting in Sunday schools. When the two men met, they immediately saw how their ideas complemented each other.[23]

Rev. Vincent was schooled in traditional ministry and believed Sunday school instruction was exclusively for religious education. His notion of a lesson plan was to have everyone of all ages study the same passage of Scripture on the same Sunday. He believed a good Christian foundation would ensure good citizenship. A charismatic and emotional speaker and aware of his persuasiveness, he used it to his advantage to get his point across about education. Akin to Lewis, Rev. Vincent wanted a child-centered approach to learning. He incorporated singsong geography lessons and other mnemonic devices that placed him at the forefront of emerging educational trends at that time. Together, Rev. Vincent and Lewis knew they could make significant changes in Christian education.

In the summer of 1872, at a religious meeting entitled the "The Promotion of Holiness," Lewis shared his thoughts with two long-term childhood friends, who were sisters from Canton. Both were Sunday school teachers as well. Lewis suggested that they establish a Sunday school convention where people interested in Sunday school work could meet for three weeks for Bible study, classwork, and general instruction. Lewis expanded his idea further and suggested musical entertainment lectures, recreation, and devotional exercises. He thought it would provide them with rest and a holiday while preparing for the following year's classes. Both women agreed it was an excellent idea, however, they thought it would be an enormous undertaking. Lewis viewed these meetings as potentially beneficial and having far-reaching influence. The two sisters thought it was a splendid idea and recalled an idyllic spot they had once visited near upstate New York. The two sisters were so taken with the wild beauty of the place that they suggested to Lewis it would be an ideal place for his idea. Lewis thought that if he offered this to Reverend Vincent, an influential and rising star in the Sunday school education and the Methodist Church, the concept would become a reality.[24]

Lewis was eager to share his vision with Reverend Vincent. But before Lewis had an opportunity to reveal his dream about an outdoor convention, Rev. Vincent articulated his own concept of an annual convention for Sunday school teachers. The conception for his model was that it should be held in the winter. The Reverend wanted to pay homage to Lewis and suggested that the first one be held in Akron, then imagined the convention moving from one city to the next each year. Rev. Vincent openly sought Lewis's endorsement of his idea and requested his financial backing unabashed. Undeterred by his friend's enthusiastic presentation, Lewis expounded on his outdoor idea and told the Reverend he would call it an "Assembly." Initially, Rev. Vincent could not conceive of an outside gathering because it was evocative of the hysteria surrounding revival camp meetings that were in vogue at that time. However, Lewis refused to give up on persuading him and further asserted there would be literature and science taught connected to the Bible. Unconvinced that it would be successful, Rev. Vincent thwarted his idea and did not believe it fit with religious study.[25]

The following summer, the sisters, who had not been regularly kept abreast of Lewis's plan, were anxious to know what was to become of the outdoor Assembly. Regrettably, Lewis expressed that he would be unable to take on the monumental task without the support of Rev. Vincent, whom he needed as the head of the Department of Instruction.[26]

Regardless of their disagreement surrounding their particular ideas about the Sunday school learning convention, Rev. Vincent had become a more frequent visitor to the Miller home in Akron. One afternoon Lewis invited Dr. Vincent to attend Mount Union College's commencement. It was located in Alliance, Ohio, thirty miles away. It would take many hours to travel by horse and carriage. Lewis and his brothers were benefactors of the school and, therefore, involved in various policies at the institution. Their beneficial work earned them naming rights to the men's dormitory and a long-standing seat on the Board of Trustees. During that long journey to commencement that evening, Lewis ultimately convinced Rev. Vincent to become his partner and build a learning institute in a setting of natural beauty.

Rev. Vincent agreed to head the Department of Instruction, and Lewis attended everything else. This task included considerable amounts of money, time, and labor. Nevertheless, Lewis effortlessly channeled the formidable organizational skills he used in his business toward his new project. All his actions and virtues came naturally to Lewis and seldom with a complaint. Lewis was utterly focused on the success of his new Assembly.

That summer, Lewis and the Rev. Vincent traveled to the future home of the Sunday school learning convention. In the southernmost part of New York, not far from Ohio, was a large campsite that touched Lake Chautauqua. The acres upon acres of bucolic grounds extended to a sizeable glistening lake. The myriad of trees offered shady spaces to rest, and the large grassy knolls added ample spots to take in the surrounding natural beauty. When they saw it for the first time, they immediately agreed it was the perfect place for their educational aspirations. What started as an academic discussion in Lewis's parlor was developing into a reality. Rev. Vincent realized that the Assembly would be an excellent concept. The first meeting, called an Assembly, opened in Chautauqua in August of 1874 and met for two weeks.[27]

After a successful grand opening, Lewis and Rev. Vincent began looking toward the following summer's Assembly. Rev. Vincent thought having a celebrity attend would bring excitement and perhaps more members. So, Rev. Vincent called on his old friend and congregant, Ulysses S. Grant. From 1859 to 1861, Reverend Vincent served the Bench Street Methodist Episcopal Church of Galena, Illinois. During that pastorate, Vincent met and befriended Ulysses S. Grant. Immediately following the siege of Fort Sumter, Grant raised a volunteer company of soldiers known as the Jo Davies Guards. In 1861, as the troops assembled to leave Galena, Vincent delivered a farewell address in the presence of five thousand onlookers.

The president, who was vacationing in Long Branch, New Jersey, was happy to accept the invitation. The Ulysses S. Grant Cottage on the shore of New Jersey was also referred to as the Summer White House. The president started spending summers there in 1875, and he spent three months of every summer there until 1885. He held cabinet meetings and composed parts of his memoirs at the cottage. The president traveled four hundred miles by train to Jamestown, the town adjacent to Chautauqua. Once he arrived in Jamestown, he was escorted up the lake by a fleet of eleven elaborately decorated steamboats by the Jamestown Methodist Church. He followed on his own yacht, the *Josie Belle*, which was also draped in presidential regalia. Sitting in an armchair at the bow, President Grant waved to the throngs of crowds who greeted him with shouts of joy. Theodore Flood, the first editor-in-chief of the local newspaper *The Chautauquan*, recalls that when the president disembarked, "Chautauqua seemed to form itself into one mammoth handkerchief and one throat that sent up shout after shout."[28]

President Grant enjoyed a pleasant weekend at the Chautauqua site, hosted by Lewis Miller and his family. His visit achieved Rev. Vincent's goal—the Chautauqua Institution was catapulted to national publicity. The Associated Press published a dispatch expounding on Chautauqua's programs, attractions, and picturesque grounds, ensuring steady growth for the years to come. The following two years proved steady growth for Chautauqua. Enrollment more than doubled each year. The two-week session quickly grew into three weeks and eventually into an eight-week program. With his adored speeches and charisma, Rev. Vincent would become the public face of the Chautauqua movement.

Hebrew and Greek were added to the curriculum, as was a four-year study program of guided reading. This group would be called the Chautauqua Literary and Scientific Circle. Rev. Vincent's goal was to promote reading and study habits in nature, art, science, and secular and sacred literature. In addition, he intended to encourage individual study and open the college world to persons unable to attend higher-learning institutions. The reading list for the four-year course included books on history and literature, two books on the Bible, one on astronomy, one on physiology, and a study guide for each of them.

Over 8,400 people enrolled in the first year. Of those original enrollees, 1,718 completed the reading course and the required examinations and received their diplomas on the first Chautauqua Literary Scientific Circle Recognition Day in 1882.

Members who lived far away from the original Chautauqua Assembly in New York banded together to create something analogous in a more accessible spot. These "Little Chautauquas" popped up all over the Midwest. They varied in size, but all had the same basic features in common: healthy fun, wholesome recreation, religious reverence, good taste, and honest inquiry. Midwesterners seized on the opportunity for self-education. Within a few years, nearly every community of any size in the United States had at least one person following the Chautauqua reading program as a Literary and Scientific Circle member. A monthly magazine was established for the members as well.[29]

Drawn from a different cloth than the Reverend Vincent, Lewis worked tirelessly behind the scenes to situate Chautauqua on a sound financial and legal footing. Much of the financial backing came from the Millers themselves, and Lewis did all the administrative work to ensure it was a well-run organization. Individuals from throughout the Midwest embraced the opportunity for self-improvement and trusted as unbreakable the Miller-Vincent partnership.

Ten years later, by 1885, there were one hundred thousand members following the Chautauqua reading program. But, unfortunately, that very same summer, Mina would discard Rev. Vincent's son George for Edison. The Miller family could only hope that Mina would not rupture an alliance built on unwavering work that spanned almost fifteen years.

That September, only six days after breaking off her courtship with George, Mina bought tickets to Boston and New York to meet up with Jennie and roam various shops. According to Mina's 1885 account book, her fall purchases included silk gloves, collars, shoes, silk stockings, slippers, and assorted items for her new life as Mrs. Thomas Edison. She attended the symphony and dined at fine restaurants as a respite from shopping. Mina was given a generous allowance from her parents and spent lavishly on dresses and many items for her trousseaux.[30]

While Edison felt confident the Millers would accept him as their new son-in-law, he knew he would have to write a formal letter to Lewis and request his daughter's hand in marriage. On September 30th, Edison sat down to write at his desk and attempted to seem as unpretentious as possible as he wrote his letter to his future father-in-law.

My Dear Sir,

Some months since, as you are aware, I was introduced to your daughter, Miss Mina. The friendship which ensued became admiration as I began to appreciate her gentleness and grace of manner and her beauty and strength of mind. That admiration has on my part ripened into love, and I have asked her to become my wife. She has referred me to you, and our engagement needs but for its confirmation your consent. I trust you will not excuse me of egotism when I say that my life and history and standing are so well known as to call for no statement concerning myself. My reputation is so far made that I recognize I must be judged by it for good or ill. I need only add in conclusion that the step I have taken in asking your daughter to intrust her happiness into my keeping has been the result of mature deliberation, and with the full appreciation of the responsibility I have assumed and the duty I have undertaken to fulfil [sic] I do not deny that your answer will seriously affect my happiness, and I trust my suit may meet with your approval. Very Sincerely yours,

Thomas A Edison[31]

3

A Girl Born to Luck

THE WEDDING DATE, SET FOR FEBRUARY 24TH, SEALED EDISON'S acceptance into Mina's family. The new union and name recognition would propel Lewis Miller's business and regional fame to new heights. Mina's older brothers, who perceived themselves as the company's successors, were overjoyed—counting the future profits that would line their pockets. But, although Mina's mother appreciated the windfall that would flow from Edison's name, she harbored reservations about the match.

Brandishing her familiar obstinate character, Jennie was the sole holdout of ten siblings and remained firm about postponing the wedding. Believing it her particular duty, she voiced her concerns: "It is still my opinion to wait a few months before marrying.... I would not promise to be married in February.... It seems to me that Mr. Edison should wait for you a year or six months at least." Hoping to soften her hesitance, she admitted to Mina she wanted to ensure her sister was both happy and married. Mina became tired of her older sister's cautions and did not engage with her; the date remained as-is. The squabbles between the two sisters often escalated. Mina preferred to avoid them reoccurring. Placing a simmer on the heated argument, Mina agreed to meet Jennie in New York to shop for Mina's new wardrobe. Jennie stood confident about which boutiques should clothe the future Mrs. Edison. Jennie always needed to be correct. It would be effortless for Mina to accede to Jennie's clothing suggestions in this sphere.[1]

While they were in New York, Jennie inquired whether Mr. Edison liked her. Jennie began to realize that Mina might care more about his thoughts than Jennie's. Upon hearing Mina's report that, indeed, Mr. Edison liked Jennie, the deluge of her opinions came pouring out again: "If you truly love Mr. Edison, I cannot help but feel if you wait one year [you] will know [him] so much better . . . one so often makes a mistake, and you are yet so young." Querying deeper, she did not doubt that Mina loved him, but is it "because you love him for himself or because he loves you?" Assessing her sister's observations at every juncture exhausted Mina. At this point, she disregarded them.[2]

Jennie, still hoping to be a guiding force, addressed her sister's other remaining insecurities. Jennie assured Mina, "I wouldn't worry about the Vincents anymore." If Mina did not like the family enough to be one of them, it was perfectly reasonable to be a little unkind to them to make herself happy. Feeling confident, she gave her younger sister good advice, and she was bold enough to confront another open issue. Jennie was still dismayed with Gilliland's role in making the new match and incessantly debated both sides of Mina's case. Jennie, never ashamed to reveal her dissatisfaction, accused them of swaying her impressionable sister. Their interference influenced her to choose Edison over George. Holding her ground, Lillian Gilliland, pleased with the outcome and a more seasoned woman, decided not to debate Jennie but emphasized that Mina's decision remained the best.[3]

Mina hoped the predictable emotional disturbance Jennie caused would disappear once Edison arrived at Akron in the coming days. He made preliminary plans to visit the Millers at their home for a short visit before Christmas. Mina expected his visit to Akron would dispel any remaining misgivings that her mother sheltered.

When Edison appeared, the children followed their mother's instructions and overcame their gawking. Mina's mother was curious to see Edison interact with her younger children and Mina in a less formal setting. Edison loathed leaving his laboratory, yet he knew he needed to perform as the doting and interested fiancé in meaningless familial affairs. Nevertheless, he stood wise enough not to appear rude and feigned interest in what he believed were the banal pursuits of the Miller family.

The magnificent home and grounds were so breathtaking that they muted Edison's public disregard for conspicuous consumption. Named Oak Place, it hosted countless parties for the Akron community— the Miller mansion was remarkably impressive. Lewis hosted a family reunion for 250 attendees a few months before Edison's visit. In addition to extensive outdoor activities, a fifteen-piece band serenaded the guests while they enjoyed all the festivities. Mina and her siblings were accustomed to large and gracious gatherings by her parents. While Edison did not attend the party, he noted the magnitude of the home's grounds and architectural beauty. He knew Mina would desire a house comparable to the one he entered and was obliged to visit.

When Lewis Miller sought a location in Akron to build a new plant for his expanding business, the newspapers were swift to divulge his activities. The headline read, "Lewis Miller and his interesting family will be a valuable accession to our population." Miller enjoyed his creature comforts. Before this home, he purchased the nine-acre estate in Canton from Christopher Parsons Wolcott, the assistant secretary of war under President Lincoln. That property was where Lewis perfected his skill for landscape gardening—a fondness and passion he passed on to many of his children. Oak Place's many gardens were even more striking.[4]

Increasing his property almost threefold, Oak Place sat on twenty-five acres overlooking the city of Akron. He paid $48,000 for it in 1870 ($986,000 in today's money). There were winding driveways and wooded lawns of beautiful, lush acreage. In the rear of the house were stables, greenhouses, and a brook that poured into a larger stream. Even with this impressive home, Lewis was never smug regarding the business wealth he amassed. His wealth never turned him into a lazy aristocrat. It just spurred him to turn and help the surrounding community work. He felt humbled by the respect and affection of those who worked for him and with him.[5]

Oak Place existed as a beacon of hospitality. In the colder months, the Millers beckoned the visitors to sit by a blazing fire in the sitting room. Mina's many spirited brothers and sisters filled the library, formal drawing room, and kitchen. There were ten in all. The magnificent attic on the third floor included a playroom, gymnasium, and a children's stage for family productions and winter circuses. Moreover, a printing shop for Mina's younger brothers self-published the family newsletter, called *The Jumbo*.

Lewis regularly brought home guests from his various businesses and church matters. The children were instructed how to engage with the company and were included with their parents and all guests. Good-humored banter and familial give-and-take enlivened every dinner. The children learned to appreciate and emulate their father's energetic engagement in the nation's economic life. They all admired and hoped to mimic their father's pluck and persistence, which they believed made him successful—adding a gentleness of manner and a unique comradeship that endeared him to all his households. He earned eternal loyalty.

The staff arranged provisions handy in the butler's pantry for an unplanned visitor. The children were not to enter the dining room and eat later if there was not ample room for them and the guests. Certainly not made to feel as lesser or irrelevant, the children were encouraged to bring home friends as often as they wished. They understood that continual hospitality existed as the chief guiding principle of the household. After her husband, Mary Valinda found her most noble cause in serving her children's needs. Her endless love gave each child the opportunity to discover themselves and let their character permeate the family dynamic.[6]

The year Lewis and Mary Valinda bought their house, they had seven children paired with a staff of seven, including three domestic servants, two dressmakers, a gardener, and an additional man as a styler whose work changed with the needs of the day. The oldest four children—Eva, Jennie, Ira, and Robert—attended the finest boarding schools. The three youngest—Lewis, Mina, and Mame—anticipated their planned return. Despite their varied ages, the children were close and lively when together. The endless manicured grounds enabled infinite pursuits. Only the seasons dictated their activities. In winter, they were racing their sleighs down the knolls; spring and summer summoned a competitive game of croquet or lawn tennis. Domestic animals of all kinds were loved and cared for by the children. Both the animals and children walked along the many graveled footpaths. They would visit the peacocks on the grounds and admire lush gardens with their unusual flowers for the Midwest. Lewis took pride in the beautiful gardens, in which he took a deep personal interest. During the day, the children played on grasses, providing extra care their voices would not scare the various waterfowl who lived in the duck pond. Lewis Miller was a passionate man. He worshiped and loved on a primal level with an intensity his peers could not match. He and many gardeners attended the greenhouse. While relaxing, Lewis could be spotted cultivating flower buds and blooms from season to season. He would admire each plant as though it were his only child. He tended to their blossoming in a kindhearted way.[7]

By the time Edison visited in 1885, three more children had been born into the Miller clan. Grace, John Vincent (named after Rev. Vincent), and Theodore, the youngest. John and Theodore were three years older than Edison's sons, Tom Jr. and William. The Miller parents fostered the boys' enthusiastic nature. Lewis and Mary Valinda raised all the children to be go-getters regardless of their varied interests. Lewis saw each child differently and wrote down their most prominent trait in one of his sketches for the garden. Eva Smart, Jennie Proper, Ira Dignity, Edward Independent, Robert Joker, Lewis Friendly, Mina Lover and Lively, Mary Go-Getter, Grace Scholar, John Follower, Theodore Best Liked Organizer. Unfortunately, Miller's high standards caused the family's daughters to suffer from routine self-doubt. They often revealed to their sisters that they felt "blue" yet hoped the mood would soon pass.[8]

While Edison stayed with Mina's family, he witnessed the hubbub and noted Lewis Miller's reputation and standing in the Akron community. The local paper reported Lewis's philanthropic nature. Adjacent towns were aware of his largesse as an earnest business leader and a Methodist. Less than forty miles away, in Alliance, Ohio, a fellow Methodist, Orville Nelson Hartshorn, established a small college known as Mount Union College. Hartshorn recruited notable leaders to add to his board of trustees. Hartshorn approached Lewis, who accepted the invitation due to his impassioned interest in practical education. Lewis inhabited his role with delight and expanded the school's enrollment. Lewis remained on the board, but he prioritized addressing students on the benefits of education frequently.

Lewis donated $75,000 ($1.2 million in today's money) to build a men's dormitory. Then an additional $25,000 ($400,000 in today's money) to endow a chair at Mount Union College. Lewis was consumed with the future of Methodists and their ability to obtain a well-rounded education. His vision was that all ambitious young people needed the opportunity to reach their goals regardless of their standing in society. He insisted faculty coordinate their teaching with the many students who also worked on their parents' farms and did not have the luxury to leave the farms due to their work. He stayed sensitive due to his upbringing and lack of formal education.[9]

Edison understood how enmeshed the Millers were in their devotion to family and Methodism. He recalled how his mother forced religious belief on him, although he unequivocally rejected all of it. As an inventor, he claimed he could not believe in things that he could not see with his own eyes. Regrettably, this matter would be a source of contention that Mina and Edison endured their entire lives. No matter how hard Mina tried to persuade Edison to join any church or see benefit from belief, she would never succeed.

Edison enjoyed his stay at the Millers' and made a vivid impression on Mina's two younger brothers, Theodore and John Vincent. He often connected well with children who were not his own. Mina's younger brothers possessed an innate love of learning and showed great aptitude for understanding new concepts. This combination mirrored Edison's abilities. While Edison interacted with the boys, the Millers witnessed a kindhearted side of his personality. Observing their interaction dispelled reservations about the wedding being two months away. Jennie and her mother and other members of the family who were too timid to voice their concerns were lulled into a false sense of security that Edison possessed a nurturing soul and his marriage to Mina would bring it forth.

Perceptive of the two last holdouts in the Miller family, Edison needed to secure the February wedding date. So, he sent the two youngest boys a lengthy letter describing the accompanied Christmas presents he shipped them—"an electric shocking coil . . . [and] a telescope which shows the rings of Saturn. . . . I hope it will suit you . . . hoping you will have a merry Christmas and not watch me and Mina so closely when

I come again." With the gifts came detailed instructions and explanations for their use. The letter and gifts formed a mutual bond between the young boys and Edison. But, as with all Edison's close relationships, it subsisted on a displayed interest and propensity for electrically powered devices—something his own sons lacked.[10]

The letter and gifts soothed Jennie and her mother's apprehensions about Edison's affection, intentions, and warmth. However, Edison contained one more trick up his sleeve to woo the Millers. Edison needed to locate and purchase a house for his new bride. So, he asked Mina if she would prefer to live in the city—a mansion on Riverside Drive near one of his financiers, Charles Schwab, or in a country home. Mina worried that a house in the city might keep him in a business meeting at all hours of the night; she chose to live in the country, confident it would mimic a lifestyle with which she was familiar.

Three weeks after his departure from Akron, on January 12th, Edison was considering purchasing a property in Llewellyn Park in Orange, New Jersey (currently known as West Orange). Llewellyn Park was one of the first planned residential communities in the United States. It was set on 350 acres and was twelve miles from New York City. Llewellyn Haskell, a drug manufacturer, and partner, Alexander Davis, a landscape architect, designed the community. They mimicked several aspects they admired of the famed landscape architects Frederick Law Olmstead and Calvert Vaux. They designed large areas with overgrown trees, vibrant bushes, winding roads, and a mountain stream. Gates and large, sloping lawns separated each home to create aristocratic country estates; each property owner comprised a fifty-acre plot for their estate.[11]

Edison bought his home from Henry and Louisa Pedder. The house was built in 1880 and designed by famed architect and writer Henry Hudson Holly. His most famous popular book, *Modern Dwellings in Town and Country*, expressed his attitude toward architecture. A strong proponent of the Queen Anne style, he chose many verandas placed on the east side of the home, where they would receive the most shade. The family's parlor, or room most used, stood on the sunny south side, where it would shelter from winter wind yet be cooled off by summer breezes. The conservatory held numerous plants—the dining room was placed in the west so the family could enjoy the sun setting while dining. The library was on the northern side for its exposure to continual light, and the kitchen remained positioned in the least-desirable direction. However, Holly advocated humane treatment of servants and made their quarters airy, with a hall and separate sitting and dining areas for the staff.

Named Glenmont, the house was one of the largest in Llewellyn Park. It boasted many gabled structures surrounded by manicured lawns and colorful shrubs. It was positioned on a knoll facing the east and covered ten acres. Part of the ground was wooded and comprised of extensive greenhouses and stables.

Henry Pedder worked in New York City as a confidential clerk for the large department store Arnold Constable & Co. The Pedders bought the house for $271,000: $36,000 for the land and $235,000 ($6.3 million in today's money) for the improvements made throughout their years living there. In 1884, Pedder was caught embezzling hundreds of thousands of dollars from his firm and ran off to Europe. When he returned to the United States, he paid restitution and handed his entire Llewellyn Park property to his firm for $1.00; then, he fled to St. Kitts.

Arnold Constable & Co. acquired all of Henry Pedder's land, totaling twenty-three acres. In addition, it received all the fixtures, furniture, and personal property within the building. The company retained ownership of the house for one year and five months.

In the spring of 1885, the company decided to sell the home. Edison showed Mina the house at the end of 1885. Days later, Edison received a letter from a real estate agent that they would like to "submit our services, learning you consider the purchase of Real Estate and would suggest the property recently occupied by Mr. H.C. Pedder in Llewellyn Park. . . . The property has cost some $400,000 furnished ($11.8 million in today's money). It can be bought fully at half its cost, either furnished or unfurnished."

Unknown to the broker, Edison bought the property directly from Arnold Constable & Co. the day before. He paid only $125,000 ($3.6 million in today's money) for the twenty-three-room house, the outside buildings, and the land. A separate contract for $1.00 included all the

Pedders' furnishings and personal possessions listed in a thirty-six-page itemized inventory.

Edison took a mortgage from the seller for $85,000 ($2.5 million in today's money), which he paid in two installments: $10,000 ($295,000 in today's money) in July 1886 and the second for $75,000 ($2.2 million in today's money) years later in 1890. When the press heard of Edison's most impressive latest acquisition, he attempted to earn favor from his audience: "When I entered this, I was paralyzed. To think that it was possible to buy a place like this, which a man with a taste for art and a talent for decoration had put ten years of enthusiastic study and effort into—the idea fairly turned my head, and I snapped it up. It is a great deal too nice for me, but it isn't half nice enough for my little wife here."[12]

Hundreds of papers raced to print Edison's purchase of his luxurious new home. Mina delighted in reading phrases such as "Edison would be electrifying his friends by bringing a blooming and beautiful bride to occupy the enormously expansive house." Countless letters arrived at Oak Place, remarking on Edison's generosity when it came to his future bride. As a result, Mina's restless mind took a hiatus from its frantic state. The hectic pace surrounding planning an enormous wedding in a short time frame took on a more relaxed sheen.[13]

The latest events placed Mina in an unfamiliar state of temporary calmness. Still not mature enough to restrain herself, she shared her happiness with her chum Louise. Mina lived as the eternal vacillator. Her inability to make decisions shaped her personality. Few women ever asked Mina for advice; instead, she sought it from others. Within the past weeks, the entire nation learned the name Mina Miller. It was an opportune time to disclose to her friends her new persona. She believed she had shed her insecure days and reinvented herself into a young woman the public would admire. Louise, a rare woman, never expressed jealousy regarding her friends' successes. In all earnest, she was pleased to hear that her young friend Mina had finally reached a state of bliss.

Louise's affirmations were most beneficial to Mina, unlike her mother's and Jennie's. The latter contained worry or ominousness. On the other hand, Louise's constructive reflections about her recent courtship and the trajectory of her life left Mina more contented. Countless years in the

Methodist Church schooled Mina to internalize constructive words when heard, allow them to permeate one's soul, and aid one through future struggles. Mina could not be happier. At that moment, she thought her life with Edison would be nothing short of a bed of roses.

Louise said Mina would be the perfect woman to be the new Mrs. Edison. So aware the role was extraordinary, it would take an exceptional young woman to fill that spot. There would be constant world travel, two homes to maintain, and industry heads to entertain. Louise, a consummate wordsmith, summed up Mina's life as "surely a girl born to luck."[14]

⚊ ⌣

Those words could not be more apt. Even as a young girl, Mina knew that the timing of her birth was exceptional. It was 1865, and Mary Valinda was in the ninth month of her seventh pregnancy. The country was ready for rebirth on a global and intimate scale.

July 4th of 1865 would be memorable in Ohio for so many. For the first time since the original Independence Day, the United States flag waved in peace over a nation of free men, turning its back on the past four years of war. The people of Ohio were thankful to God that their ears were not deafened by cannons or their hearts were not saddened by an impending battle. Instead, everyone felt confident it would be a day of celebration and joy.

Sensible families went to bed early the night of the third. They awakened with the sun the next day and embraced every moment the day would bring. Oversized flags hung prominently from porches dotting the block with hues of the nation. Smaller versions of the nation's flag darted through the streets in the palms of excited children. Visions of blurs of color appeared between untroubled strolling adults. Excited shrieks of children were at every corner.

Vessels of every size lined the rivers with banners adorning them from stem to stern. Mother Nature joined in the merriment and left the sky flawless with a few small clouds whose only task was to occasionally block the sun from squinting eyes. The souls and minds of Americans were finally at peace. The jubilant mood in the streets of Ohio floated over into the house of Lewis and Mary Valinda Miller.[15]

While many were outdoors celebrating the birth of the nation, Lewis Miller was celebrating the imminent expansion of his own family. He was known in the city for his zeal and enthusiasm in life, and he could not contain his joy; he was by no means finished procreating, in his mind. Moreover, his wife ceaselessly enticed him. Her distinctive kindness and mutual respect delighted him in ways that he acted upon in the privacy of their bedroom.

When the celebrating died down across the country, it was reborn in the Miller household; the seventh child was a baby girl. They named her Mina. She would bring the number of the Millers' daughters to three. The staff of seven provided Mary Valinda with more than ample help. The local newspaper, satisfying the gazers in town, reported his salary. Lewis Miller's income for 1865 was $55,821 ($903,000 in today's money). The Miller children were not denied any material goods in return for exceptional manners and faithful adherence to Methodism.[16]

By Mina's twelfth birthday, eight years since Eva died, Miller's eleventh and last child, Theodore, was approaching three years of age. The family had entered somewhat of a daily routine. The oldest daughter, Jennie, age twenty-four, still not married, traveled on an extended trip to Europe. Jennie molded herself into a woman of impeccable taste and used her varied experiences in Europe to impart knowledge and behavior to her younger siblings.

Knowing someday she would be traveling abroad, Mina was keenly interested and inquired about cultural landmarks, museums, and architecture. Mina, ten years younger, was still in public schools and had yet to leave Ohio. Nevertheless, Mina knew it was valuable information to have at one's fingertips for social situations and took care to review her letters. Mina's mother welcomed Jennie's role in the family; she never possessed the opportunity to travel extensively before having children. Jennie's personality lent itself to this position, and she effortlessly styled her siblings in her preferred model.

Mina's older brothers displayed other traits she wanted to emulate. At college, Ira, eighteen years old, wrote about the merriments that accompanied university, yet he included his grades to reinforce the importance of high achievement. Each family letter to and from their school stated their siblings' academic standing. Top grades and other successes were always shared and celebrated with the family, illustrating the value of academic accomplishments. These exchanges fostered closeness and mutual dependency throughout the family.[17]

European travel was not exclusive to Jennie. Lewis Miller had once traveled in Spain with his son Edward and then, on a whim, decided to meet Jennie in Paris while she was there for the year. Thus, the family absorbed the varied European culture while maintaining their Midwest mores.

While the older children toured Europe mimicking the idle knickerbockers of the day, Mina spent the weekends of her early teenage years memorizing the Methodist doctrine at their church. She recited *Heathen Woman's Friend* to the local devotees who crammed the pews every Sunday. Careful to enunciate every word, Mina described the conditions of church mission fieldwork. She documented their successes of Christianizing heathen women in her proudest tone to fellow believers.

Not once had Mina questioned the harsh doctrine of Methodist teaching, and she unequivocally accepted the law. On the contrary, she believed God sent it from above. Her letters bear witness to a fleeting moment of spiritual questioning when Mina reached her teens. As an adolescent, she commenced to think and feel for herself. Trusting her mother, Mina dared to question the severity mentioned in a sermon that terrified her. To avoid retribution, her mother remarked, "I do hope my dear ones will always be worthy of a good name." Those words remained in Mina's mind for the rest of her life. When at a pivotal crossroad, Mina would recall how vital it is to be known for a good name, works, and moral standing.[18]

Many Methodists interpreted idle gossip as a divergence from the religious dogma; the Miller family, however, sanctioned its use once a year when they consorted with the superficial aspects of society and shifted their focus to fashion, money, and social standing. New Year's brought opportunities for the Millers to hold court among Ohio's high-minded individuals. Mina and her sisters hosted an annual New Year's Day open house. Dressed in their recent lavish acquisitions, they received guests and good wishes. Predictably, the newspaper's description of the Miller parlor was nothing less than sumptuous. Other advantaged ladies who desired to go along with this annual rite parked their perfectly tailored dresses the appropriate distance from the Miller girls and plastered a well-trained smile on their faces for friends and interlopers alike. It was unambiguous to fifteen-year-old Mina that her surname earned a coveted position. Mina was confident and well-respected at that very point in her life. Faith and status were the two sole building blocks that defined her self-identity and worth; however, at that point, Mina's world contained little else. She was not sophisticated enough to understand the varied shades of life and believed Lewis and Mary Valinda coveted little else.

The Summit County Beacon further buttressed Mina's mistaken perceptions of what remained essential. The local paper was keen on building its readership and, in due course, triple its profits based on the appetite for local gossip about the upper crust of Akron. Knowing the Miller father's lifestyle sold many papers, the children's happenings would undoubtedly produce the same if not better results. During the Gilded Age, there was a stark divide between the wealthy class and the have-nots. Those without were anxious to read and glimpse how the others lived. The activities of the famed Miller clan and their ilk sold papers by the pound. A reporter was dispatched at once if they got wind of a Miller function or incident.

One such story relished by readers started that June. It reported that "Nine Akron young ladies with uniform hats were on the square last night shopping and attracted attention." One of these young ladies was Mina. The other eight were Mary Hopkins, Bell Ruggles, Clara Simbers, Emma Sierberling, Cora Wise, Hattie Seiberling, Mattie Henry, and Anna Upson. After numerous reports in the "Social Notes" column, the group of nine young ladies earned the moniker of "The Decimal Club." The group was deemed exclusive, which inflated their already-outsized egos. Still elevating the Miller family above other prominent families in the region, the newspaper reported that "the social event of 1881" was hosted by Jacob Miller of Canton. His brother and wife, Mr. and Mrs. Lewis Miller of Akron, his sons and daughters, and two hundred guests were in attendance. For Mina, life couldn't be more sparkling.[19]

That June, Mina once again stood out from her peers in her ivory-colored Venetian lace gown among the twenty-five other graduates at the commencement exercises of the Akron High School Class of 1883. Superintendent Findley was pleased to boast that ten of the twenty-six graduates would continue their education. Mina and two of her classmates were headed east to be "finished" at prestigious seminaries rather than a traditional college. There is no record of Mina receiving any academic honors; however, she once again proved her ability to speak comfortably in front of a large crowd and recited a short essay at the afternoon ceremony.[20]

With three months to prepare for her upcoming move to Boston, Mina arranged plenty of time to do what she enjoyed most: socializing with girlfriends. Her parents chose her finishing school for its academic standards, but it was clear to the family that being close to George at Yale would benefit Mina if she needed any emotional support. That summer, Mina appeared confident and mature while surrounded by familiar things. She spent most of her summer visiting friends in Indianapolis or hosting them at Oak Place. From her letters, one can picture a cheerful young woman hoping to marry her childhood sweetheart as soon as possible. Back then, wise-minded Louise cautioned Mina; it was too premature for thoughts or discussion of a wedding.

It was not easy for Mina to focus on school when her sister was constantly sending silks and lace from Europe, and her mother's chief concern was using the best dressmaker in town. As a result, Mina preferred parties and teas, and she said little about her upcoming classes. Instead, she mostly spoke of improving her piano skills and finding a girlfriend with whom to attend church service.

Mina's school year began that October and brought feelings of excitement and fear of the unknown. Her first letters home reveal a young girl slightly homesick. To suppress her sadness, she visited her high school classmates attending other schools in the area. The Millers reassured Mina that her feelings were typical of a child who leaves home for the first time. Her older brother Robert cautioned her to take advantage of "all the opportunities" Boston and the school offered. Assuming a parental role, he reminded her of the enormous expense of sending her East, hoping the sheer guilt would shake her of what he understood to be navel-gazing and complaining about nothing.[21]

Her younger sister Mame took a more female tactic to lessen her loneliness. First, she told Mina in no uncertain terms that George would make life "more pleasant" for her if she visited him. Then, quoting from the week's previous sermon, Mary Valinda instructed her daughter, "the world is a schoolhouse, and the one teacher gives us some hard lessons to learn." Despite all the encouragement, Mina could not locate her muscle memory of her previous carefree days of life in Akron.[22]

Jennie, who spent time between New York and Akron, was dispatched to Boston to spend a Sunday with Mina, which boosted her spirits. Subsequently, the Vincents invited Mina to spend Thanksgiving with them, which was agreeable. Further mollifying her worries, Jennie instructed her to enjoy the various boutiques of the area and search for just the right hat and collar for her visit with the Vincents. However, in Mina's following letter, the outing to the shops of Boston only posed negligible effects on her mood: "Oh, how I would love to be home today; it is so stupid here with no one but strangers about you." Mina admitted she had one solace: her new "peculiar looking" friend, Helen Morgan, whom Mina assessed, "from her dress you would think money not too much." Nevertheless, she made up for her fashion deficiencies by making Mina laugh "when she imitates Miss Johnson," the headmaster.[23]

Mary Valinda counseled her with her well-meaning and ever-predictable religious phrases: "the creator will give you the guidance if you let him to help clarify your thoughts." A careful appraisal of her mother's reflections reframed Mina's attitude. Unsophisticated in understanding her thoughts, Mina struggled to understand her mixed feelings. She needed direct advice to mimic rather than go through the complexity of analyzing herself and her needs. Mary Valinda knew all her children and their varied personalities, and she applied the most fitting comments in each letter that left her home: "It is pretty nice to have a good and smart husband; Folkes will notice you . . . on his account." Mary Valinda's intention to include this anecdote could suggest ambiguous readings. Mina tended to interpret life in its most literal form and understood it as a criterion in choosing a husband.[24]

Mina's recent joy with Edison felt similar to the best days of her younger life. She was sauntering around town with her chums, greeting varied guests on New Year's, and speaking at her graduation. Basking in the limelight thrilled Mina. While at school in Boston, the other girls barely noticed her. No one understood or cared about her prior importance. She did not have the wherewithal to prove her worth academically. Mina, conscious not to compete with the wolves from Boston, averted a feeling of loss. She preferred to hide like a sheep. One decision altered her trajectory. Applying her mother's aphorisms aided her in finding her true path. Mina felt mature once she decided to become Mrs. Thomas Edison. Now, to be sure, there was no challenging Mina's new mindset; she would rise above all others and revel in fame for the rest of her life.[25]

4

Becoming Mrs. Edison

WHILE THE MILLERS WERE MAILING THE LAST WEDDING INVITATIONS, the press got wind of the news. The editorial board of the *New York Tribune* deemed it front-page news. By the end of the first week of February, newspapers nationwide picked up the story, placing it no deeper than page two. The prominence of Lewis Miller and the more celebrated name of Edison made the marriage of great interest. Copious congratulatory wishes poured in. The country's appetite for the Edison and Miller courtship could not be sated.[1]

Filled with happiness, Mary Valinda basked in her finest milieu. Her husband would lead the first of ten children to the hymeneal altar. Lewis Miller's fortune at present stood at $2,500,000. ($70 million in today's money). The rumor mill churned with no expense spared for this affair. Lewis Miller held no intention of disappointing his admirers.

The next three weeks' papers carried all aspects of the upcoming merger—Mina was introduced with brown hair, medium height, a well-developed figure, and a peach-like expression. Nine days before the wedding, the news of the courtship traveled to London, Scotland, and Australian papers. The Miller family felt firsthand the scope of Edison's fame; the experience was overpowering. Even before the wedding took place, the world could describe the greatest inventor's future bride.

For the next three weeks, pre-wedding activity absorbed the Miller household. They reflected that their fame would be put off to a late date. Mary Valinda finalized the detailed one-hundred-person guest list. Lewis

Miller hired H. M. Kinsley, Chicago's finest caterer, along with fifteen waiters, for a sumptuous reception dinner, and he purchased Prince Albert suits with matching gloves for his sons. Mary Valinda and her daughters wore different-colored silk accentuating their features and adorned with endless lace trim, in keeping with the times.

Mina's gown presented the epitome of elegance. The most delicate white silk and long veil embroidered with Duchesse and point lace, finished with a corsage square neckline, complemented her physique. Her diamond and pearl necklace filled her neckline, glistening and glimmering when hit by the sunlight. Mina was confident her dress would make a lasting impression. The glamorous appearance of a fairy tale–like wedding would make great copy for the papers.

Back in New York, preparations for the wedding ensued as well. Edison disliked the winter months and decided to depart from Akron on the evening of the wedding and honeymoon in Florida in his new home. Mary Valinda wanted Mina to convince him to remain a few days before leaving, but Edison's overpowering personality remained closed to negotiations. The pre-fab homes he and Gilliland had designed were sent down by a schooner from Maine. The houses were scheduled to be delivered and built before his arrival. Edison planned to remain in the South and work there through the winter, then return to his new home in West Orange in late April.

A decision needed to be made regarding Edison's three children. Edison possessed no regret in excluding his ten- and eight-year-old sons from his plans. They would not attend the wedding nor see their father and new stepmother until they returned two months later. Although ample guests could have accompanied the boys to and from the wedding, the boys' involvement in his daily life remained of little concern to Edison. Arrangements were made for the boys to be watched by Edison's brother William, known to the family as Pitt, and his wife, Ellen. Sixteen years Edison's senior, he and his wife were empty nesters. The pace of their life allowed them to care for Edison's boys for a lengthy period. Their daughter Nellie, eleven years younger than Edison, had married William Poyer, a grain merchant from Ohio. Nellie made a habit of corresponding with her famous uncle. Her numerous letters rewarded her with an invite to the celebrated wedding. Her younger brother Charlie had also rubbed elbows with his renowned uncle. Years before, he had worked in Menlo Park, proving himself worthy, and subsequently he was sent over to England to demonstrate the Edison telephone. Unfortunately, his luck turned sour; he contracted peritonitis and died before his twentieth birthday.

In order to keep the boys on a regular schedule, they remained in school while Pitt and Ellen stayed with them at their new home in Glenmont. After settling in, the boys thrived and drank in the much-needed attention their aunt and uncle bestowed on them. Fastening their heart to their stepmother's photograph, they told her, "We kiss our new mama every night be fore going to bed." Then, hoping to find favor in their father's eyes, they added, "Willie and I goes [sic] to school every day I was promoted in higher room in the fifth reader and willie is in the second reader and I am in long division, and willie is in subtraction." The boys were "well"; they each played with their rabbit and pigeons on the lawn while "uncle and antie give us all the candy."[2]

Well aware of her father's pecking order, Marion remained outspoken and tended to be provocative, believing this remained the best tactic to stay in view in papa's universe. The winter after her mother's death, her father moved the family to an apartment in Manhattan but retained his mother-in-law as the housekeeper. Marion "loved being wanted" and never complained that she missed the ponies from her New Jersey life. Marion spent her days after school procuring cigars, cashing checks, and listening in on her father's meetings, requiring love over traditional childhood. No one dared to question his parenting skills. The local paper once reported that Marion sat aboard a train with her father, who was so preoccupied with his next idea that he left her sitting alone when he exited the train and began walking home. The conductor recognized her before the door closed and brought her to her father's side.[3]

When plans were made about the wedding and trip to Florida, Marion exhibited no intention of being pawned off on her family and missing the subsequent events. Reflecting on those days in her memoir, she claimed: "She never missed a trick."[4]

Yielding to a convention, Edison enrolled Marion in school. However, all the recent activities made her fall behind at Madame Mears boarding and day school in New York City, where she was registered. The headmistress wrote Edison and regretted "this interruption to her studies, as she has been making very satisfactory improvement [and] would like to know when to expect her again in her classes. Her Music lessons are also interrupted, which is a real loss to her." Edison did not put much stock in his daughter's education, often taking her out if it did not suit his schedule. This was not the first time Madame Mears "requested that [Marion] could be with me altogether in boarding-school, as the regularity of her study would tend greatly to her progress." Last October, she hoped to "persuade" Edison to board his daughter at school to avoid the distractions of "engagements at home." Edison entertained no intention of boarding his daughter at that juncture and arranged that his secretary inform the school she would not be returning for the rest of the year. Making a mental note of her time away, he refused to pay for the balance of the year's tuition.[5]

Edison's mind focused only on one thing at that juncture: indeed, not the pomp wedding, nor Marion missing school. It was the new home and laboratory in Fort Myers. While winning this month's battle but not the war, Marion was permitted to join the Gillilands as they traveled to the South. Edison instructed Ezra and Lillian to take Marion and a maid down to Florida, circumventing the wedding entirely. He needed someone he could trust to oversee their new homes and ensure the laboratory arrived safely. Edison hoped to commence experiments in their new laboratory as soon as he arrived in Fort Myers. Significant planning and finances were involved in the transport, and leaving the arrival to chance would not do. Safeguarding the bride from feeling slighted on her special day, the Gillilands made a brief visit to Akron before the wedding and extended their good wishes.

There is no record from any correspondence that Mina agreed to host her stepdaughter during her honeymoon. The Gillilands bought their own home and would not infringe on their intimacy. Marion, however, would be residing with them. Mina would be forced to fare with the arrangements made by her future husband. Recalling her mother's advice, she kept her feelings to herself and appeared "a good and happy help mate—a wife he may be proud of."[6]

Before Edison's arrival, his colleagues planned the bachelor party for Saturday evening, February 20th. Ensuring Edison would attend, it happened at his favorite dining haunt, Delmonico's. Known for its rich cuisine and opulent surroundings, Edison and nine of his closest colleagues toasted their kingpin while imbibing fine wine and devouring steaks and twenty bottles of champagne. After the others wished him farewell, he and his best man, Frank Tappan, a retired Navy man from Massachusetts, traveled toward Akron. Following him in the next car were many presents for the new couple. The remaining guests would be returning to work. They would arrive on the Tuesday evening train for the nuptials on Wednesday.[7]

Upon his arrival in Akron, Edison gained a chance to catch up with various family members who had made the journey to toast him and his new wife. His sister Marion attended with her husband, Homer Page. Twice Edison's age, she and her husband, Homer, still lived in Milan, Ohio; they were fond of the town and remained committed to its landscape. His uncle Simeon Edison and his wife came from Cleveland to attend. Simeon was Edison's father's half-brother and worked as an iron dealer; he was as industrious as his nephew. Although he had recently established the Edison Lock Co., he remained savvy enough to stay close to his wealthy nephew if ever came the point in his life that he would need Edison's assistance. This occurred in August 1890, when Edison gave Simeon $10,000 to start a business and also put him on the payroll at $125 a month for the next three years.

Conspicuously absent was Edison's father, Samuel Edison. He had not yet experienced an opportunity to travel to Europe and explore his ancestry. Aware of his father's desire, his son offered to pick up the tab in 1878. Various circumstances prevented the trip from coming to fruition. Regardless of the wedding, Samuel Edison, now ninety years old, finally took his son up on his offer. Arriving in London, Samuel Edison, trading on his son's name, as well as his line of credit, was a "select guest" of the Prince of Wales and "enjoyed himself accordingly."[8]

Lured by the fragrance of rose blossoms, the guests yearned to discover the source of the lovely scent. The florist had built walls of roses displayed throughout the home—lavish décor designed by florists from

Cleveland and New York. Gazing eyes took in a vast floral bell that suspended over the foot of the staircase. Garlands of shiny deep-green smilax vines adorned the bright chandeliers. The effect made the room spectacular. Blooms and potted plants were placed in every inch of the house. Oak Place was transformed into an indoor botanical garden for everyone to enjoy.

The nation's recent prosperous and unprecedented growth in industry and technology allowed the hosts and invitees to enjoy extraordinary wealth and opulence. Each woman's dress was adorned more lavishly than the next. Confident the papers would not miss a detail, the guests were eager to exhibit their spoils. Mrs. Goodman King, one of the heirs to the famous jewelry house Mermod Jaccard & King in St. Louis, arrived wearing white satin with lace trimming and diamonds. Mrs. Jacob Miller, the bride's aunt, wore pink silk with pearl trimmings and diamonds, and Mrs. G. C. Berry of Akron, whose husband ran a successful home-furnishing company, wore white satin square lace trimming and diamonds. As the ritual appraising died down, the guests took their seats, anticipating the occasion that had brought them there.

The last stroke of three on Wednesday, February 26th, 1886, brought a hush to the one hundred guests and the bridal party's entrance. A member of the church choir played the "Wedding March" by Lohengrin, and the notes echoed throughout the home. Emerging from his widowhood, Edison was the first to enter, accompanied by his best man. Hair slightly gray yet still with a youthful groom appearance, Edison wore a black Prince Albert coat and tie but left his hands ungloved. Noticing the glaring omission, the traditional crowd did not have an opportunity to comment. Within moments, the triumphant Miller family walked down the aisle, Mrs. Miller leaning on the arm of the oldest son, Ira. Jennie followed with Edward, then Mame with Robert, and finally Lewis Jr. and Grace. Then, rising and turning to the rear, the crowd witnessed Mr. Miller walking his daughter Mina down the aisle toward Thomas Alva Edison; one of the most notable weddings in history was about to take place.[9]

Despite the decision to remove his gloves and prove to the world that he was a working man, not a man of excess, he willingly knelt on a velvet cushion with his bride, presided by Reverend Doctor E. K. Young, pastor of the First Methodist Episcopal Church. Adorning the altar was another canopy of palms, the back of which overflowed with calla lilies. The piano played once more Mendelssohn's wedding march as the recessional.

The couple received their friends under a floral wishbone made of roses with white and pink carnations forming the initials *E* and *M*. Numerous gifts were displayed in the parlor for their purview: ruby and sapphire pins, a column of gold and onyx, silverwork of all kinds; diamonds in great profusion and endless tables of sterling silverware. Once the ogling subsided, the guest enjoyed a six-course dinner.

Edison believed he had devoted more than ample time to the Millers, their religion, and their social status, and less than four hours after making his entrance, he made his exit. The pair climbed into a new, handsome cab and traveled down the hill onto the main thoroughfare of Haward Street. They paused a moment to climb the steps of a photographer's office to pose for pictures. Then, within moments, Edison, along with his newest and most attractive business acquisition, boarded the 6:48 train in a private car. The optimistic Mrs. Edison was now heading toward Cincinnati, later making scheduled stops in Atlanta and Jacksonville, then proceeding to Fort Myers to begin the next stage of her life.[10]

In the course of his travels, Edison, while stretching his legs at a station platform, used the opportunity to promote his final destination: "Fort Myers is at the extremist point of the Florida Peninsula . . . 150 miles further south than most tourists go." Accenting its seclusion, he added, "the railroad goes to within twenty-eight miles of the place, and I have a steam yacht to get me there." With little time to reboard, Edison cut short the questions shouted at the couple. Keeping up his public image, he ended the interview with the flair of a ringmaster: "Sharks eighteen feet long . . . fish that weigh 500 pounds . . . perfect white sand strewn with beautiful shells . . . I am sure Mrs. Edison will be enchanted with it."[11]

Farther down the rail line, fields laden with cotton pickers soon ensnared Edison more than his wife's reflection. Mina realized her husband was preoccupied with the foliage and, in particular, the "peach groves in bloom." Thursday brought the newlyweds to stay at the Kimball Hotel in Atlanta. Edison readily engaged with the encircling press and several locals who had learned of his arrival. Attesting to his newest interest, he queried, "how much cotton can a hand pick in a day?" Then, producing a current sketch out of his pocket, he went on: "I have a cotton picker here. See … I've been studying the question, and sure as I live, I got the idea here." Claiming he would revolutionize the industry, he relished their adoration of the onlookers. Amateur inventors came from the state to catch a glimpse and bask in the glory of the man whom they dubbed a genius. "Giving away a great many autographs" and attending to their patent ideas, Edison enjoyed the zeal of his admirers much more than making small talk at his wedding. Separating the enthusiasts from their wizard was the 3 p.m. departing train toward their ultimate destination. Few things rivaled those satisfying moments for Edison. It would take many years for Mina to learn that lesson.[12]

The St. James Hotel in Jacksonville made Mina feel more at home. First, it was one of the state's finest hotels. Then, within the past few years, a different story had confirmed its respect by tourists and locals. The Stick-style structure could accommodate five hundred guests by this time and boasted, among other features, telegraph offices, a passenger elevator, steam heat, electric lighting, an orchestra, and "plenty of agreeable society."

Meanwhile, the unfamiliar experiences were piling up and cramming Mina's head. Desperate for an outlet and connection to her home, she wrote her mother: "This is Sunday, and I now know right where you are … I see you all at church." She longed to hear the hymns that brought serenity to her family on the Lord's Day. Edison did not appreciate Lewis Miller dropping the *Book of Discipline* into his coat pocket. Confronting Mina, he "asked her if [she] married him to convert him." Mina was not mentally astute with a master wordsmith and recoiled. Witnessing his wife's posture, Edison restrained himself but continued his campaign. "He wants to believe but … has such an inquiring mind that he cannot believe what he cannot see." Softening further, he did not want Mina "to be influenced in the least by him nor believe anything he says on the subject." For the time being, the couple realized a heated debate on their honeymoon did not bode well for the future; therefore, "No talking or arguing on the subject will do any good."[13]

So far, the honeymoon was nothing like the young bride envisioned. She was not comfortable with her lodgings or the new surroundings, and she told her mother she "hardly leave[s] my room until we leave again, that is I do not go to my meals . . . but Mr. E. has taken a drive about to see the sights." Endeavoring to share interesting facts, she disclosed, "we saw peach groves in bloom. . . . The orange trees all seem to have been killed." Oblivious that she was the product of the cloistered world, she "has seen nothing yet resembling the jungles read and seen illustrated in books. . . . You would or will be surprised when you see how they live here in towns! Nothing to them whatever and a dozen or so of colored people living in a house with probably but one room and no windows. All the men of color are so black here; nearly every one of the darkest shade."[14]

Freely admitting the accommodations were not up to her standards, Mina declared, "This is a miserable hotel and a worse city. . . . I am not as well . . . but nothing serious." Remaining optimistic, "a few days will bring me out aright again." The tone of her letters was filled with longing for her previous life in Akron, and she wondered "whether all the beautiful decorations have been removed. I wish I might see them again. I shall never forget what a beautiful sight you all made . . . nor can I ever forget when we as a family were in the Sitting room." The tenor of her letters changed again when Mina admitted, "People stare at us so; all knowing that the person with me is Mr. Edison who was just been married . . . [it] causes quite a stir." [15]

Edison telegrammed Ezra Gilliland frequently, requesting updates on the status of their new houses. Upon discovering the houses were not complete, Edison became frustrated. The Gillilands and his daughter were forced to stay at the nearby Keystone Hotel. Besides cabling Florida, Edison kept in constant contact with New York. A flurry of telegrams from his workers kept him abreast of work being completed in New York. Mina, now spending entire days with Edison, recognized what took precedence in his life, even on his honeymoon.

Arriving in St. Augustine for a week, they lodged at the San Marco Hotel, which boasted picturesque vistas of the island and river. Privacy eluded the couple once more after arriving in the city of Palatka and reading the headlines, one of which read: "America's Greatest Inventor Thomas A. Edison of electric fame of New York is at the Putnam accompanied by his bride." Edison stayed in town for two days and planned a private excursion to Ocklawaha. The guidebook described the ride on the river as an unforgettable night on a mysterious journey. Mina and Edison spotted colorful birds and alligators of the Florida jungle while the captain glided their steamer through the vibrant tropical fauna.[16]

In Akron and no longer planning her sister's wedding, Jennie managed her own emotions surrounding her younger sister's marriage. Still unsure of her devotion to Mr. Marvin, she lived vicariously through her younger sister's life. Keeping Mina abreast of Akron news, Jennie wrote her every few days, desperately waiting for a reply. Finally, hoping to curry favor, she packed up the wedding gifts and shipped them to New Jersey. Unlike Jennie's previous letters, these were upbeat and optimistic: "When you get this letter, you will be at your destination. I hope you will find everything beautiful and lovely and that you will be happy." Unfortunately, the new family dynamic differed, and Jennie admitted, "sometimes I feel so discouraged and that Everyone is against me, but then I think it is all my own fault and try to brace up and do the best I can."[17]

Mina, confronting her new role, could no longer return to her former identity. She needed to navigate her new life, which did not allow excess energy to aid her sister. Her circumstances altered her relationship with Jennie, which forced her to cope. Mina had no choice but to look forward and focus on her new family.

After returning to Palatka for a day, Mina and Edison boarded their train for the last leg of their long journey before reaching their winter home. When the Tampa railroad tracks proceeded no farther, the couple boarded the *Manatee*, the city's steamer. By no means was it a private steamer; the newlyweds traveled with the local cattle ranchers and others who were headed to Fort Myers.

The citizens of Fort Myers were overjoyed to welcome Edison back to town with his new bride (he had traveled there with Gilliland after his previous wife died), and they planned a public gathering upon his arrival. However, knowing the construction delays and the long journey would elicit an angry response from Edison, Gilliland, acting as an intermediary, suggested the city alter its plans. The revised plan, more agreeable to Edison's needs, included creating "a sixty-foot avenue" from his home to the city's edge.[18]

After eighteen days of travel and lodging, Edison and Mina were eager to see and sleep in their own new home. Unfortunately, on March 15th, they learned that neither the Edison nor the Gilliland home was finished. Much to Mina's dismay, they were forced to endure staying in another hotel. This one was far worse than the previous one she'd criticized. It featured no electricity, gas, or indoor plumbing. The trip was far more unpleasant than Mina had ever imagined. Mina read her mother's letter that imagined her daughter "locked in [Edison's] arms . . . and making plans for the future." Nothing could have been further from the truth.[19]

The plan for the sixty-foot path did not materialize as promptly as the town boasted. Instead, Mina traveled the mile-long trail into town on a donkey car with her feet dangling off the side and sand blowing everywhere. Although shipments and supplies continued to arrive north for the home and laboratory, both houses were still weeks away from completion. One home was further along than the other, and after three nights in the dreadful hotel, the group decided to move into the nearby finished home. The large group consisted of Mina and Edison; Ezra; his wife, Lillian, and her sister, Jeanette (Nettie) Johnson; Edison's daughter, Marion; and two maids, Nora and Helena (Lena) McCarthy.

Although the home was completed, Mina remained distraught that it possessed "no running water, no sewage, no ice, Tough beef—no other meat—making it almost imperative to have food shipped from the north." In addition, Edison had yet to install electricity, and the kitchen was detached from the rest of the home, with no protection from the constant wind. "There were many times when the bread and other foods were blown out of [our] hands and carried out of sight." During the evening, the group read or talked by kerosene lamps or candles. Although wires were installed, the generator was still not operational.[20]

The group, save for Edison, was bothered by the absence of basic amenities. However, what made it worse for Mina was the proximity to her contentious stepdaughter. Marion had inserted herself into this honeymoon trip when she should have been in school or with her brothers and tutored at home. Mina exhibited annoyance that Marion was treated as an adult when she acted like an uneducated, petulant child.

Edison, meanwhile, possessed the ability to ignore domestic inconveniences, and he returned to work. Even without a finished laboratory, he wrote every day in his notebooks, filling six of them with his ideas and drawings for older projects, such as incandescent lighting and railway telegraphy, as well as a host of new inventive projects. His mind seemed to expand, matching the expansive, undeveloped tropical landscape. His new winter home became a place of active research rather than a vacation.

Mina concluded that Edison had pawned his bride off on his friends, and his daughter made her utterly cheerless. Receiving mail from her family helped her mind escape the misery of her honeymoon. In contrast to Jennie's persona, Robert's witty and easygoing style cheered his little sister as he shared life from Oak Place. Mina savored every word of her brother's entertaining multipage letter. Confessing that he was occupied with his own work and never privy to news around Akron unless someone stopped to share it with him, Robert further suggested that Mina probably knew more about recent Akron society than he did. Robert revitalized his sister and announced that their parents had begun their journey down South to join her. He was keenly interested in his parents' impression of the South, and he reminded Mina his letters were scarce as "I am a much better listener than relater" and "remember me to our Bro Mr. Edison."[21]

Although uplifting and semi-frequent were the letters from home, there were many more hours in the day during which Mina remained desperate for a connection with her husband. Unfamiliar with her husband's workaholic behavior, she stood unsure how to engage with him. Whether of her own volition or whether she was biding her time until her parents arrived, Mina joined her husband in his work.

For the next two weeks of their honeymoon, Mina followed him to his makeshift workshop and discussed his future inventions with him. It pleased Edison that his new wife could be engaged and more intelligent than his first wife, whom he referred to as "Popsy-wopsy who can't invent." Mina participated in his inventions by writing or recopying some of his entries. Then, deciding to humor Mina and break from his more profound ideas, Edison allowed them to experiment together. He attempted to shock an oyster out of its shell with an electric current. Edison thought the electric current would paralyze the shell muscle and force the shell to fly open. Recording the bleak results in the notebook, Edison wrote, "Dead failure."[22]

Any irony from the results remained lost on the couple. At Mina's most lovely point in the marriage, she would be unable to yank her husband from his shell-like laboratory. No one stood to control Edison, who was adamant in his opinions about a wife. He had once told his father, "My wife does not nor never can control me." Marion, forever the interloper, also pushed her way into her father's notebooks, copying a few news articles and a telegram message.[23]

The reunion between Mina and her parents happened not a day too soon. The two homes were practically finished, giving both families the privacy they desperately craved. Edison could continue to work uninterrupted now that the Millers were present to occupy their daughter. They were swapping "war stories" of their exhausting trip, which included traveling by horse and buggy over empty trails for miles. The Millers' tales shocked the group when they spoke of the night they slept in an abandoned shanty, and Mary Valinda slept on a door placed on the floor.

Finally settled, Edison began to think about the much-needed landscaping for the barren area. In a seventh notebook, he detailed instructions on plantings for surrounding his new Fort Myers home. With his father-in-law present, who appreciated the fine art of designing lush grounds, Edison flaunted his ambition for the estate and a working botanical knowledge of the region.

Concerned about local citrus, he planned orange and grapefruit groves between the two homes and lemon and lime trees on the opposite side. Optimistic about his choice of groundskeeper, Eli Thompson, Edison requested to have every type of berry grown, from strawberries to gooseberries. He wanted the trees to be just as varied, requesting peach, mango, guava, apricot, and many others. Nut plants were also to be scattered throughout. Once the enterprise was planned out on paper, he instructed the groundskeeper to protect all the plants, even purchasing beehives to help pollinate. A fence was required to keep out the roaming cattle of the area. Edison hoped to show off to the locals "the grounds best manured in Florida."[24]

The locals observed the new residents from afar, warned by the towns-men not to intrude on their privacy. Restraining the residents became a daunting task, however, and Edison laid down his scepter for the town elders to enter his environs. They wanted to entertain their famous neighbor and his family with the town's brass band. Ever gracious in public and skillful at investor relations, Edison praised the gentleman calling their music ethereal.

Once Edison had accomplished enough on this visit, he sent word to the secretary up North that he intended to leave Fort Myers on April 26th and arrive in Akron to drop off his in-laws on the 29th. Following the order from above, the group began packing their belongings. Edison's craving fans were sated when the press reported he would return next winter for a more extended period. Avaricious landowners were formulating their ads and cashing in on the town's newfound fame. By the end of the summer, the papers read, "The great electrician, after a thorough look, over the entire state, has chosen FORT MYERS as his WINTER HOME. . . . IT CANNOT BE EQUALLED ANYWHERE."[25]

Before her departure, Mina sent two small live alligators up to her little brothers, John and Theodore. Closer to them than to her new step-children, she wanted to send them a souvenir from the jungles of Florida. Her parents, who were with her on the trip, did not discourage Mina from sending the extravagant gift.

Arriving in Akron at the end of April brought up the same wistful feelings that Mina had encountered at the outset of her honeymoon. Surrounded by her siblings, Mina remained comfortable. She was still uncertain whether she could fill the role of Mrs. Edison away from the support of her family. Although the amenities Mina had lacked for the past two months were restored, a more daunting challenge lay ahead. Mina now had to mother three children, one of whom would not be amenable to any management style. Sensing she would be doing this on her own made her anxious. Unfortunately, Mina's anxiety would never diminish.

5

An Arduous Adjustment

Two months shy of her twenty-first birthday, Mina walked through the entrance of her new home. Dark and cold, the house stood crowded with items that were not of her choosing. Edison had purchased the house and its entire contents. Unfortunately, the home had been previously decorated by a thief who had absconded to the Caribbean Islands. Mina frowned at the mere thought of such behavior. In truth, the furnishings were fine quality but not necessarily the ones Mina would have chosen. Everything from the gravy ladle to the bedroom drapes lingered as a reminder of another woman's taste. The house felt like a dress handed down from an older sister that did not quite fit right but would be wasteful if thrown away. Looking around and feeling disappointed with most of the décor, Mina kept sentiments to herself.

Higher on her list of concerns were caring for Edison's children and hiring a staff to help run the sizable house. Her first thought was to turn to her husband for guidance in these matters. Unfortunately, this presented itself as a miscalculation; neither subject was of any interest to him. Furthermore, he had no intention of aiding his new wife—a task he believed was beneath a man of his stature.

It was no more than five months ago that Mina had first seen Glenmont resting on rolling hills; she marveled at its magnitude and architectural beauty. Mina envisioned her mother in Oak Place and planned to mimic her life, with many children scampering about growing up in a loving environment. Still getting acquainted with Edison, she felt confident she had a bighearted husband and believed he was generous with his money. Likewise, he would be generous with his time. Now she was not so sure. Her husband's recent actions contradicted his behavior during their courtship. When seeing the house with fresh eyes, her anguish intensified, forcing her to second-guess her assumptions about the man she'd married.[1]

Days before their arrival in New Jersey, she and Edison dropped her parents off at Oak Place. Her siblings greeted the newlyweds as they would a king and queen. Recognizing familiar smells made Mina's heart ache, knowing she was no longer a resident but a mere visitor. Her brother Ira, who had recently proposed to her friend Cora Wise, had bought a house blocks away from Oak Place.

Similarly, when Robert and Louise eventually married, they lived nearby in Canton. Mina, on the other hand, was starting anew. Her uneasy character did not have the resilience of sturdier women in the face of new challenges. Moreover, it would be daunting without any family there for help. Pessimistic, she left Ohio and headed to New Jersey with her husband and stepdaughter, forced to confront her situation alone.[2]

Within days of taking up residence in Glenmont, the new reality alarmed Mina. It was clear that Edison had no desire to partner with his wife to build a home together. Instead, he had countless other partners with whom he chose to collaborate, and those relationships took precedence over Mina.

The attention and genuine interest he'd initially shown her remained a distant memory. The leisurely, at-ease character she'd fallen in love with was replaced by a man consumed with work and his next invention. Mina endlessly ruminated whether his initial feelings were a mere façade. Did he even love her, or had it been a farce to get a wife? Confused by the change in his personality, Mina existed in constant distress, yet societal conventions forced her to put on a jovial face for the public and her new husband.

Mina subsisted as a good actress. Her husband did not notice her sadness; he ignored it if he did. Her family back in Akron, however, knew the truth. They were eager to come to her rescue and began writing to soothe lonely Mina.

As the days progressed in her new home, Mina tried to rekindle the bond from the courtship. But Edison did not care for small talk. He had finished wooing Mina. There was no additional need to keep her entertained in his mind. Edison informed her he had complete confidence that she could run the house by herself. After all, his previous wife from a lower stratum had done. And this was comparable to other positions in which Edison had "appointed" a manager. Edison believed that people were given tasks and were expected to follow through. A particular man was placed in charge of the lamp factory; Mina Miller was in charge of Glenmont.

Eager for her husband's praise, Mina began to view herself as any other employee of Edison and strived to do the best in her position. But she was fueled by fear and thought any blunder would ignite Edison's rage. Moreover, the new, uneven power dynamic stalled any potential coziness between the newlyweds. Although Mina was raised to demand respect from men and her peers alike, Edison's high self-regard precluded him from thinking they were equals.

Wandering through the rooms of Glenmont, Mina's thoughts turned to her mother. As a young girl, she saw the ease Mary Valinda displayed in running a large home. She remembered when her mother felt challenged or distressed about a domestic matter, she could always rely on her father's unwavering support. Her parents' unified vision buttressed her mother's strength—their singular worldview stemmed from their faith. Their view informed his work and, by extension, raising a family. Edison's opinion on religion was opposed to Mina's. The matter was swiftly closed and no longer up for debate. Mina doubted she and Edison would duplicate her parents' marriage.[3]

Trying to untangle her range of emotions, Mina remained restless. Her faith pulled at her soul. Mina's thoughts vacillated: She was honored to be married to the famous Mr. Edison, yet she was distressed her husband was so detached from the family. Hopelessly complicated was tending to Marion. She displayed her dislike for Mina as a badge of honor. Besides teasing her brothers incessantly, she developed a disdain for Mina's requirement for proper manners.

Moreover, Edison had recently jettisoned Marion from his daily life; the laboratory and his meetings were no longer welcome to her. Belligerent that she was now under the auspices of her stepmother, Marion grew increasingly hostile. Having inherited her father's strong-willed nature, Marion was not timid about upsetting Mina or criticizing her methods.

Both sons' behavior was anathema to Mina. They were as unkempt as their father and argued with each other incessantly. Their attitude was appalling, and Mina could not conceal her disgust. Every day she begrudgingly attempted to undo years of poor rearing. However, what started as simple daily lessons turned into quarrels. Eventually, they all reached a point where everyone around her in the new home was unhappy, including herself. Bonding with the children was close to impossible.

Having little patience with the children, Mina could not suffer any longer. Fearful that she did not know the first thing about training the children, Mina complained to her mother about her grim circumstances. Mary Valinda interceded, wishing "she could write one word that brings her daughter cheer." She encouraged her daughter to infuse the children with church teachings, suggesting that "Love joy and peace should be their motto." Mina's despair was tinged with guilt; her Methodist upbringing had always infused her with culpability, and she felt selfish she was complaining. Mary Valinda assured her daughter that "I don't think there is one selfish spot about you . . . unselfishness which is the true way of making a happy home." Mina was reminded of what her mother told her when they were together in Florida, far from the distractions of her busy family, that "she found [Edison] to be a kind husband that would stand by her if needed."[4]

Mary Valinda sent lessons from her perch in Akron, and Mina tried to embrace them with their loving intent. Her siblings' many accomplishments were proof that she was a wonderful mother. Mina admired her siblings' successes and hoped her mother's advice would transform Edison's children to become more "Miller-like." The positive encouragement bolstered Mina's mood for a time. She shared her better mindset with Edison, hoping it would provoke a positive response. But he was indifferent to her mundane concerns, and Mina was crushed.

While Mina held down the children's rebellion, Edison controlled his own. Within two weeks of his return to New Jersey, his workers at the Edison Machine Works organized a strike. The labor force contention involved hours, overtime pay, and shop rules. Rather than manage the conflict, Edison controlled the result. Instead of giving in to the workers' demands, he closed the factory and moved it to Schenectady, New York. Uncaring about the local workers' satisfaction, he announced to the press that the move was "to get away from the embarrassment of the strikes and communists." Although overwhelmed with her new duties, Mina should have seen this as a warning: If you differ with Mr. Edison, he will have no compunction in sending you into the wilderness.[5]

Edison's long days in New York often ended with him sleeping in his office and returning home sometime the following evening. Mina could not fathom why he would not want to be home for dinner and see his new wife or children. Each day, she put all her energy into their appearance and manners. Mina foolishly dressed up the parlor for his arrival and had the cook prepare lavish meals. The dress worn less than an hour returned to her armoire, and the food was placed in the icebox for the following day.[6]

Mary Valinda needed her weekly update from New Jersey. When one did not arrive, she believed her daughter had become too depressed to write. Jennie was summoned to dispatch a costly telegram to ensure all was well. Confirming her mother's suspicions, Mina felt more profound loneliness and isolation than ever before. Mary Valinda immediately instructed her children to write their sister, taking turns to lift her spirits.

Jennie was the first to take the reins, jealously remarking, "with all you have, it seems dreadful that you are not happy." She further noted that her sister's attempts to hire a staff did not deserve much sympathy. Mina possessed a smaller family than the Millers and enjoyed access to better-quality staff in New York City. If employment decisions were difficult for her, Jennie claimed that Mr. Edison surely could recognize that Mina was struggling and come to her aid. Jennie believed Edison was very patient, loving, kind, and fond of Mina, but she had little familiarity with the circumstances.[7]

The most mature and level-headed of her four older brothers, Ira, and Robert, worked for the Millers' various companies. Both young men made it clear they were ready to settle down with their soon-to-be wives, put down roots, and follow in their father's footsteps. Mina adored both brothers; each chose to marry friends of hers. Their cheery letters shared the everyday activities of life in Akron, an existence she'd once thought she was destined for; however, it was one she was now mourning.

Her two other brothers were still sowing their oats; Edward, Mina's older brother, was endlessly seeking a wife. It was clear from his correspondence that he did not lack attention from the local young ladies of Ohio. He expected to continue his carefree days in no rush to settle down. A handsome young man of means, he shared his summer plans to go west for five or six weeks, or maybe to Mexico or join a friend on his yacht for a cruising expedition on Long Island Sound. Then, when he returned, he would perhaps make a stop at Glenmont and stay for a short visit.[8]

Lewis, the last of the older four, was in California enjoying Yosemite Valley. More sensitive than Edward, Lewis expressed some guilt about "his lively lifestyle while his sister is so unhappy." To assuage his conscience, he reminded his sister that their parents would eventually visit and "she won't be alone."[9]

Mame, the intellectual of the family, was studying at Wellesley College. She believed Mina's life was "glamorous" and "thrilling" and that she'd married the "most famous man in the country, if not the world, and lived like a queen in a mansion." Mame reminded Mina that her own life was "often dull and unexciting." Hoping for juicy stories, Mame asked if many visitors were "part of fashionable society" and if Marion and the boys liked her.[10]

Feeling stung by Mame's comments, yet knowing they were well-intentioned, Mina invited her to visit at the end of the semester. Declining this offer, Mame suggested instead that Mina cheer her up by visiting the family in Akron, wishing she could "put her arms around [her] give you a good kiss . . . and good wishes for happiness in your new home."[11]

Cherishing all her siblings' letters, Mina often reread portions of them to Edison. In those short moments they shared, she used the letters to engage him about something other than the children and the staff. Their comments went unnoticed, but he did tease Mina's sister Mame, who was studying at Wellesley, suggesting she find a suitable husband. This moment opened up a small window into her spouse's nature. An uptight person herself, often touchy when teased, she made a mental note to learn to connect with her husband through his sense of humor.

Although scarcely three weeks had passed since she had seen her family, it seemed like decades to Mina. Desperate to be with them, she wanted to invite them to Glenmont, but pondering the idea of approaching Edison made her anxious. He often accentuated their age difference, judging her needs as infantile. She feared this request, too, might be rejected. Deciding it was too risky, she demurred.

Cognizant of the uneven power struggle between the newlyweds, Lewis Miller set a scheme to travel to New York at the end of May and drop in on his daughter. His business dealings often took him north, and the trip could appear as a convenient stopover before meeting with suppliers. Edison admired Mina's father and his thriving businesses. Further, he appreciated his desire to be frugal and stay at their home rather than at a costly hotel. The spontaneous trip was a much-welcome relief for Mina.

Jennie suggested another way for Mina to spend much-needed time with her older sister—take Marion, Tom Jr., and William to meet her in Boston for a two-week vacation. They could visit historical places of interest and consider it an educational trip. Attempting humor, Jennie added, "Mr. Edison could spare you not being around for a bit." Unfortunately, Mina did not have the fortitude to ask Edison about the trip. Mame, however, changed her mind, realizing the dire need for her sister, and she decided to visit Mina after her exams in June.[12]

Mina put her energy into planning her father's upcoming visit to escape all else, telling her trained staff to be diligent in making Glenmont sparkle for his arrival. She and the cook were meticulous in purchasing the foods her father preferred. It was the first opportunity to make her parents proud; the positive reinforcement would fill a void in her ego that her husband kept enlarging. Everything needed to be impeccable, ensuring her father's desire to return. The triumph of this visit reflected who she was as a person. Mina was not a scholar like her sister Mame or an independent world traveler like Jennie. Instead, Mina would reveal to them that she exhibited the qualities of a consummate hostess, using every fiber of her being.

After his visit, when Lewis returned to Akron, he promptly told Mina how enjoyable his stay at her home was. The meals, the children, and Glenmont were "wonderful." Mary Valinda was so pleased with her husband's report and commended Mina. Once Lewis regaled his wife and daughter with luxurious aspects of Glenmont, she and Jennie visited within weeks of his return. They, too, were looking forward to seeing Mina and enjoying her hospitality and "the splendor of Glenmont."[13]

Basking in the encouraging words, Mina was jubilant. Whether it was intentional or unconscious, Mina had built a mental blueprint. First, she would make her home so appealing that guests could not resist a visit. It would start with her family. Then, feeling more confident, she would branch out to her husband's colleagues and the greater society. Mina's life began to take on a new form at this juncture. She would reveal a friendly and generous nature, hoping to be adored. That admiration would strengthen her for a life as Mrs. Edison while her husband would not.

While visiting Glenmont, Mary Valinda assessed the family dynamic. She noticed that Tom Jr. needed some loving guidance. She suggested sending him to Akron to spend time with Mina's younger brothers, John and Theodore. If the visit proved beneficial, he could extend his stay and travel with them to their lake house in Chautauqua for part of the summer. She believed the home environment at Lake Chautauqua would provide him with the religious foundation he so desperately needed.

Agreeing that an alternate surrounding would do the boy well, Mina decided to allow the trip. Considering that Tom Jr. would gain extra attention from her family, she sent him to Akron without William. William would manage fine under the guidance of Edison's brother and his wife, who owned a farm in Port Huron, Michigan. Still not adequately healed from the emotional scars of their mother's death, they wrote gushing letters to Mina whie they were away. William enjoyed the carefree life of a farm rather than the formal rules of Glenmont. Riding his uncle's mules and playing with pigs kept him content. His only concern was that he deeply missed his brother, Tom.[14]

Destiny placed another test before Mina; George Vincent traveled to New York and visited Mina at Glenmont. It had been ten months since Mina had seen him face-to-face and broken his heart. One could not comprehend why he would put himself through this agony after being jilted. It might have been sheer curiosity, or perhaps his mother's urging prompted the visit. Regardless, George traveled to West Orange and visited Mina, who had married another man.

This meeting would be a tug at the depths of her heart, but it was too late to turn back the clock on her life. Each trait she admired in George was absent in Edison. Her courtship with Edison was a farce. Mina, now lonely in her marriage, left only with her husband's shadow, was floating around their mansion, lost in her thoughts. The daily struggles with his children still encumbered her. Even with her family's recent visit and adequate staff, she could not rise above her despondency. Letting George sense this would be a catastrophe. Speculation would pass through society that Mina Edison had made a mistake—a humiliation that neither her parents nor her family would survive. Forced to put on her best face, Mina curtailed any suspicion of discontent. Focused on a seamless meeting, Mina survived the reunion. In a later social visit, the flawless performance was mentioned to Mary Valinda, and both mothers agreed that George should find a more suitable match. This personal victory bolstered Mina once again. Gradually coming into her own, Mina felt proud of her accomplishment.

Mina was overwhelmed and confused about what should be a priority in her first year of marriage. Receiving Edison's approval was her most significant concern. Each day, she made sure to greet her husband at the train station when he returned. Edison did not appreciate the gesture, considering it unnecessary. In addition, clothing and external appearances were never a priority for Edison, who wore the same suit days in a row, sometimes without bathing. Mina soon learned that he refused even to take an umbrella, no matter how hard it rained. Not interested in wasting time at a tailor, he refused to go. Finally, his threadbare suits were sent, and a new one was measured off the existing ones.[15]

Despite Edison's unmistakable unsociable nature, Mina's parents expected a letter from him. The Millers were always forgiving of Edison's poor manners, yet they never seemed to realize that he possessed no intention of becoming a loving member of the Miller family. The siblings wished to call him Thomas, but Edison created an unsurmountable remoteness. Only Robert, the most uninhibited and playful, took it upon himself to call Edison "Bro." The scant letters sent to her various brothers were always of a business nature and usually initiated by the Millers.[16]

That summer, Marion joined her brother Tom at Chautauqua; she slept in the tent with Mina's youngest sister, Grace, only a few years older than Marion. Both midway through adolescence, they enjoyed each other's company. But, in a few years, Marion would grow bored with their proper Methodist way, and the relationship would sour.

With the children away, Mina was largely alone in early August. She had begun to master the flow of her home of six months, and the staff understood their new roles. Glenmont was now fully stocked with clothing purchased by Mina and the family. Yet, her days were left empty. Her family had all come and gone, and she had no immediate travel plans that required planning or packing. Mina had yet to make new friends in her new community, and she had nothing to occupy her days.

She hoped to rekindle the positive impression she had made on her husband in Fort Myers at his laboratory. She resorted to almost anything to be noticed and started hand-copying her husband's experiments that involved increasing the life of electric lamps. Whether they were written at the Lamp Factory in East Newark or brought home to Glenmont, it is remarkable that she wrote out the entire experiment in the lab book. Mina continued her work on these experiments every day from the third to August 9th, save for August 8th, which fell on a Sunday—a day she attended church. She returned on Monday to finish her task.[17]

Edison must have been rather pleased with his wife's diligence and conscientiousness since he agreed to accompany her to Chautauqua in mid-August. Chautauqua was a religious retreat and a place to mix with polite society. Mina hoped that once Edison was away from his work, he would return to a state of leisure. This trip would be an opportunity for her to attend the religiously enlightened lectures and stroll around with her famous husband. He might telegraph his workers from the Lake, but he had no laboratory where he could escape to work.

Edison, however, found ways to avoid polite society and small talk. Indifferent to Mina's humiliation, Edison told the reporters he had no intention of going to the lectures "as long as I can smoke my cigar and read the lecture in the newspaper the next morning, I see no object in attending them. What is the use." His public display of impolite conduct astounded Mina.[18]

The Edisons stayed with Mina's parents for two weeks. When September arrived, Mina dreaded leaving the warm cocoon of her parents' summer home, despite her mother's encouragement that Mina had the "best possible boys ... at this point ... she should be so pleased with them." But unfortunately, Mary Valinda's Methodist magic wand did not turn Edison's children into charming, well-behaved offspring. Instead, trepidation stared at Mina while she attempted to bond with Edison's three wayward children in the months ahead.[19]

Jennie returned East with the Edisons but did not visit her sister. Unable to settle in New York or Akron, she headed to Europe with the Vincents, including George. Mina went to see her sister off at the ship's landing. She allowed another furtive, longing glance at George as he boarded with her sister. George's mother whispered something to Mina on the dock that caused her face to grimace, and Jennie witnessed the transformation. Mrs. Vincent still harbored terrible feelings toward Mina and was not shy about telling her so when she would hide from rebuke while touring Europe for the rest of the year.

Across the Atlantic, Jennie enjoyed traveling with the Vincent family. Rev. Vincent was considered charismatic. Even if Jennie was captivated by him, it was, indeed, surprising that Jennie went off to Europe for such a lengthy time. Choosing to be with the Vincents rather than attend her brother Ira's wedding demonstrated Jennie's inner emotional turmoil. Jennie should have been married to Richard by now. Attending another Miller wedding that was not her own was too much to bear.

Jennie confided in Mina about matters of her heart, divulging her doubts about going to Europe and missing the wedding. Also, Richard Pratt Marvin, Jennie's longtime, "on-again, off-again" suitor, disclosed to Mina's mother that "now that Jennie has sailed to Europe, he will never have a chance to wed her." Jennie told Mina that Richard had finally dropped the idea of marriage. Jennie had been witnessing her sister's struggles with her marriage and stated that she never wanted to marry Richard, but at the same time, she wanted him as a friend.[20]

Jennie's struggles did not distract Mina from her own. She was having a "battle within herself" about her choice, which she shared with her older sister. Ironically, Jennie was spending every day with George. Jennie was confident that Mina "would not have been happy" had she married George instead: "There are always things you want to change about others." However, Jennie definitively stated that George was not the one for Mina, who had a loving and devoted husband. "Don't think of the past; your family loves you, and yours [you] should live in the present and stay there . . . you are strong and [have] enough . . . character and [can] stand on your own. You are just a beginner, and you are doing everything splendidly, and you must not expect to do things like an older person would."[21]

Word got back to Mary Valinda of Mina's continued unease, and she returned to Glenmont to visit Mina for two weeks. Jennie told her sister that a visit with their mother would do them both good. Furthermore, Jennie suggested that it would be better for Mina to go to Akron a little earlier than Ira's wedding and perhaps set up flowers or arrange things in Ira and Cora's new home. Ira and Cora were having a small wedding. If Mina needed to feel appreciated in life, Ira and Cora would express gratefulness for Mina's help at this time.[22]

In a rare moment of self-evaluation, Jennie admitted how impulsive it was for her to go to Europe during this time. A moment later, she quickly returned to her familiar maternal tone and commented on her brother Edward, who was not settled and perhaps floundering, wishing his hopes would be realized. Pondering about her own life, Jennie admitted to Mina that she wrote Richard a long letter but once again was vacillating on whether she would mail it.

After Ira and Cora's wedding, they, too, planned to visit Mina at her home after a brief honeymoon in Boston. Everyone in the family had a desire to see the splendor of Glenmont with their own eyes. They hoped Mina would show them around the shops of New York. Shopping in Manhattan was a temporary salve for Mina's emotional ups and downs. During her excursions, she had unfettered access to the finery of New York City. With access to Edison's bank account, she reinvented herself as a woman with a beacon of taste and purchased extravagant gifts for her family. Mina learned that Cora had joined the church and could only wallow in sadness over her husband's disinterest in joining the Church in West Orange.

Jennie continued to write to Mina from Europe, primarily about Richard, who had been seen in Akron as reserved and quiet. He was depressed that a Miller wedding was approaching that was not his own. She also inquired about Marion. Mina had not decided what to do regarding Marion's future education. It was unclear whether she would have a tutor or be sent away for school. When Mina complained about her husband's actions, Jennie said, "you must make Edison be good to you." Even with constant reassurance, Mina did not have the inner fortitude to confront Edison about her needs. Jennie also suggested that Mina invite Louise to do her pre-wedding shopping in New York to distract Mina from her sadness. Soon Jennie herself began to feel what Mina felt daily and admitted she was slightly homesick. She told Mina to tell both Louise and Cora to write her as well.[23]

Feeling guilty, Mina decided that Marion would remain home and have a tutor instruct her, and the boys would attend the local West Orange school. As a result, the children did not join Mina and Edison in attending Ira and Cora's wedding.

When Mina returned to Orange, she continued to struggle with the children, who were inherently rambunctious. Mina constantly felt they did not enjoy her company, and she could not relax around them. She complained to her mother about the coldness she felt from them. Finally, her mother, who was warmhearted, told her, "Sit with children and read to them and sing with them don't stop for a minute to win them to you try to make them smarter and play with them anything to make them happy that will help them to love you. Buy them things that you think will make them happy." Mary Valinda attempted to teach Mina to be a warmer, more relaxed stepmother. She believed if Mina behaved differently with the children, her mind would turn and become happy and content.[24]

Mina tried to have a positive outlook but could not sustain it. Marion's new tutor enjoyed church, and the two of them went regularly. Mina was planning to go back to Fort Myers the following February and hoped to send the children to Akron to be with her parents, which pleased the children as well. Mary Valinda tried to implore Mina not to focus "on things that make you sad or feel hurtful to you or unpleasant it only makes you feel older." Finally, admitting to her daughter that it must be "hard for you to manage a husband that is so short and cares less about friends that visit."[25]

Thanksgiving was approaching, and Mina's parents and younger sister Grace would be joining them. Mina was consumed with the holiday and how it could set the proper tone for all others to follow. Agonizing over the details, she wrote a memo that listed the seating chart and the table decorations. What was of utmost importance was to seat her father next to Edison. Her father would keep her husband in the proper spirits, and she hoped Edison would remain at the table throughout the meal.

The end of the year brought great news from Mina's dear friend Louise. She and her brother Robert had set a date to get married on January 25th. Louise made it clear to Mina that it "would not go off right without you so must not fail to come." Louise was aware of Edison's propensity to skip social occasions and informed Mina in large, underlined words that "if he does not come, I will never forgive him" and then added, "perhaps that will scare him." The letter must have lifted Mina's spirits even though Louise shared her regrets that she could not join her for Thanksgiving.[26]

Being aware of the third Miller wedding, Jennie was still deliberating about marrying Richard. She certainly had misgivings both about living with her parents and wanting her own home. In addition, Jennie was concerned about Richard's finances and whether he would have enough money to buy the large house she desired. Mina was still overwhelmed with her duties and could hardly bear more of Jennie's indecision.

As Edison's first wedding anniversary approached, all three children were in Akron for Edison and Mina to spend quality time together. Mina could have used this time to step back and take a breath. Regrettably, Mina and Edison were not destined to reflect on their first year together. By New Year's Eve of 1887, Edison had fallen gravely ill with pleurisy.

6

Inability to Bond

With each breath, Edison's chest ached with brutal pain. Likewise, his body temperature fluctuated between high fever and chills. His appetite decreased significantly. What scared Mina the most was watching her very highly energetic husband become incapacitated. Her only experience with a family member having a sickness this acute was when she was four years old and her oldest sister, Eva, died of pneumonia. Mina's vague memory of that experience was based more on family tales than recollection. Seventeen years later, Mina, barely twenty-one years old, was relegated to care for a gravely ill husband. Less than a year before, Mina had been shopping for her trousseau and daydreaming about a life married to the world's most famous man. She could never have envisioned this, at least not this early in her marriage.

"Pleurisy" refers to an inflammation of the membranes lining the chest cavity. Injury and overwork—commonly seen in middle-aged patients—could have been attributed to Edison's disease. In addition, Edison may have suffered from an acute form manifested by fever, coughing, shallow breathing, and pain. However, initially diagnosed in December, his illness continued well into January. For most of January, Edison was confined to his bed and unable to rise. The doctors informed Mina that the lining of Edison's chest was completely inflamed. His illness simply did not want to leave his body.[1]

During that time, Mina was pregnant with her first child. Edison's illness, combined with Mina's condition, caused excessive anxiety.

Regrettably, Mina was inept at juggling all the tasks that ensued. But instead of asking for any sort of relief from family or friends, Mina buried her anguish deep within herself. Having been raised as a strict Methodist, she believed suffering was something one was obligated to endure. The public, however, never caught a glimpse of her pain and falsely observed a contented life. Mina's mother knew the truth and provided her daughter with weighty verses she had heard in the previous week's church sermon: "The greater the cross, greater the blessing, the richer the crown." Mina and her siblings believed that their mother had a tailor-made Bible verse for every hardship in life.[2]

Mina tried to internalize her mother's words and looked to her religion for solace, a task that proved grueling. As the newest member of the Edison family, Mina was the only one connected with religion. Her three new stepchildren were unruly and constantly bickering among themselves. They did not grow up in the Methodist church—or any church. The values their biological mother had instilled in them held no regard for decorum of any kind. Edison was no better; he mocked religion relentlessly. So, Mina had to search for solace on her own.

Mina's mother was deeply affected by her daughter's anguish. Previously when a problem arose, her family was typically on the next train from Akron, destined for an extended visit to West Orange to remedy the situation. This time, however, she was unable to visit. Mina's brother Robert was to be married to Louise Igoe within weeks, and there would be far too many preparations for the wedding. So, an excursion to New Jersey was not an option.

Mina longed to attend her brother's wedding. This was not just any new sister-in-law. Louise was her closest friend, whom she had confided in from the start of her courtship with Edison. It was a profound emotional hardship for Mina to miss this wedding. More so, it would have been an occasion to return to Ohio. Mina would have relished catching up with her childhood friends and extended family members. But instead, she remained at her husband's bedside, miserable as she consulted with doctors about treatments and medicines.

Before Edison's illness, his children stayed at Mina's parents' home in Akron. They were sent back to West Orange in early winter with their tutor, Sarah McWilliams, an Ohio native. Mina's mother shared her regret at sending them home to a house filled with illness. Mina rigorously tried to emulate her mother's well-known saintly behavior and sought to attend to everyone's needs. However, Mina could not mimic her mother's natural goodness and often felt anger and resentment when everything did not go exactly the way she intended.

Additionally, Edison deprived Mina of her incessant need for positive reinforcement. He did not comprehend why anyone needed a verbal reward every time they did something good. On the other hand, Mary Valinda would help others simply out of the goodness of her heart, never once requiring gratitude.

Mina's youthful, thin frame prevented her pregnancy from remaining a secret to her stepchildren upon entering her second trimester. Likewise, this caused Mina to fret about her already strained relationship with Marion. She nervously asked her mother if she thought Marion would even like the new baby. Fourteen-year-old Marion habitually provoked Mina. She had opinions about everything and was never bashful about sharing them. Upon first meeting Mina, Marion had told her father that he should marry the beautiful blonde—Louise Igoe, the other young woman visiting Winthrop, Massachusetts. She was the same Louise, Mina's closest friend, who was about to marry Mina's brother Robert. Marion never elaborated on why she favored Louise over Mina, but Mina knew Louise was educated and witty. Everyone in the Miller family loved her. Even Mina believed that Edison considered Louise more interesting than herself. He certainly thought she was beautiful. When he'd first met Louise, he cleverly described her as a "fresh invoice of innocence and beauty."[3]

Regardless of Edison's thoughts about Louise's beauty or personality, it was Marion's conduct that needed curbing. However, neither Mina nor Edison had the slightest bit of interest in investing the time or love to curtail her behavior. Instead, they remedied the Marion situation the most effortless way they could—by pawning her care off to the hired help. Then they naturally blamed them for the predicament when they did not obtain the desired results.

Although Edison was sick, he was unable to be idle. He tried to manage preparations for an upcoming visit to his winter home and laboratory in Fort Myers, Florida, arranging for the shipment of lamps and equipment for lighting the buildings and grounds, and scheduling the delivery of the supplies, including groceries, distilled water, fishing gear, photographic instruments, and a gas machine. He also made some experimental notes on lamp filaments.

Edison's condition had improved enough for him to travel by early February, but then Marion became ill with congestion of the lungs, which further postponed the trip to Florida. Mina had to tend to her until she recovered. Finally, in mid-February, the Edisons traveled to Fort Myers. Mina, Marion, and a private doctor secluded themselves in a railroad car. Edison had received at least one hypodermic injection of morphine, resulting in his arm and hand being "badly swollen" when his train reached Savannah.[4]

When they finally reached their winter home in Fort Myers, the Edisons greeted their dear friends Ezra and Lillian Gilliland; Mina's sister Mary; her brother Robert; and his new bride, Louise. Robert and Louise knew how much Mina would appreciate adjusting their honeymoon plans to spend time with her. They understood Mina was devastated to have missed their wedding. Edison, who had no intention of being inactive, was expecting six experimental assistants to join him as well.

Edison's fame kept numerous newspaper reporters waiting for the latest update on his life. When word spread that he was ill, Ezra Gilliland, his friend and colleague, took it upon himself to update the world on his health, stating that Edison's respiratory condition had triggered heart troubles, and "it was found necessary several times to administer hypodermic injections of morphine." Cognizant of keeping up good relations with the town of Fort Myers, his new winter home, Gilliland instinctively added that the Fort Myers weather was so beneficial and recuperative that "he is now as hearty and as well as ever." Edison agreed and declared he "never felt better in [his] life." Edison, thoroughly enjoying camaraderie with the working man and simultaneously showing disdain for formality, showed the reporters "an ugly little sore" on his arm from his last morphine injection. The press loved conversing with Edison, constantly hurling questions and persuading him to chat more.[5]

Mina and Edison shared their first wedding anniversary in Florida. She had severe doubts about the marriage and his love for her when

Edison returned to work when he recovered. She could not fathom why he would work rather than spend time with his wife after she had just nursed him through a terrible illness. Mina was unaccustomed to this level of obliviousness and insensitivity. Mina could only interpret her husband's actions to mean displeasure with her company. She swiftly apprised her father of the situation and begged him to come down to Fort Myers to spend time with her husband without her presence and find out if he loved or valued Mina at all.

When Mina, Marion, and Sarah McWilliams left for Akron to spend time with Mina's family, Lewis went down to Fort Myers to become better acquainted with his new son-in-law. Marion had vastly different experiences at Oak Place than at Glenmont with her father and stepmother. Mina's parents were affectionate and exuded kindness to all who visited. Mina's parents were sensitive to blended families because of their own parents' deaths and subsequent remarriages. Mina's parents considered Marion and the boys to be their own grandchildren and had the children refer to them as Grandma and Grandpa. They showered them with gifts and wrote frequent letters during the year.

However, the tension between Marion and Mina continued to grow. Marion would refer to Mina by her first name, although the boys called her Mama, and she called Mina's parents Grandma and Grandpa. Mary Valinda was acutely aware of her daughter's scuffles with her stepchildren. To lighten Mina's load, the children had an open invitation to stay at her home or join them at Chautauqua for the summers. Mina's parents implored her to be patient and encouraged her to love the children and see the good in them. After all, they were only children who had recently lost their mother. However, this was a steep learning curve for Mina at twenty-one years old. She wanted to be a newlywed and stroll on the arm of her world-famous husband while basking in high society. However, she loathed her reality of being a mother of three boisterous children and the wife of an absentee, workaholic husband. In Mina's mind, she was slighted and snubbed.

While in Ohio, Mina wrote Edison four letters; he did not reply to any of them, further validating Mina's impressions of her husband. Marion also wrote her father in Fort Myers, primarily of her opinions of her large family. Marion, notorious for her flair for the dramatic, told her father that the journey was disagreeable in that "some of our party would have died before we got here if we had not stopped over at Lake Wier and Jacksonville."[6]

"You may well be glad that you did not come north with us, it is as cold as an Iceberg here, and the trees have hardly commenced to bud yet, I think if it keeps on very long, you had better buy your tickets for July." Marion was also quite shrewd when it came to her audience, and she mentioned her desire to continue to study with her tutor as she did in Fort Myers.[7]

With all the commotion around Oak Place, Marion overhead Mina complaining about her father not responding to Mina's letters. As always, Marion overstepped her bounds and impetuously commented about the situation to her father. Finally, worried about it getting back to Mina, Marion pleaded to Edison, "please, for my sake, do not tell her that I said anything about it, but I really think you ought to write her very often if you don't intend having a cyclone soon."[8]

There is no existing record of Edison writing to Mina, but Mina's father shared his first one-on-one impression of Edison. His encounter was quite different from her experiences. He had a delightful time with his new son-in-law and perceived that he had a sincere concern for Mina. The more time he spent with Edison, the more he was impressed with his prominence. Mina's father thoroughly believed that Edison would always be faithful to her. Edison's strength was his ability to command a room with his tales. Lewis Miller relished those interactions and reported to his daughter that he understood Edison to be "socially . . . superior to most any one I know."[9]

Mindful of his daughter's concern about Edison's constant critical remarks and opinions, Lewis construed them as "genuine innocent wit" and noticed that this was how Edison often spoke to those with whom he felt closest, whether friends like the Gillilands or his wife. Lewis found Edison so jovial and charming; he kept the group in a good mood the entire time with his quips and tales: "I have purposely watched him to see if any remarks which might accidentally drop would show any kind of different feelings towards you. He seems to me just as he did a year ago. Kind an[d] affectionate in all his way."[10]

Lewis implored Mina to be more realistic about the situation, implying that Edison had a fully matured mind while Mina was still forming. Mina needed to give it some time for the marriage to evolve. The children had undoubtedly improved their overall conduct from her father's perspective. Edison's sister-in-law, Ellen Edison, the wife of Edison's brother, William, believed it was most fortuitous that Mina had entered the Edison family and would have a constructive impact on the children. Mina needed to understand her husband's witty remarks as his attempts at entertaining and amusing. Edison was used to talking this way and could not change the habit to alter the way he interacted with others. Mina should not respond to his comments when he came home and should not share anything about the household matters. Edison had no interest in those things.

Lewis also instructed his daughter on how to bring up the children. Regarding Marion, he said Mina could positively influence her. Lewis informed his daughter that Marion knew Mina was aloof and suggested that if she didn't stifle those feelings, Mina would lose her. She enjoyed Mina's friends and enjoyed being with Grace and Mary. Mina needed to change her interactions with Marion. The boys also must learn from examples because lecturing them would have no lasting effect. Lewis knew precisely where the boys learned the naughty behavior; he told her to undo it before it became second nature: "I am very anxious that you show your true Christian influence. Your life, not your talks, will impress the true character you have shown. . . . Jennie is so much troubled in this direction that s[h]e is constantly unhappy."[11]

Mina's father hoped his lengthy epistle would have a lasting influence. After reading her father's letter, Mina presumably took his advice to heart. She certainly appreciated that her father was candid with her about her sister's unhappy existence. She now was looking forward to a pleasant reunion with her husband.

Edison returned to Llewelyn Park at the end of April and worked in his laboratory the next day. His swift departure was devastating to Mina, making it challenging to consider what her father said about her husband being faithful. Regardless, Mina attempted to make constructive changes in how she interacted with her family.

Amid her loneliness, Mina looked forward to any mail as a salve for her emotions. Trained to write regularly, she relished each letter as a much-needed, warm embrace. Knowing Mina would be looking for letters, Mina's mother shared Mina's troubles with her siblings, knowing they would write her sympathetic letters. So, when Jennie received word of her sister's pregnancy and Edison's illness, she wrote Mina immediately. Jennie was traveling abroad for most of the year to expand her cultural self for the third time and, at the same time, resolve to marry her longtime suitor, Richard Marvin. She stayed at the Hotel D'Angleterre, which accommodated foreign travelers in luxury a short distance from central Athens. Jennie was thrilled that Mina was pregnant yet was "sorry you have been obliged to go through so much this winter. I imagine your trouble was quite enough to go through with patiently without having severe illness to worry you. I hope, though, my dear, you will have an easier time from now on." Jennie was also keenly aware of the friction between Mina and Marion and suggested that if Mina confided in Marion about the pregnancy, she would see that Mina wanted to be allies of some sort and would love the new baby. Hoping to lift Mina's mood, Jennie said she would buy a crib when she arrived in Paris, as well as some dresses for Mina at Madame Joyeuse, a famous Paris dress shop at Rue du Colisee. Furthermore, Jennie hoped Mina was happy and cheerful about being pregnant and ventured to add that even if Mina was not pleased, she needed to put on a good face; otherwise, the child would feel neglected. The baby was due in mid-June, and Jennie, sailing from Liverpool at that time, asked if she could spend a day or two with Mina before going back to Ohio.[12]

Keeping within character, Jennie assumed her tough-love approach and said Mina must join the Church in West Orange. If she didn't, she wouldn't feel connected with people, and she wouldn't feel settled. Jennie felt obligated to share a conversation she had had with Rev. Vincent, George's father. The Reverend thought that Mina would not join a church once she moved to West Orange. Mina might have believed that her sister's conversation with the Reverend was prompted by her rejecting George and marrying a heathen like Edison. The Reverend thought she would discard all those years of spiritual upbringing, too. It was a sanctimonious suggestion about Mina, but she might have believed this was one more reason her sister was so attracted to Rev. Vincent. They both were exceedingly smug and self-righteous.

Unaware that her comments often hurt Mina, Jennie wished Mina would write more often and tell her how she was getting along. "I am sure I want you to feel that you can write me anything. Often times when one feels a little blue or a little worried, if they can tell one person, they soon feel better. Now write me and tell me a little of your plans and expectations. I want to do anything I can for you, so don't hesitate to ask me."[13]

Mina tried hard to make Glenmont as social as her parents' home. Mina had her parents visit in June for an extended stay. Mina was entering the later stages of pregnancy and had been busy fixing up a room for the baby. But Mina, unable to keep to herself her mumblings about her husband's inattention, still complained to her mother. In contrast, Mary Valinda ascertained him to be "as happy and as nice as anyone could be." Edison was fond of Mina's parents and had great regard for her father and his accomplishments. Edison purchased five tickets to an open-air charity entertainment at the home of J. Hood Wright, who was part of the New York banking firm Drexel, Morgan & Company. Edison had plans to approach him later in the summer for startup capital to build a large industrial complex in the Orange Valley near the new laboratory site. The factories Edison hoped to construct would turn out highly marketable inventions from the lab.[14]

The construction and furnishing of the new laboratory in West Orange were one of Edison's chief concerns during the summer, and he needed to travel to Philadelphia to visit electrical and chemical apparatus dealers. He invited Mina and her sister Mary to travel with him to Philadelphia as a goodwill gesture and an attempt to create familial closeness. Mina and Mary went sightseeing while Edison shopped for new laboratory equipment.

Edison wanted to flaunt it to his competitors after the workmen finished the laboratory. Edison considered it his home, and he was very proud. The press relished visiting the site and accessing a research and development establishment unrivaled in the United States. Initially, scientists and entrepreneurs alike from all areas worldwide were curious to see how Edison worked. It was visited weekly and almost daily.

Edison built a series of substantial brick buildings that made up the laboratory. The main one, directly on the corner, was an impressive structure, three stories in height. The first floor had a magnificent library finely finished in artistically carved oak. It had the upper tiers of bookshelves; the shelves had valuable works on electricity and associated subjects from the bottom to the ceiling. A large open fireplace was a highlight of this room. Near the library's center was Mr. Edison's private deck connected by electric call bells and speaking tubes with all portions of the series of buildings. Eventually, Mina added a bed in the corner; Edison often slept there rather than returning home, even though his home was just a ten-minute walk away.

In the rear of the library, on the first floor, was the storeroom. There were skins, hair, horns, hoofs, and teeth of almost every known domestic and wild animal, including tusks of elephants, hide of rhinoceros and hippopotamus, antler of deer, sharks' teeth, llamas' wool, and specimens of many other beasts.

The facility also housed almost every known variety of grain and cereals, fishes from all quarters of the globe, the rarest and most costly of drugs and chemicals, and ore of gold, silver, copper, and tin. In addition were flour, sugar, and many other products found in a grocery store and a collection of iron and tinware. Edison's desire for constant experiments necessitated this. There was no telling when he used them.

On the second story of this building were several small rooms in which Edison's assistants were doing experiments, conducting research, and completing work under his direction. Finally, a large hall displaying phonographs was on the front section of the third story. They tested the machines regularly for flaws and improvements. When the machines passed the requisite tests, there were frequent exhibitions for exclusive guests.

Behind the hall were small workrooms, a well-fitted phonograph gallery, and a room devoted to displaying Edison's telegraph and telephone inventions. To the north of the main building was a long, one-story brick structure filled with instruments measuring electric currents.

North of this building were chemical rooms, where other experiments were done.

Seeing Edison spending freely on his beloved laboratory, Mina decided to extravagantly redecorate Glenmont beyond what she had initially planned for outfitting the nursery. In early July, she purchased a long list of items from the New York interior design company Pottier & Stymus, including Spanish tapestries, paneling, curtains, furniture, and several electroliers. In addition, Edison wanted to furnish Glenmont with four hundred electric lights with power drawn from his laboratory. Edison also agreed to provide electric lighting for several Llewellyn Park neighbors at cost. He also gave Mina two $500 checks ($2,500 in today's money). She donated one of them to the church. After that, she joined the Ferry Methodist Church in Orange.[15]

In early May, Mina traveled to Ohio to visit her parents. After seeing her family for a few days, she made a brief excursion to Chautauqua with her father and traveled east to West Orange. The local family newsletter, entitled *The Jumbo*, was happy to report that Mary Valinda and her daughter Grace traveled to Glenmont because Mina was about to give birth. Unfortunately, complications arose, and Mina suffered a miscarriage. Her mother shared the unfortunate news with the family in Ohio. Mina's mother, Grace, and Mary remained with her at Glenmont until mid-June to soothe her during this distressing time. The loss devastated Mina. She thought she was doing everything precisely for her unborn child. The result was another emotional step backward in Mina's quest to build a family with Edison. Mina's older brother Edward also made a brief visit to West Orange to check on his younger sister. Once Mary Valinda and Grace returned, Mina's father traveled to West Orange to be with his daughter during her recovery. Mina's sister-in-law Cora, who had married her brother Ira, wrote her when she heard the news: "Please accept my love and my warmest sympathy. All present wish you have a safe and speedy recovery. We should all be so happy that the unseen hand [of] death was gentle . . . it was God's wish that it should not be so. Man proposes, and God Disposes." Jennie, expected to arrive home from her trip to Europe, stopped in West Orange to spend time with Mina. In addition, John and Theodore came from Ohio and stayed with her at

Glenmont. When Jennie and her brothers returned to Ohio, they took Tom Jr. to spend time with the Millers and give Mina a further respite. Days after the last of her family departed, Mina turned twenty-two years old.[16]

After the miscarriage, Edison and Mina decided that Marion would benefit from some formal education. Accordingly, Marion was enrolled in Bradford Academy in the fall of 1887. The Bradford Academy, thirty miles north of Boston, was situated on twenty-five acres along the Merrimac River. The school offered a broad curriculum that included theology, Latin and modern languages, literature, mathematics, art, music, and piano instruction. Its principal for twenty years was Abby H. Johnson, who had run the Boston school that Mina attended.

Marion's first time away from home with other young ladies made her feel more mature, and she attempted to engage in newfound experiences. However, Marion was never considered an intellectually serious or studious girl. When her mother died, she switched from various schools and tutors during her primary years of education, leaving very little structure. Headmasters informed Edison that his daughter needed consistency during that time, but Edison never heeded their advice. In his mind, Marion's education could not interfere with his business travel plans. She would have to muddle through school with various tutors accompanying her while trailing behind her father.

Mina still believed that Marion did not like her regardless of her efforts to win her over. They both desired Edison's attention and competed for any scrap they could catch. Mina's parents wanted her to follow her father's instructions and be a loving "Christian" with her stepchildren, but living under the same roof with Marion continued to make that an ongoing struggle. Mina knew that once Marion was away at school, it would be the teacher's and headmaster's job to smooth out her edges. Mina hoped to concentrate on building closeness in her marriage without any distractions from a petulant and moody teenager in the house.[17]

Mina knew she would have to bite her tongue and appear like a loving family in public. She played this part well when taking Marion to Bradford Academy. Edison had no intention of leaving his laboratory for an extended period to drop his daughter off at boarding school. So, it was up to Mina to present herself as the caring and dignified Mrs. Edison. According to Marion's first letter home, Mina succeeded.

Marion knew her father had little interest in reading mail, so she crafted her letters carefully. Marion was slowly mastering the ability to get her father's attention, albeit in a short time frame. Initially, she echoed his words about being grateful for this opportunity to study hard and practice piano. Then Marion inquired about his beloved laboratory. She had received a check for $200 from her father in July, and if she anticipated additional funds, she would have to add something positive about her stepmother. However, Edison knew there was tension between his wife and daughter. Marion needed to prove to her father that she had matured in the short time she was away at school and that those feelings were a thing of the past. Marion effusively stated, "Mina was very kind to me when she was here, and I think papa that I love her truly and that every day she takes more and more the place of my mother, you ought to be very happy in having such a noble woman to love you and I hope it will ever continue so." Still yearning for her father's affection in earnest, Marion ended her letter to her father stating she sincerely "hopes that I shall be such a nice woman and so accomplished that you will not altogether think that I am undeserving of all you have done for me I study all day now and not only for knowledge but to show you that I love you." The letter was a success. Edison instructed his bookkeeper John Randolph to send Marion a check for $3 every week ($80 in today's money).[18]

With Marion away and the boys in school during the day, Glenmont finally took on a rhythm that Mina could manage. Mina was again pregnant, and still trying to adapt to her husband's lifestyle. Edison realized the household was less stressful since his daughter was away. Pleased with her personal growth of late, she wrote her sister Mame about her much-improved life. Essentially flaunting her husband's work ethic, she declared to her sister that he begged her to stay at work and eat at his laboratory so as not to interrupt his inventive thought process.

Heeding her father's advice, Mina put on a maid's cap and a large white apron and served lunch on a laboratory office table. Still desperately craving adulation, Mina presented an elaborate lunch consisting of cold ham and roast beef, baked potatoes, bread and butter, quince jelly, olives, cheese, mince pie, coffee, and chocolate milk. She received numerous compliments. Mina executed her plan flawlessly.

Unaware that her husband only needed a few hours of sleep a day, Mina altered her sleeping schedule to coordinate with Edison's. She unwisely thought his round-the-clock schedule would soon cease after they began to manufacture the phonograph and let the experiments have a rest.

Edison wanted a wife who was not too sensitive to every josh or jest. Edison was pleased when Mina dressed in the maid's cap and apron, and he kissed Mina in front of the workmen. He relished the fact that she had dressed up as a maid more than the food itself. Mina, totally missing the point of what made him happy that evening, attempted to seduce her husband back home with delicacies for years to no avail.[19]

After Mame returned to college, Mina needed other friends to keep her company while isolated in her large mansion. So, once more, Mina followed her training. First, she created a fictitious show for her friends and acquaintances to see how she lived so happily in opulence while her husband changed the world for humanity. Initially, reaching out to Miss Johnson, the headmistress of her school, Mina needed to prove that she left the school for a life with a higher purpose. Miss Johnson believed it was her mission to prepare her graduates to marry industry titans. Mina could show how well she had succeeded. Then she invited an old classmate, Helen Nichols Hall, to visit for a repeat performance.

Mr. Marvin would also visit Mina. His purpose was more to keep in touch with the family and convince Jennie to marry him. He went as far as to send gifts to Mame at Wellesley. Further inserting himself into the Miller family, he traveled to Boston and treated Mame and Marion to dinner. For Thanksgiving, Mina sent an opulent culinary gift to Mame at school, letting the young ladies of Wellesley know how kind and generous Mina Edison was.

Still unsure of her husband's unwavering affection, Mina did not have enough self-esteem in her emotional vault to act so selflessly without any bitterness. Mina's true wish was to live near her mother to better cope with her sentiments and moods and get much-needed perspective. In the meantime, she lied to herself and others, claiming that she was getting on famously. Unable to enjoy her pregnancy with concern for what the future would hold with another child in the house, she revealed to her sister Mame that she would be disappointed if she were to have twins. However, Mina did hope "the baby would be beautiful in every conceivable way and above all, extremely intelligent."[20]

Although the sisters were less than two years apart, they lived vastly different lives. Mary was planning a trip to Europe with her French teacher. Feeling bored at college and needing a change, she considered leaving school early. Having never gone to college, Mina emphatically told her she would regret dropping out. Speaking to her sister and at the same time trying to persuade herself, Mina stated, "Nobody seems contented but always wanting something different than what they have . . . we must try to be contented. . . . Let us both think we are doing the best we can and be happy." Mina confided in her sister that her "second year of married life is going to be my happiest. But I am happy now, and I am going to enjoy it while I may. I only want to gain a little more confidence in this dear kind husband of mine, and then I think all will be right."[21]

On the last Wednesday in May, Mina gave birth to a baby girl. Family members immediately called her Grace in honor of Mina's youngest sister. Marion, studying at Bradford Academy in Massachusetts, was not invited to meet her new sister at home. Nine-year-old William, who was attending the local day school and still lived at Glenmont, told one of the many reporters who were swarming around the house, "Papa has been experimenting with my new sister. He is all the time experimenting." To be exact, Edison used his daughter to show the world how well his new phonograph worked. He lifted the newborn from her deep sleep to elicit cries so he would be able to record her voice. Edison publicly referred to his new phonograph as his "new baby," and he wanted to show the world its capabilities. He planned to make recordings of his daughter at three-month intervals, but he seems not to have executed this plan. Perhaps Mina showed some courage and put a stop to this practice.[22]

Once Mina was on her own, she complained to Mame about Edison returning to work on his beloved phonograph so soon after she gave birth. Mame replied, "Thomas is a very bad husband to desert you just at the time you need the most sympathy and husbandly love. If I were there and got to see him . . . I should give him a piece of my mind."[23]

Consumed with his phonograph business, Edison accused one of his closest friends and business allies of disloyalty in a dispute over phonograph patent rights. Angered, he could not contain his rage and said, "Here after, I am going to be a hog myself and look out for myself." His behavior might have been news for some regarding his business dealings; however, it was no surprise to Mina.[24]

Weeks later, his temper turned even more caustic when he was caught off-guard by the utter betrayal of his dear friend Ezra Gilliland. Gilliland had left his management position in the Bell Company's research department to join Edison at his laboratory in what he likely believed to be a relationship of equals. To Edison, they never were. During the phonograph negotiations, Gilliland had made a side agreement with Edison's attorney, ultimately diminishing what Edison would be paid for his invention. Edison's fury had no bounds. Nothing would repair that friendship despite Gilliland having introduced him to Mina and building a house next door to Edison's winter home in Fort Myers. The camaraderie was ended and never restored.[25]

Mina was inundated and dazed by all the family and business chaos. As the boys started their school year, Marion returned to Bradford. She hoped to gain favor and told Mina that she enjoyed her elocution lessons. Mina, highly interested in how Marion spoke, wrote a personal letter to ensure that the teacher took a particular interest in Marion's success. But that personalized attention and care did not produce constructive changes in Marion's behavior or study habits. By mid-October, Marion had resumed her frankness and the rude comments toward Mina. Marion wanted to leave school and join Grace and Mame in Europe by October. Mary Valinda, however, was concerned that a sixteen-year-old girl might be too young to be so far away.

At baby Grace's baptism on November 28th, Edison changed his daughter's name to Madeleine. Edison knew his wife had chosen Grace after her beloved youngest sister. The entire family had called her Grace for the first six months of her life. Yet, Edison decided to exercise his might against her without cause. Mina did not dispute her husband and accepted the name change without contention, even concerning personal matters. This event solidified the power dynamic for the rest of their marriage.

Mina, hoping to turn her attention to more pleasant things, was looking forward to Christmas at her parents' home. She decided to stay at the Hotel Normandie in New York City to do her Christmas shopping and clear her mind of the boys and Marion's insults and various requests. The entire family headed to Akron to spend the Christmas and New Year's holidays with Mina's family at Oak Place. That year, they had a massive Christmas tree decorated with forty incandescent lights. Away from his laboratory, Edison was free to give interviews to reporters about his upcoming inventions. Mina knew these interactions kept her husband happy and the center of attention, where everyone could venerate his accomplishments.

Mary and Grace had already sailed to Europe with their French chaperone. Marion, just past her sixteenth birthday, refused to return to Bradford. Jennie, who had been home from Europe since June, graciously offered to escort Marion to join them. Mina hired an additional chaperone to accompany Marion while touring Europe. Yet Mina did not plan for Marion to return to the United States. Mina and Edison had plans to travel to Europe for five weeks for the celebrated Paris Exhibition in August. Perhaps they would decide on her return date when they arrived.[26]

7

If You Want to Succeed,
Get Some Enemies

MARION, ORNERY AS EVER, COUNTED THE DAYS TO LEAVE NEW JERSEY
and travel to Europe with Jennie. Mina was unable to comprehend the
return of her stepdaughter's demanding behavior. Mina thought that
Marion's time at Bradford, albeit cut short, had taught her about good
judgment when making wise decisions. Marion, however, reverted and
was impetuous as ever.

While she was away at school, she admitted in arguments with Mina
that "I have I fear been doubtless many times in the wrong." Phrases
such as those gave Mina hope that Marion had grown up and become
more respectful of her parents. Also, Marion said she wanted to repay
her stepmother for her "kindness by being good and grow up into such
womanhood as will show you that your good bringing up has not been
wasted and underserved." The lines in these letters were the impetus and
deciding factor in allowing Marion to return home to travel to Europe.
When learning that Mina and Edison had allowed her to return home,
she assured them that "I will never cause you to regret letting me go, and
I shall try and study hard and be good." Yet with all those platitudes,
Marion could not contain herself and disturbed the family to an extreme.[1]

After Mina purchased Marion's tickets, she refused to travel second class. Instead, she proclaimed to anyone who would listen that if it
was "not good enough for Papa's servants, it is not good enough for his

daughter." When she went to talk to her father about it at his laboratory, he did not give her more than one or two seconds of his time because he knew the conversation was regarding money. Edison attempted to inflict his self-image and way of acting on the rest of his family. His children and wife refused to adopt his manner. They knew their father was wealthy. Why should they rough it just because he preferred to adopt that lifestyle when it suited him?[2]

Before Marion's departure, Lewis visited Glenmont and witnessed Edison's indignation toward Marion. Giving up the task of bringing the family together, he admitted to his wife, "I do think it will be a good thing for Mina and the boys to have her (Marion) further away. . . . She had the boys, especially all unsettled. Mr. Edison said he wanted her to get away from here, as he put it, and thinks her going to Europe is really the best thing. He did not go to the steamer to see her off and [did not] want Mina to go." Mina had intended to go, but she gave it up through Edison's persuasion.[3]

Edison never required a reason to remain at his laboratory for extended periods. However, his heightened anger toward Marion gave him fewer reasons to return home. In addition, Edison had recently begun buying land around Bechtelsville, Pennsylvania. He was planning to build a large plant to recover workable quantities of iron from lower quality for commercial purposes and visited an iron ore mine he had recently purchased.

In the meantime, Edison's phonograph was becoming as famous as his light bulb, yet his longtime adversary, Westinghouse, still enraged him. George Westinghouse became rich and famous from his railroad air brake and manufacture of railroad signal devices; he also became involved in manufacturing electric lamps in Pittsburgh and made significant profits in generating and distributing alternating current (AC). His central stations could illuminate 350,000 lamps, and he received more orders in a month than Edison had in the past year. In addition, the local companies found that the thin-wire high-tension system was cheaper to install and operate. With his recent successes, he became a competitor of Edison and his enemy by extension.

Edison could not tolerate America choosing Westinghouse's alternating current over his DC system for their lamps. Although told by many engineers that alternating current was superior because it could distribute power at higher voltages and serve more extensive areas, he refused to adapt. Edison believed the higher voltage was dangerous and would have adverse effects on the entire industry.

Westinghouse, focused on his beloved alternating current, feverishly strengthened his number of patents. As a result, his firm was granted over thirty patents in electricity in one week. The firm was also in the process of securing an electric meter, which would be critical for furthering its commercial success.

Besides the AC/DC dispute, Edison and Westinghouse were involved in dozens of patent suits infringing on incandescent lamp patent claims. Edison published an eighty-two-page pamphlet titled "Warning from the Edison Electric Light Co." underscoring Edison's patents and warning consumers against patent infringements. Moreover, he restated his arguments against the Westinghouse AC system. The Edison company also circulated a "confidential" memorandum advising his agents that the Westinghouse firm had suppressed the results of a commercial trial of their lighting system against Edison's in Philadelphia.[4]

George Westinghouse heard that allegation and used a Pittsburgh newspaper to respond: "exposure is so complete that one wonders how the Edison company will get out of the hole in which it seems to have been put." But, like enemies sharing a jail cell, Edison could not escape the entangled destiny he inhabited with Westinghouse.[5]

Inherently a stingy man, Edison did not believe in high salaries for his workmen. On the contrary, he reasoned their long hours in the laboratory would be better rewarded with stock. However, this business model, coupled with the market fluctuations, never made his employees rich men. Numerous long-term close advisors and friends suffered due to Edison's business model. Edison's tendency to be impatient and impulsive made corporate decisions that cut out men who had been loyal to him for years. Edison made decisions that were never reconsidered. Men who devoted the most productive years of their lives to the newly crowned "Inventor of the Age" spent their remaining years poverty-stricken.[6]

By this point in his career, Edison had business interests in many companies. Edison Lamp Co. manufactured lamps; Edison Machine

Works manufactured dynamos and electric motors; and Bergman & Co. manufactured electric lighting fixtures, sockets, and other electric lighting devices. In addition, J. P. Morgan and the Vanderbilt family financed the Edison Electric Light Company, which provided financial support for Edison's electric light experiments and controlled the resulting patents. Around that time, Drexel Morgan & Co., founded by J. P. Morgan and Anthony J. Drexel, continued to finance Edison's experiments.

Henry Villard, an investment banker, was an early backer of Edison's electric light in the United States and abroad. After moving to Berlin, he became associated with Deutsche Bank. Helping Edison blend the interests of the French and German Edison electric companies, he returned to New York as the American investment advisor and manager for Deutsche Bank. Villard understood that Edison was fatigued by years of conflicts with financiers and managers in the electric light businesses and no longer wanted to give outsiders control of his affairs. So, discussions about consolidating the companies were brought to Edison's attention.

Villard worked out the details for the merger of the Edison entities into a new company with fresh capital. Villard organized the financing, mainly among German investors. One of Edison's chief concerns was to prevent Drexel, Morgan & Co. from gaining a controlling interest. Reassured that the American banking firm would be a minority investor, Edison trusted Villard and established Edison General Electric. The new company also acquired Sprague Electric Railway and Motor. Yet again, employees who had valuable positions in the smaller companies were cut out due to minor disagreements or misunderstandings and replaced. When asked about the restructuring, Edison, unashamed, revealed the man "possesses my entire confidence and is in full accord with my views."[7]

Notwithstanding Edison's moods, many lower-level employees venerated Edison. When he turned forty-two, they bought him a "complete new phonograph made of gold, silver, and steel" and restored his old clock, now regulated by a telegraph signal from Washington, D.C.[8]

Despite all that was transpiring around him, Edison devoted much of his time to the phonograph and experimented with significant changes to the sensitive parts.

Jennie and Marion left for Europe by steamer in March in first-class accommodations, including sitting at the captain's table for dinner. The glamour of travel was thoroughly enjoyable for Marion, and she relished every day of it. However, when men aboard the ship became aware that Edison's attractive sixteen-year-old daughter was onboard, the suitors began swarming around her with bouquets. Although Marion was tempted to share her exciting adventures with Mina, she remembered her stepmother's cautionary remarks about remaining humble, modest, and calm.

Once Marion's initial delight in the ship subsided, she resumed her judgmental comments describing the passengers and what she alleged was inappropriate behavior. Marion knew she had to frame a new narrative about her incessant flirting aboard the ship, which caused unwanted advances from young men. She hoped Mina would believe her side of the story before Jennie reported back to Mina.[9]

When Marion arrived in Paris and visited the Exposition, she was delighted at how it paid tribute to her father. She exclaimed that the Parisians were utterly enthusiastic over the phonograph and confessed to Mina that "she enjoys living in a time when it is better to be the daughter of a genius than to be the daughter of a Prince." Marion enjoyed her many encounters as the daughter of a celebrity. However, Marion's impulsive behavior kicked in, and she soon claimed she was bored with France and desired to venture to Great Britain.[10]

The reason behind Marion's departure had more to do with her inability to get along with others—a pattern that followed Marion wherever she went. In this case, the struggle was with the once-beloved Mary and Grace. In the past, she seemed to go along with them fine, but that was a ruse. Marion simply wanted them to like her so they could convince Mina and Edison to let her leave Bradford and travel to Europe. Now that they had to live together, she admitted that she did not care for them. It was clear that Marion could not conceal her privileged and dishonest side for the long term. The duplicity was semi-tolerable, but what Mary and Grace would not endure was the raucous and unbecoming behavior that followed. The three of them constantly fought and bickered about decorum, hotel accommodations, and table manners. Mary accused

Marion of walking in the street unaccompanied, flirting with strange men, spending extravagantly on dresses and hats, and then simply changing her mind and returning them. Unaccustomed to someone with such audacity, Mary could not cope with it. Mary, already with a propensity for anxiety, had a delicate constitution. The multiple yelling matches with Marion were hurtful and nasty. Mary was utterly unable to calm herself and remain with Marion. Finally, after numerous altercations, Mary took leave to a retreat in Spa, Belgium, to calm her frazzled nerves at a doctor's suggestion.[11]

Marion, undisturbed by the altercations, sent a telegram with an air of entitlement: "Papa may we visit London for a fortnight send money reply today." Mina received multiple letters from her sisters and Marion outlining what had transpired. The situation was of great concern to Mina. Once again, the Edisons were at a crossroads on how to manage Marion's upbringing. It was well within their power to insist she come home and put effort into bettering her character. But Edison could not be bothered. Nothing could interfere with his determination to perfect the phonograph. Mina, also exhausted by Marion's actions, let the chaperones remedy the situation. Marion was triumphant; the next week, she was in England, away from the Miller sisters. Edison ordered his secretary to forward Marion $984 ($24,000 in today's money) through Drexel, Morgan & Co.[12]

Once Marion arrived in England, she reported that she liked the English much better than the French. "The French I simply detest I think them immodest, irreligious, fickle, and insincere I could tire you with a list of their many faults." Without a tinge of regret or thanks for the recent infusion of cash, she added she was "awfully afraid you will get to Paris before we do. One cannot possibly do Scotland in less than ten days." Marion claimed disappointment but had no interest in curtailing her excursion. Using her newly developed sense of prominence, she warned her father, "You must expect Papa to be bored to death in Paris with invitations." Hoping to gain her father's favor, she concluded the letter stating, "It makes me so proud to think that I am your daughter I only wish that I was half worthy of such a father."[13]

The Paris Exposition was a world's fair that celebrated the centenary of the French Revolution. From early May to early November, it was held in Paris, drew more than thirty-two million visitors, and made eight million francs. The American exhibit, organized by the United States Commission, included areas set up for fine arts, education, industry, machinery, agriculture, electricity, and minerals. The entire exhibition covered more than two hundred acres. Edison exhibited 493 machines taking up about 9,000 square feet. It cost him at least $100,000. It was the largest exhibit at the Exposition, and his new phonograph was the highlight. The exhibition brought tens of thousands of visitors each day and was situated adjacent to where the famed Gustave Eiffel had just built his famous tower.

Mina was looking forward to this trip immensely, except for leaving her daughter behind. Without the laboratory's usual pull, Edison mixed with European society, well aware the French favored form over function and had many lavish events planned in his honor. Mina believed she'd earned her moment to shine among European society. In the meantime, she still had to manage the persistent troubles at home.

As Edison and Mina began to plan their trip, they assumed the boys would stay with Mina's parents in Akron. However, when the news of the altercations with Marion reached Oak Place, it seemed to precipitate a decision that Tom Jr. and William would remain with Edison's brother on his farm in Michigan instead. Madeleine, who had recently turned one year old, stayed in Akron the entire time.

The Edisons planned to stay at the Hôtel du Rhin while in Paris. They tried to keep their departure as private as possible to avoid overwhelming crowds and the press. On August 3rd, they boarded the *La Bourgogne* in New York and sailed with an Edison colleague, Francis Upton, and his wife, Margaret, who were traveling to Paris for their honeymoon. Edison had purposely kept his name off the passenger list and arrived at the dock in a closed carriage at the last minute. Although Mina enjoyed the ship's first-class amenities, including dining at the captain's table, she was pretty unsettled over her separation from her daughter, Madeleine, and she used her photographs as bookmarks. She was so lonely without her daughter that she looked for other babies in first class. When none were found, Mina went below to third class, where she could visit other passengers' children. While in Paris, her heart further ached when told by her mother that the baby called out, "Mama, Mama," in response to hearing Mina's recorded letter played on the phonograph.[14]

Fretful about external appearances and concerned with the formal manners of the French, she insisted she and Edison review their customs and eating habits. She knew full well he would mortify her with his boorish behavior if he were not aware of their protocols. Edison never agreed to lessons in formality, but he knew he had to somewhat play by their rules for the financial health of the business.

The ship arrived in Paris a week later, and associates immediately greeted the Edisons. French officials and journalists came out to the ship aboard a tugboat. As reported in the press, "The party convened with Edison in the gaming room of *La Bourgogne*. Everything was said in English because Edison only knows two words in our language, 'bien' and 'merci.'" As the ship arrived, passengers cheered, "*Vive Edison!*" No longer pressed for time as he was before his departure, Edison greeted the press in his usual approachable manner, apprising all who would believe that he wanted "to rest and relax."[15]

"It is in some fashion a pleasure trip, a honeymoon trip, I come like everyone else to see the Eiffel Tower." After his public remarks, they were escorted into a private section on the train toward their next destination. Edison and Mina were met by Mina's sisters, Mame and Grace, and additional Edison associates. Still attempting to avoid the overflowing crowds, the Edisons and their guests hopped into four waiting carriages, which brought them to the Hôtel du Rhin in the Place Vendôme. The hotel was located near the Tuileries Garden, which had been the Paris residence of Napoleon III as president of France. The beautiful, oversized windows allowed them to look directly out where the Prince of Wales stayed while visiting Paris. The rooms were spectacular salons decorated in red velvet and gold and an abundance of mirrors. Opulent bouquets were situated throughout the room. Reporters continued to inundate Edison. His secretary, Alfred Tate, was purposely positioned around the corner at the Hôtel Castiglione and acted as a go-between for the countless aspiring young inventors seeking advice or endorsement from the famed inventor.[16]

The hotel staff escorted Edison, Mina, and her sisters into a suite on the hotel's first floor. The hotel was mainly visited by princes, ambassadors, and heads of state. Marion arrived days later, but Mina informed her mother that Marion had been writing letters all morning, probably to keep a low profile and not engage with Mina's sisters.

Although Mina had the opportunity and pleasure of choosing fabrics from the finest dressmakers, visiting museums, and enjoying the inherent beauty of Paris, she was not content during the trip. Mina complained to her mother about how little time she got to spend with her husband. She wrote her mother, "I see almost nothing of Mr. Edison." Despite her concern about the French and their formal practices, she noted, "the people are simply unbearable," and "they are thoroughly immoral. I would not live here if they presented me with a palace all the days of my life to live in." She believed that her husband was enjoying himself despite all the adoration. Edison had the keen ability to concentrate on the people he was interested in and refrain from focusing on others.[17]

Mina knew her complaints about the French would be looked upon favorably by her mother. Regardless of her husband's fame and subsequent travel, she would never stray far from her Midwest Methodist roots. Proving her older sister Jennie's strong influence, many receipts confirm that Edison spent thousands of dollars in Paris. Many of the bills are not itemized but came from shops specializing in clothing, fabrics, and personal effects.

Notwithstanding the spending, Mina's fantasy of her and her husband receiving admirers together was quashed. Instead, he was dragged from her at every possible moment, leaving her with her sisters. The aggressive and immodest French society she encountered on this trip bore little resemblance to the experience she had during the trip she'd made years earlier with her siblings.[18]

The most glamorous experience occurred at the outset of their visit. Gustav Eiffel's son-in-law, the engineer Adolphe Salles, brought Edison and his party to the top of the tower. Waiting there to greet them were Gustave Eiffel and his sister. Edison was honored with a party in Eiffel's private apartment just below the highpoint. Attending the festivities were Russell Harrison, son of president Benjamin Harrison, the Count and Countess of Mareuil, and the Italian count Giuseppe Primoli, who took photographs of the event. Gustave Lyon, president of the Pleyel Piano Company, prearranged a small concert in the Eiffel apartment.

They dined on chicken and truffle sandwiches, cakes and bon-bons, and the finest of wines, which Mademoiselle Eiffel herself passed to the guests. While they ate, they listened to music by three of the finest musicians in Paris. The entire event was recorded on one of Edison's new phonographs, which had been carried up. Thus, all the guests could hear the concert again. Numerous tubes attached to the phonograph allowed several people to listen at once.

Edison also had the opportunity to meet the Native American members of Buffalo Bill's Wild West Show, which performed just outside of Paris for the crowds to enjoy as they headed toward the Exposition. Chief Rocky Bear led the Sioux tribe in a series of what was reported to be "war whoops" when they greeted Edison. Edison and his entourage, including Marion, Mary, and Grace, attended Buffalo Bill's Wild West Show in a Paris suburb. Edison, who complained about the richness of French cuisine, was given an "American breakfast" of pork and beans, steak, hominy grits, apple pie, peanuts, corn bread, and biscuits.[19]

Italy's King Umberto I, so impressed with Edison, named him an officer of the Order of the Crown. He then sent his representative, Cavaliere Enrico Copello, to Edison's hotel and formally made Edison and Mina an Italian count and countess. Edison, who abhorred any type of pretentious formality, chuckled as he received the honor. However, Edison's snicker flabbergasted Cavaliere Copello. Conscious that he was insulted, Mina remedied the situation and hosted the entire party for a celebratory luncheon at one of Paris's finest restaurants.

The Edisons also spent several evenings at the opera and the theater, where they quickly became the center of attention. They received standing ovations from the audience at the Paris Opéra while the orchestra honored them with "The Star-Spangled Banner." Edison also met President Sadi Carnot, the president of the French Republic; Mr. Bartholdi, the sculptor of the Statue of Liberty; the French astronomer Jules Janssen at Académie des Science; and Louis Pasteur. Edison was quite impressed while visiting Pasteur's Paris clinic and laboratory, where he observed rabies victims being inoculated. Edison and Mina also made an excursion to Versailles with her sisters.[20]

Before departing for the second leg of his European trip, Edison donated 10,000 francs ($150,000 in today's money) to the city to distribute among the poor. The following day, Edison, Mina, Marion, and Mary left Paris by train for Berlin. Edison arrived in Berlin at the Hotel de Russie near the Imperial Palace. He was honored at a dinner at the Union Club hosted by Werner von Siemens of the legendary manufacturing firm and Hermann von Helmholtz, the famed physician and physicist. Another more intimate and lavish dinner in Edison's honor was held at the Siemens family villa in Charlottenburg. Elizabeth Leisinger, a soprano of the Berlin Court Opera, entertained and recorded on the phonograph.[21]

They then departed for London, where Edison, Mina, and Mary were guests at Cray's Foot, the country estate of longtime business associate Sir John Pender in Kent. All the travel and interactions with others caused Edison to catch a severe cold and painful sciatica. Despite his condition, Mina and Edison accepted a luncheon invitation with the Lord Mayor, Sir Henry Isaacs. They made a quick return to France and arrived at the Hôtel du Rhin. Whitelaw Reid, the American ambassador to France, presented Edison with the insignia of a French Legion of Honor commander. Learning from his past infraction, Edison visited his home and thanked him for the award personally.

Marion chose to continue her travels throughout Europe, and neither Mina nor Edison objected to her decision. The miles between them would be favorable to the family. Mina was eager to see Madeleine; the extended separation had been agonizing for her. Edison was keen to get back to work in his laboratory. He had mixed and mingled and dressed up more than he had ever imagined.

Despite his aversion to all the formality of his European tour, Edison had his colleague William Hammer purchase a marble statue displayed in the Exposition's fine arts section. He paid about $1,700 ($51,000 in today's money) for *The Genie de le Electricite* by Aurelio Bordiga of Rome. The human sculpture was six feet tall and then mounted on a three-foot-tall pedestal. At the feet of the statue were symbols of the telephone, telegraph, battery, and dynamo. Situated in the raised hand of the figure, Edison inserted a light bulb. Edison had the sculpture placed near his desk in the library's center, so it would be the first thing visitors saw as they walked in.[22]

Before his departure, he also purchased a painting by contemporary American painter Abraham Archibald Anderson for $2,500 ($76,000 in today's money). The oil painting, titled *Le matin Après le Bal* (Morning After the Ball), was shipped to New Jersey and placed over the main stairway at Glenmont. This painting depicts a young woman reading about her success at the ball on the society pages. She is lying in bed, scanning the society pages for mention of her debut at the ball. Her ball gown is tossed in the right-hand corner of the painting. The woman who posed for the portrait was a ballet dancer at France's "Grand Opera" ballet.[23]

Anderson also painted a portrait of Edison working on a tinfoil phonograph owned and exhibited by the National Portrait Gallery Smithsonian Institution. The painter later recalled serving as Edison's translator on numerous occasions during the Exposition and said that the inventor often visited his studio in search of quietude.

The woman in the painting still dressed in her nightgown would be considered immodest by Mina's standards. Mina was proud to admit she never wore a dress above her ankles. If Mina had any influence on her husband, the painting would not be displayed so visibly. Nevertheless, Edison, far from a prude, must have insisted on its purchase. While on his visit to the Louvre, he stated his low opinion of Old Masters paintings. This painting suited Edison, and in a letter to Anderson when they returned in November, Edison's secretary remarked that the painting "now occupies a prominent place in Mr. Edison's residence, where it is much admired by everyone who sees it."[24]

Prior to Edison's return, he instructed his colleague Adelbert Wangemann to remain in Europe and continue to promote the phonograph. Of German descent, Wangemann composed music, played, and occasionally performed at the piano. Familiar with the European landscape, he produced a successful exhibition in Berlin. A savvy businessman, he enticed the famed industrialist Werner von Siemens Simens company to invest in his future manufacturing.

Traveling easily through the highest echelons of German society, Wangemann showed the phonograph to Czar Alexander III at the Russian embassy in Berlin. Siemens further aided Wangemann in recording the voice of Otto von Bismarck. Following the successful public-relations presentations, he traveled to Vienna to further publicize the phonograph before returning home and reporting back to Edison about his triumphs.

Julius Block, businessman and music lover, demonstrated the phonograph in Russia much to the same success as Wangemann. The czar was seeing it for a second time and sharing its marvels with his family, and members of the Russian Musical Society, which included Pyotr Tchaikovsky and Anton Rubenstein. Block anticipated recording Antonin Dvořák in Moscow. Block, an avid music lover, kept bound autograph books in which he collected testimonials from those who had attended his phonographic soirées. He called these his "Edison Albums."[25]

On the ship home, Mina had another bout of seasickness and had to stay below for most of the trip. Edison fared better and remained on deck. After five weeks of very little solitude, he enjoyed the isolation of the deck, smoking cigars. Reverting to his aggressive self, he safeguarded his freedom; he "would give a big puff, and they would go away."[26]

Eager to return to his beloved laboratory and get back to work, Edison quickly crossed the harbor onto a launch to the Jersey shore and rode by carriage straight to his workroom. Hoping to surprise the couple, Lewis had brought his two young boys to the dock for a reunion. But unfortunately, in Edison's determination to get back to work, he missed them entirely.

Upon hearing famous musicians and politicians enjoying his mechanical baby, he arranged to send an engraved phonograph to the Russian czar, as he did for the president of Mexico, the royal heads of Korea and Japan, and prominent Chinese leaders.

With the recent promotional success of the phonograph, Edison desired to improve and market it more strenuously. So Wangemann returned to the laboratory and began to invite musicians and singers to record there. The musical recordings were used to analyze and improve the phonograph as a sensitive recording device. Edison instructed that some recordings be sent to phonograph distributors in the United States.

Between the phonograph improvements, the recent consolidation of his various companies, and visiting his new mines, Edison was still keeping very late hours. One night in November, the press reported, "Edison left the laboratory for his Llewellyn Park home at 4 a.m. . . . in a buggy."[27]

The carriage was pulled by "a pair of fine grays." The horses were "restless," but Edison took the reins from his coachman. Unfortunately, he lost control, and the horses were "soon dashing along at a terrific rate." Eventually, the buggy overturned and was "dashed to pieces," with both men ejected from it. Edison only received a few bruises, but the coachman was "badly cut and injured internally." One of the horses was killed.[28]

A few days later, the papers noted that Mina was involved in a similar incident. The horses drawing her carriage bolted down Main Street in Orange after a rider carelessly bumped into them. Though skillfully managed by the driver, her team eventually crashed into and overturned another carriage before thundering "along up Mt. Pleasant Ave." Neither Mina nor her driver was injured. The paper stated she was "not at all agitated by the fearful peril she had been in." Admitting resilience at that time was effortless for Mina. Had modern medicine been in a more advanced state, she would have known she was pregnant with her second child.[29]

At the end of a tiring year, Edison and Mina and the children, Tom Jr., William, and baby Madeleine, traveled to Akron to spend Christmas and the New Year's holidays with Mina's family at Oak Place. Beneath "a mammoth Christmas tree," again decorated with forty incandescent lights, Edison held court comfortably while being interviewed for the local paper. This time they wanted answers about Edison's baby—the new phonograph. Edison said it would be "used chiefly in offices for correspondence. And then actors use it; singers use it." Animatedly, he added he already had 350 men and boys working at the new Phonograph Works in Orange and expected to hire 150 more in anticipation of a booming business. He had in hand, he declared, a single order that would require the production of eighty-five machines a day for the next six months.[30]

Edison heard that his adversary Ezra Gilliland was traveling to Fort Myers when they arrived back in New Jersey. Edison immediately instructed his secretary to inform William Hibble, the groundskeeper at Fort Myers, that they were no longer business associates. Furthermore, if Gilliland did go to Florida, he was "not permitted nor any of his party to enter the Laboratory or go about the premises belonging to Mr. Edison. Neither must any of Mr. Edison's property be used by them for any purpose whatsoever." The fracture in their friendship consumed so much rage in Edison that he did not return to his beloved Florida home for the next twelve years.[31]

8

Out of Sight, Out of Mind

A MONTH BEFORE CHRISTMAS, MINA FORCED HERSELF TO KEEP BUSY with plans for the upcoming holiday. She was still unsure whether Marion would be returning home from Europe to be with them. If she was to return, Mina had to consider which events and social circles Marion would join. Marion would need to be presented to society befitting her last name despite their lack of mutual esteem. It would not be difficult marrying her off. Although her manners required significant improvement, her bold personality and above-average looks would capture any man's heart.

Mina knew that Marion continued to galivant through Europe, allowing her father's name to open otherwise-restricted doors. Marion relished the nonstop attention. Her blond hair, blue eyes, and keen ability to learn foreign languages allowed her to soak up the local culture. After Marion jettisoned the tedious and uptight Miller girls, she toured Europe only with her chaperone. However, in early spring, Marion's chaperone, Mrs. Earl, needed to return to New York to attend a previous obligation.

The Edisons and the Millers trusted Mrs. Earl completely. She was initially friends of Jennie and had subsequently moved from Ohio to Brooklyn in recent years. Jennie thought she would be a suitable governess for Marion and described her as "a charming lady and one who has had experience with young ladies" and who came "from an excellent family." Moreover, she "is a very good musician and is fully educated." When

Marion arrived in Paris the previous spring, she thought Mrs. Earl was plain-looking but "a good conversationalist and all in all very clever."[1]

Mrs. Earl found a suitable replacement, Miss Brigham, and informed Mina that she was "a lady, of culture and refinement, high principled gentle, patient, wise, affectionate and sympathetic." Prior to Mrs. Earl's departure, Miss S. W. Brigham met the energetic Marion in Europe in 1889. Pleased with the new chaperone, Marion told Mina that she was "simply charming. . . . She is about forty and not at all good-looking, well-informed, and knows just what to see and when to see it. She is quite well acquainted here in Paris, and many of her friends have already asked to be introduced to me."[2]

Marion updated Mina on her travels. Now with her father's new line of credit and the Miller sisters off her back, Marion developed into a snarky sixteen-year-old. After not receiving any mail from home, she accused Mina of having "entirely forgotten poor me or that your letter was lost." Marion, however, never getting her fill of upsetting her stepmother, further admonished Mina that a lost letter was "highly improbable."[3]

Marion wrote from Italy, shared her adoration of its cities, and high-lighted its vast difference from England, France, and Germany. Then, with another nasty stab, Marion pitied Mina that she did not have a chance to see its unparalleled beauty and had to return home. She continued to request money and assured Mina how careful Miss Brigham was with the accounts. Not returning home for Christmas, Marion informed Mina she was invited to the Rathenau family in Berlin. Emil Rathenau was an industrialist and engineer and a European colleague of Edison. Marion wanted to remain in Germany after the New Year's holiday and wait for her beloved Mrs. Earl to return. She hoped they would continue what was left of their planned travels together.

Mina, unaccustomed to sensing signs of manipulation, suffered pangs of guilt despite their frequent disagreements. Mina was aware of Marion's tendency to be dramatic and wrote her dependable sister Mary in Europe to discover the truth about Marion's state. Mame had an opportunity to speak with Miss Brigham and thought it best for Marion to remain in Europe. However, if she remained in Europe, Mrs. Earl must take charge. Marion had taken advantage of Miss Brigham's leniency and often behaved in an unbecoming manner. Marion knew Mrs. Earl's "word is law," and with her around, Marion would "do the right thing." Mame further disclosed, "Marion is not interested in the museums or architecture and does not appreciate in the least and rather shop." Even the opera glasses that Mina sent her from home were left at the last hotel and never used.[4]

Despite Marion's carelessness and lack of gratitude, Mame told Mina that Marion was saddened that Mina did not write to her often. Mary implored her sister to realize that her "advice has more weight than you think." Mina heeded the advice and permitted Marion to stay for Christmas, yet she hoped she would return shortly afterward with Mrs. Earl. Mina surely thought this time away had matured Marion, and she could come back and live with the family, behave accordingly, and enter society correctly. Despite the recent unpleasant news from Europe, Edison granted a $3,000 line of credit ($88,000 in today's money) to Marion. It was more than a sufficient amount to cover expenses until Marion returned home.[5]

Fate intervened, and Edison's line of credit was unused. While Marion was on a train en route to Berlin from Vienna, she became ill. Miss Brigham panicked and whisked Marion from the train station in Dresden to the city hospital. Upon arrival, she was diagnosed with smallpox.

Edison and Mina were also traveling simultaneously, and it is unclear when they heard of Marion's illness. Mina and Edison spent Christmas in Akron with her family, then traveled to Norwalk, Ohio, to spend New Year's Day with his niece Nellie Poyer and her family. Having heard about the smallpox before her daughter, Mary Valinda wrote to Mina on January 2nd, concerned about Marion's illness.[6]

Mina and Edison did not return home until January 3rd, but the news about Marion was spreading fast all over Germany. Then, the telegrams came flooding into New Jersey. The first was from Miss. Brigham stating that Marion was being cared for in a Dresden hospital. There was still no improvement, but she was receiving the "best attention." The following day, Marion was "no worse, quite comfortable but crisis not yet reached." The severity of her illness and its contagiousness put Marion into quarantine. Her only method of communication with Miss Brigham was through notes. Miss Brigham reported that Marion was "brave" and her "fever moderate by the sixth day."[7]

Although Edison was incapable of displaying sympathy, his colleagues were quite willing and able. Within days of the onset of her illness, Josiah Reiff, a railroad financier and a longtime business associate of Edison, had "just learned" about Marion and had "deep regret about the serious illness of Dot (Marion's childhood nickname) in Dresden let us hope the next few days will bring encouraging news." In addition, Fredrick Siemens used his clout and ran interference between the hospital staff and Edison. Karl Ludwig Alfred Fiedler was the head physician at Dresden's municipal hospital and personally attended to Marion. Siemens assured Edison that Marion was receiving the "best attention," but her "state [was] critical." A man of his word, Siemens wrote a few days later that the "crisis was favorably sustained."[8]

Mina's mother wrote her daughter again, wondering who would retrieve her from Europe. It was anathema to leave a seventeen-year-old girl alone in the hospital. Although there were competent doctors in Germany, smallpox was a dangerous illness, and her parents should unquestionably be there to comfort her during this difficult time. Mary Valinda fretted that "It must be very hard for her to be alone, no dear hand to soothe her fevered head or say one cheering word."[9]

The news of Marion's illness spread across the nation. Edison's brother Pitt wrote from Ohio, "with much regret we learned of Marion's illness" and falsely believed that his brother was experiencing "great anxiety." But neither Mina nor Edison had any intention of retrieving her. Instead, Elizabeth Earl was summoned to Glenmont and met with Mina on January 7th at the Edison home. She planned a trip to Dresden to attend to Marion and ultimately bring her home to the United States. Edison authorized a $1,000 advance ($30,000 in today's money) to her in cash and credit to cover all the expenses.[10]

When American newspapers picked up the story, Mina acknowledged Marion's illness but denied the smallpox diagnosis. Mina was thoroughly embarrassed to admit to the press that she and her husband had abandoned his daughter in Europe with a severe disease. Either the countless conflicts precluded her from feeling sympathy toward Marion, or she was following Edison's default position: Why exert energy in doing something you do not want to do when you can hire someone else to do it instead? Regardless of Mina's inclinations, it was clear that Edison had no intention of retrieving his daughter from Dresden himself. While receiving his telegrams regarding his daughter's health, he was in the lab writing in his notebooks about his newest love interest—ore mining.

Miss Brigham continued to report to the Edisons about Marion's slow recovery. Finally, Miss Brigham realized that Marion had not received a letter from home. And in a rather bold but necessary act, she informed Edison that he needed to send one directly to his daughter. Edison, a well-known agnostic, complied and scribbled a well-known phrase more in line with Mina's beliefs than his own: "We all thank heaven" that Marion had passed the crisis. In addition, Edison learned that the doctor feared Marion's face could be permanently disfigured from the illness. He, therefore, told Marion to "obey the Doctors in every respect so you may not be marked." Edison assumed the ordeal would ensure Marion's prompt return and added that Mrs. Earl would be coming to retrieve her when she was well enough to return home.[11]

Marion's demeanor improved after receiving her father's telegram and, by extension, she felt a slight confirmation of his love. Miss Brigham noted Marion's recent "cheerful note" and added that Dr. Fiedler said Marion's fever was going down. Thus, Marion had survived the worst and was slowly improving.[12]

Ten days later, Marion's fever broke, but she was not yet ready to be discharged. Edison, however, wanted his colleagues and well wishers to know Marion was better. The Edisons were looking forward to Marion moving out of the hospital in three weeks and returning home. So, Edison instructed his secretary to inform his European colleagues of the news. The press got wind of the story through various channels and started printing that Marion had completely recovered. Now that word of Marion's recovery was circulating, Edison's ability to travel for business would not be considered callous.

Unfortunately, the daily telegrams from Miss Brigham experienced an unusual hiatus, prompting Edison to inquire about his daughter's health.

Edison was made aware that Marion's recovery was not going as well as he had previously thought. The doctors said that Marion's abscesses would prolong her stay in the hospital until the end of January.

Upon Mrs. Earl's arrival in Europe, she apprised Edison of the severity of his daughter's serious condition. There was an abscess "on her back that inflicted permanent injury to the spine . . . when they lanced it, she bled so profusely they feared for her life."[13]

After seven weeks at the hospital, the staff believed Marion was well enough to be released. Although she was expected to return home to Glenmont, Marion took Edison's money, as well as her physical and emotional health, into her own hands. She headed down to French Riviera Côte d'Azur near the Italian border with Mrs. Earl. They both believed the abundant sunshine would help with fading her numerous scars.

Mrs. Earl informed Mina that Marion's smallpox had left her weakened and that her appearance was "still dreadful." She further described Marion's entire body as "spotted like a leopard" and her face still having a "beefy redness." They remained at the Hotel Cosmopolitan under the care of doctors and nurses, where Marion's strength was "gaining slowly."[14]

Mina was embarrassed that Marion did not choose to return home to recuperate. Edison, more indifferent, found out about his daughter's whereabouts while in North Carolina. He had left New Jersey to scout ore milling sites. So, again, Mina was left with Madeleine, now an active toddler, and Edison's two rambunctious sons, just as she was entering her sixth month of pregnancy.

Marion's time in Europe and her recent negative experience with her parents provided her the courage to express herself to her stepmother. Mina cared about etiquette above all else. Marion knew her target and began her first letter home with, "I hope you do not think me neglectful for not having writing before, but under the circumstances, I know you will be indulgent and overlook it." Marion had shifted the power balance and anticipated holding it for the foreseeable future. Furthermore, she was no longer going to endure her father's indifference and openly expressed her aggravation at Mina and pleaded her case: "You surely do not blame me for feeling hurt to think that I only heard from home twice during those long dreary weeks spent in the hospital."[15]

Mina must have realized her glaring oversight and sent a gift to mollify Marion. Unfortunately, Mina, too consumed with her own life, had not realized how far the damage had spread. Marion further shared, "It was quite the talk of the hospital, and you can imagine my mortification." Marion knew by then that Mina did not care for her and told her that she did "not blame you so much, but Papa is my own father, and I never thought that he would treat me with anything but kindness I know that he did not mean to add a pang to my sufferings but, it was at a time when I needed every proof of affection and two short letters in seven weeks did not prove that there was much." To intensify the sting, she added, "I wonder if I had died if you or Papa would ever have regretted not sending a few words of sympathy for those awful hours."[16]

If Marion's letters were not hurtful enough, Miss Brigham felt an obligation to admonish Marion's parents as well. In April, she wrote to Mina before her departure that Marion had "borne her sufferings very patiently" but "was a great grief and surprise to everyone that you had not written to her during this—the most awful trial—that could have come into her life."[17]

Mina, realizing the error in her ways, began to write to Marion regularly. On the other hand, Edison would not admit to wrongdoing regarding his daughter's feelings. The hospital staff was a different story. He and Mina had to preserve his reputation. Knowledge of his paternal neglect could not extend beyond the hospital walls.

Not only did Edison pay the costly hospital bill on time, but he also sent a sterling-silver service to Dr. Fielder in gratitude. Naturally, the press learned of the lavish gift, and the Edison sycophants praised his generosity. As expected, Edison arranged through Drexel, Morgan & Co. for $2,000 ($58,000 in today's money) of credit for Marion to use in April.[18]

The gift, however, did not expedite Marion's return. Instead, she and Mrs. Earl stayed in France until the first week of May, when, at the doctor's suggestion, they relocated to Aix en Provence. They planned to remain there for about a month before moving on to Switzerland for further travel. They eventually returned to southern France for the winter to allow Marion's face to continue to improve.

Both the physical and emotional wounds took longer to mend than Mina had anticipated. In November, Marion chastised Mina once again for the shortage of communication from home. At least "Mrs. Earl received a letter from you the day before yesterday, which is the next best thing to getting one myself, so at least I have the satisfaction of knowing that you are all well. I wrote to Papa last week. I wish you would please ask him if he has received my letter and tell me when you next write." In response, Edison sent another line of credit, this time for $10,000 ($300,000 in today's money) in December to cover their expenses.[19]

Mina began writing more often and even had Madeleine scribble some letters to stem future tirades. Although Marion appreciated the gestures, she still harbored negative feelings toward her. Mina's days were lonely and consisted of a monotonous routine that revolved around her small children. Marion used every opportunity to mention the rich and famous who frolicked nearby in the Riviera, knowing full well it would make Mina jealous. Marion nonchalantly said the Prince of Wales and several other members of English society were vacationing at Cannes and gambling in Monte Carlo at night. Moreover, Marion described the weather as "a day for gods, and with a turquoise sea and sky." She and Mrs. Earl would review her French lesson sitting under orange trees and enjoying the odor as it wafted toward them with the breeze.[20]

Although Edison was a failure at returning his daughter's affection, or anyone else's for that matter, his cousin Edith was sympathetic to Marion's emotional needs while she was in the hospital. Marion purposely told Mina about her cousin's frequent letters, reminding Mina of her shortcomings as a proper caregiver.

Besides Mina's dealings with the children, she was occupied with the enormity of Glenmont to manage. Since the laboratory was less than a mile away from the estate, the home proved convenient to Edison. Despite its proximity, Edison continued to work long hours at the lab and spent little time at Glenmont. When he was at home, work was never far from his mind, leaving the concern of Glenmont solely to Mina.

While the staff cleaned and cared for the physical needs of Glenmont, someone needed to do the same with Edison's brand and, by extension, his family. The newspapers were insatiable when it came to information about the inventor's life, and any reader from every class was interested in the life of the famous man. Mina would not allow any negative news to seep through the cracks.

The boys needed to appear to thrive and succeed in all endeavors. Likewise, Marion should be mastering romance languages along with various instruments, ever-expanding her cultural horizons. The Edison children's lives, in actuality, were floundering and lonely. The image portrayed in the press was a façade that Mina created. Ironically, her dower and distant personality caused their unhappiness, but she was experiencing the same feelings in Glenmont without her family or a supportive husband. Still, Mina would not allow Edison's standing in the community to be stained. To avoid any unwanted questions about the children, she diverted attention to her lovely new home.

To that point, Mina cared about keeping abreast of the latest decorating trends, and she wanted Glenmont to rival other stately homes. Her home in Llewellyn Park would receive *Harper's Bazaar*, *Life*, *Century Art Annual*, and *Country Life* magazines to educate Mina on the value of the previous owner's various purchases and decorating decisions for the house.[21]

Despite her lonely life, Mina was astutely aware of her prominent neighbors. Many were not as famous as her husband, yet they were heads of industry and had made a name for themselves in the Northeast and urban areas of the nation. She wanted her home to be as elegant as theirs. Mina knew that Glenmont was referred to as "Pedder's home." She wanted to make a name for herself as a woman of culture and taste and have the Glenmont name forever associated with Edison's.

Mina enjoyed the picturesque portions of West and South Orange. The local publications described the area as having handsome drives and romantic scenery. The well-paved streets and elegant and imposing mansions housed New York's merchant princes, leading bankers, eminent lawyers, and scientists. In addition, their presence brought the energy, public spirit, and culture of their inhabitants. Mina wanted the Edison name included among the other prominent residents of Llewellyn Park, some of whom were Orson Desaix Munn, publisher of *Scientific American*, the first popular scientific journal in the United States; George Seabury, founder of the firm Seabury & Johnson with Robert Wood Johnson I, with whom he had developed a new medical adhesive in 1874; Wendell Phillips Garrison, son of the abolitionist William Lloyd Garrison, and the literary editor of *The Nation*, a newspaper well-known to be backed by his father's vast network of contacts.

Mina made several decorating changes now that they had established themselves at home with two new children who needed continuity and beautiful surroundings in which to grow. A gas chandelier was used in the home when the Edisons moved in. However, in 1887 Edison provided electricity for the house; an electric chandelier in glass and silver gilt now hung from the mid-ceiling in the reception hall. The result was striking. It was the first thing visitors saw upon entering. In addition, there were high wainscoting and wall coverings of stamped leather, which was customary of the Queen Anne style. Also, there were carved flowers in a sunflower design featured on the doorway, staircase, and balustrade.[22]

The stained-glass window on the stairway, manufactured by a highly skilled artist, depicted a scene from Greek mythology in which Penelope, the wife of Ulysses, is waiting for him to return from the Trojan War. The well-known phrase "Penelope's Web" was derived from this story in which she continues weaving and unweaving until his arrival home. The interpretation of the image in literature could not be more fitting for Mina and Edison's marriage, which symbolizes the faithful wife and represents the ideal moral standard of a Victorian home.[23]

Although the Pedders had purchased the furniture, natural wear and tear had occurred throughout the years, and it needed updating. This project filled Mina's days. She chose Herts Brothers, a prominent decorating company in New York City, to reupholster the library sofa and install gold tapestry curtains. Gold seemed to be a favorite color of Mina's, as she purchased a gold tapestry tablecloth as well.

With the baby arriving that summer, the new nurse would be occupying the servants' quarters. A different firm laid the carpet in the servants' dining room to ensure that they would see Glenmont as a welcome and gracious home.

Mina still wished Edison would come home more often, and she went to great lengths to entice him. When Edison purchased Glenmont, there was an unfinished billiards room attached to the house. She thought finishing the room and installing a comfy window seat and accompanying tea tables would entice him to linger. She also purchased four lounging chairs with revolving bookcases, four large smoking areas, two phonographs, an Aeolian organ, and five electric lamps. Mina attempted to create a regal atmosphere, choosing green and gold accents with a green leather couch, green valances, and deeper green drapes.[24]

From the frequent terse correspondence, Mina surmised that Marion was not returning home, and she permanently moved Madeleine into Marion's room. Madeleine favored the space due to the lovely view of the property from the bedroom's porch.

In two minds with her guilty feelings, Mina continued to try to mend the relationship between herself and Marion. She shared news of baby Madeleine and informed her that her new brother was growing and improving in every way. But Marion's sardonic nature would not let up. Each week she thought of new opportunities to taunt Mina. She no longer had her brothers to tease, and Mina was an easy target. Her latest appeal requested that her stepmother go into her hope chest and send her pictures and notes that her mother had given her before her death. She gave particular instructions and told Mina not to let anyone else touch them as they were her most valuable possession.

Marion's thinly veiled passive-aggressive letters were insufferable to Mina. Her demeanor could not withstand the constant barrages. It was the start of her fourth year of marriage, and her husband only showed his affable side to strangers. The woman who cared for his children with another due in the summer was abandoned. Even when informed by others that his family was in pain, Edison never understood why they could not cheer themselves up by acting in their lives as he did with his inventions. Whether Mina comprehended her husband's psychological shortcomings, she needed to take matters into her own hands. Unfortunately, her Methodist beliefs precluded her from confronting the culprit, and she misdirected her anger and tension. Edison's innocent sons were the recipients. She decided to enroll them in St. Paul's boarding school in Concord, New Hampshire.

The boys certainly did not want to go that far away; they had hoped to bond with Mina and make her their "new Mama." But Mina would not give them another chance to prove themselves. They continued to behave recklessly around the house, and Mina no longer tolerated it. She believed someone with more patience would provide them with the discipline they sorely lacked.[25]

In a few months, she would be giving birth to her second child, and she wanted to focus on her own children. The constant barrages from Marion in Europe left Mina exhausted by day's end. Her husband's love of the laboratory and his iron-ore milling plant left Mina to fend for herself. In Mina's mind, St. Paul's would be the solution.

The school had an unmatched reputation and would turn the boys into the young men Mina hoped they would become. In addition, her two younger brothers, John and Theodore, would be attending, as well. They could keep an eye on the boys from afar, yet at the same time, be role models and ensure their success. Mina sensed she was making a wise decision with their education and their future. Now ridding herself of the day-to-day demands of Marion, Tom Jr., and William, Mina could exclusively focus on Madeleine and the health of her unborn baby. Edison's only interaction with his three children far from home was via his bank account.

The transition was challenging for the boys, and they were not given sufficient notice before their departure to fully comprehend the ramifications of their new domestic arrangements. Poor William, only eleven years old, encountered his second experience with death. In his recently mastered cursive, he must have broken Mina's heart, sharing, "One of the little fellows here whom I liked very much . . . drowned yesterday morning. I have been hurting for him . . . without any sleep." St. Paul's goal was to turn little boys into future leaders, and it rewarded William's friendship with a pallbearer's position.[26]

Tom Jr. settled into his new life at school but was concerned he would not memorize enough Latin verbs to keep up with his classmates. The boys, desperate for an emotional connection to anyone, wrote home often. Mina, on the other hand, had little room for their needs. She needed constant reminding to send the boys train fare to return home for the holidays. William told Mina he was reprimanded by the administrator when they approached the principal; they did not have money to return home for the school break. He indignantly admonished William he was not accountable to "see to the business of all the boys." Unfortunately, it would be the first of many incidents in which the needs of the boys were an afterthought for Mina.[27]

In addition, William's grades struggled. Industry and Decorum and Punctuation were continually improving, but Greek was too difficult for him to comprehend. Finally, he requested to switch to violin to get his grades up. Promising Mina "a good report" for Christmas, William would do anything for an ounce of positive reinforcement. But unfortunately, the reports never improved, nor did her fondness. At the end of the year, he was in eighteenth place out of twenty-five boys in his class. The constant frustration Mina felt with the boys precluded her from learning her lesson about writing to them. But, as with Marion, she was not concerned when William questioned her as to why she'd only written him one letter while he'd written seven since he arrived.[28]

Shipping off gifts was Mina's method of tamping down pangs of her enormous guilt. When William received the fruit, crackers, and neckties, he thanked her with "all of his love and kisses." Concerning Marion, Edison sent an additional $2,000 ($60,000 in today's money) line of credit. Mina's gifts and money reassured her that she had attended to the children's needs. However, all remained neglected and needy. Her cognitive dissonance allowed Mina to refocus her attention on Madeleine.[29]

As summer approached, Mary Valinda was anticipating Mina giving birth to her fourth grandchild. She planned to travel to Glenmont with Mame and assist Mina with Madeleine and the new baby. Unfortunately, the two boys' lackluster term was ending. Mina, disappointed they could not rise to the occasion, did not reward them with a visit home. Instead, the boys would be rerouted to Akron to be with Mina's brothers and extended family. It was only a few years since her miscarriage, and Mina did not want to tempt fate with any undue stress that the boys would inevitably bring with them. Mina only wanted to be surrounded by those whom she loved the most.

Marion used the upcoming birth as another opportunity to get under Mina's skin. With each letter, she tried to use an even more abhorrent way to distress her stepmother. Marion recently began patronizing her: "You are a lucky woman Mama, you ought to be very thankful ... you have a sweet little baby who will grow up and do you credit, money, beauty, a mother, for my part, I don't know what else you would want in this world to make it a paradise."[30]

Mina had no intention of letting the Edison boys muddy her pristine home before the birth of her second child. Instead, she made a conscious decision to have both of them spend the summer playing baseball and tennis with John and Theodore. Although Tom Jr. and William did not see their parents, they enjoyed the outdoor life at Oak Place, a home centered on their many children's needs, rather than Glenmont, which focused on one inventor's domineering nature and requirements. They would have ample opportunity to meet the new baby when Mina felt settled.

While Mina was in her last trimester, she had the opportunity to display the charming home she had created for the world-famous "wizard." A prominent reporter from the *Boston Record* wrote a lengthy publicity piece on the family entitled "At Edison's Home: Where the Great American Wizard Lives and Works." Mina could not have been more pleased with the outcome; the journalist noted all her hard work and attention to detail, yet made it appear effortless. "The interior of Mr. Edison's home is naturally quite elegant in all its appointments. . . . As you enter a spacious, lofty drawing-room, there is a beautiful painting upon the wall, many rich curios ... a Florentine table, a cabinet with Sevre vases, and Dresden figures. Many charming and valuable bits of china was [*sic.*] purchased last summer by Mrs. Edison while abroad. The furniture is crimson satin ... rich damask hangings at doors and windows ... the piano stands with dainty white marble."[31]

For the next few weeks, Mina was hopeful. Her mother was arriving imminently, and she would be bringing her second Edison child into the world. Finally, on the morning of the first Saturday in August, when the time came, the nurses carefully removed the blue silk sheets with embroidered peacocks and prepared the bed to bring a new baby into the Edison home. The infant was born in Edison's large mahogany double bed under a canopy, as was Madeleine, his older sister. In those days, the hospitals were not sanitary enough for the Edisons and their ilk.

When Mina had a chance to glimpse the baby in her bed, she found fault in his appearance. Mary Valinda, aware that Mina was impulsive and judgmental, tried to cajole her daughter into understanding that infants' appearances alter. Depressed at first, Mina was unable to bond with her son. Eventually, she found her son more appealing when he began taking a more classic infant appearance. Mary Valinda stayed the necessary four weeks before returning to tend to her own family. Mame remained in Glenmont until November. Mina had majestic hopes and dreams for this Edison heir. Even his given name, Charles, was regal. The first two males to carry on the lofty surname were not faring well, and their future did not look promising. But that was by no means Mina's fault, and she did not believe she could change their destiny. Nevertheless, Mina knew she would do anything and everything in her power to ensure this boy would grow up to make his father proud.

Heartbroken when her sister left, gloominess engulfed Mina. Not even the birth of a healthy son, Edison's older children far away, and her home featured in a prominent newspaper could cheer up Mina. Mame fretted about her sister's state: "We are sorry dear Mina, that you are so lonesome, but you must not get blue, for we all love you even if we are so far away." The Millers also left heartbroken. They were unable to alter the trajectory of Mina's life. She and Edison inhabited two distinct worlds. His days and nights were filled with activity, and he was surrounded by people who needed him; hers with long days and lonely nights with two babies. He had not the time nor the inclination to see how she was managing, and she was on her own.[32]

The world never witnessed her grief, only his industriousness. The public knew Edison was still enamored with his phonograph as he executed twelve patent applications for phonographs and cylinder records. However, even with the success of the phonograph, he was still enraged with his once-friend Ezra Gilliland. As a result, Edison formally filed suit against him for alleged fraud in negotiations with his phonograph company.

But what fully engaged his mind and identity were his ideas about ore milling. Edison believed he could develop a process for mining low-grade iron ore. He wanted to achieve this by using electromagnets to separate iron ore from rocks. At that time, smaller operations existed, yet Edison tried to do it on a larger scale. His goal was to mine five thousand tons of ore a day and have a competitive advantage over other mills, resulting in lower shipping costs than his competitors.

Establishing the Edison Ore Concentrating Company in Michigan brought his conception into reality. Unfortunately, the plant struggled due to various problems. Dust often clogged the machinery, and iron particles stuck to the magnets. Nevertheless, the plant ended up being a model to work out the kinks that occurred with an experimental ore separator operation. Edison never felt defeat. Diligently he worked out the problems in his West Orange lab. He reopened the mill but realized he lacked the capital for necessary expansion. Unfortunately, a fire burned the separators and closed the plant. Still not giving up, he constructed another ore plant in Bechtelsville, Pennsylvania. Pleased by the performance of the machines but not favoring the iron ore, he closed that mine. Edison understood those two plants to be experiments and learned a valuable lesson about iron ore technology. He was now ready to go bigger and better.[33]

He found new land for a plant in Ogdensburg in northwest New Jersey. He liked the location because it was near the New York Railroad, and it would be easy to transport supplies and equipment. He purchased the mineral rights for nineteen thousand acres and completed the mine a few months before Charles's birth. He used large crushers resembling jaws to crush the rock with low-grade iron so the iron ore could be pulled out with his electromagnetic separators and shipped to large companies like Bethlehem Iron Works and Pennsylvania Steel.

Edison was pleased and believed he was on the way to creating something new that would revolutionize the iron ore industry. The idea captivated him; there was no room for anything else in his life. He was eager for a full-scale operation to begin.

The boys returned home for a short stint to meet their infant brother at the end of the summer. Their stay was intentionally brief, and they were ushered back to New Hampshire as the season turned to resume their character building. Unfortunately, the fall term did not fare much better for the boys; they preferred to stay in New Jersey with their new brother. William wrote that he "was homesick yesterday and went up to my room and cried as hard as I could." Young William, hoping to elicit sympathy from Mina, also shared his academic progress: "I had every lesson perfect except for arithmetic which I stood out 35 out of 45. . . . I forgotten nearly everything I knew last winter." Mina, too focused on her babies, did not mind the boys and was not alarmed when they begged for more suitable clothing the next month. "It was 28 degrees yesterday morning, and you did not send any of our warmer clothes."[34]

Writing to them out of obligation, she asked routine questions. Dutiful as ever, they responded the next day, listing their teachers' names and sharing that "many boys come into our room and look at Papa and you in the picture." However, those short letters from Mina were few and far between. The majority of the correspondence from that year is laden with William pleading in any way he knew how to hear from someone from home. "I am not cheerful when I do not get a letter. Please have someone write to me, even Johnny." Johnny was a member of the Glenmont staff who often took care of William's pets.[35]

Likewise, Mina was so homesick for her own family that she decided to spend Christmas in Akron. She sent the boys directly there rather than having them stop at Glenmont and going together as a family. Mina thought of them as appendages, never considering them part of her own family. The fall term was still not relaxing for the boys, and they could not wait to see Mina: "I am so happy to think of seeing you all again. I don't know what to do." Mary Valinda, sensitive to their emotional state, felt inclined to send them an individual invitation to her home to lift their spirits.[36]

Marion blamed her disinclination to return home on her scarred face, which was taking a long time to heal. Marion played with the idea of remaining in Europe indefinitely. Her letters, however, continued to goad Mina. Although Marion adored Mrs. Earl as her new caregiver, she still needed personal items from home to soothe her homesickness. So, she requested Mina to locate, "That portrait of Papa when he was a boy is mine. It is most like that you do not know this and think it Papa's; it belonged to my mother and was very much valued by her, so I thought I would mention it in case you did not know that."[37]

Self-doubt is a strong emotion; it can debilitate one's every action. Edison and Mina were exhausted by year's end. Mina was juggling the needs of five different children, three jettisoned and two under the age of three. She could not proceed without second-guessing herself. But on the other hand, Edison was unfamiliar with doubt and had never experienced that emotion. The children and their needs bored Edison, and he never paid them a mind. Nevertheless, the energy of iron ore milling had such a substantial drag that it pulled Edison away from his home for the best part of the next eight years.[38]

9

Disturbances

UNLIKE MINA, EDISON RARELY VISITED HIS FAMILY. HIS FATHER, SAM-
uel Edison, was an energetic eighty-year-old often traveling through
the United States on his son's dime with his longtime companion James
Symington. Sam, comparable to a garrulous teenager, relished interviews
about his famous son during his travels. Edison's father was more sociable
than his son and pushed his limits as far as he could. The year his wife
died, he began an affair with his housekeeper. Despite her being fifty
years his junior, his vitality, blue eyes, and boundless energy attracted the
yearning of the seventeen-year-old Mary Sharlow. She was unaffected by
the disparity in age, and the couple lived together in bliss. It is unclear if
they were ever married. The absence of a wedding did not affect their love;
they had three daughters together while Samuel was well into his seventies. Unfortunately, Edison's brother William Pitt did not possess the
same vigor as his father. Hearing of his only brother's death at the age of
sixty of heart disease and cancer, Edison felt obligated to take leave of the
laboratory and attend the funeral in Port Huron, with Mina at his side.

Edison made a conscious decision not to inform his father of his
brother's death and instructed James Symington to withhold the news.
Symington acquiesced. The two men were in Fort Myers at the time. Edison dispatched both men to keep a watchful eye on his winter home.
While Edison was in the middle of a contentious lawsuit with Ezra Gilliland, Edison had instructed the Fort Myers groundskeeper to cut all
access to any electricity to Gilliland's adjacent home. An actual act of

vindictiveness, Edison excelled at cutting ties with those who scorned him. Edison instructed his father to report if the groundskeeper executed Edison's instructions. Gilliland received the implication clearly and decided to maintain his own house and put it up for sale. Edison put a higher premium on his winter home than on his father's need to bury his son. Had Edison telegraphed his father about his son's death, it would have pushed the funeral back days due to his travel needs. That, in turn, would have been an inconvenience to Edison.[1]

After the funeral, Edison returned to his usual preoccupied self with the scores of facets of his business. As of late, he was concerned about the possibility of impending creditors seizing his home. He, therefore, decided to transfer the ownership to Mina. The title to the property was passed to her, as well as the insurance policies. Edison first sold the property to his secretary, Samuel Insull, for one dollar, and he sold it to Mina. When Mina obtained ownership of Glenmont, Edison's attorney advised them to "have a complete inventory made of every item." However, his attorney was concerned with the legality of the transfer and stated, "articles which are already Mrs. Edison's property should not be included in the inventory . . . only those which belong to you and which you wish to have transferred."[2]

Mina savored the short yet rare time with her spouse despite traveling to the funeral. However, she was in better spirits as *Ladies' Home Journal* published a series on UNKNOWN WIVES OF WELL-KNOWN MEN. Mina was excited to be in the next issue. The magazine described her as the unchanged, placid, and quiet young lady she was while in Miss Johnson's finishing school. Although the article told how it might have been difficult to become a stepmother, Mina had succeeded in making her stepchildren her "allies and comrades," which spoke well of the strength and goodness of her nature. Furthermore, the article continued to refer to how she and the stepchildren were always practicing piano together. Finally, she was unwavering in supporting the needs of her husband's interests, discovery, and improvements.[3]

The article was a great success; it was another instance when Mina would mislead the public about her happy and loving family. In Mina's view, the Edison family mythology needed holding up. Her father had implored her to advise her husband to stop working nights and come home to the family. Unfortunately, the continued anxiety spawned from her husband's disinterest in her and his new children redirected itself to his two innocent sons. Mina continued avoiding the boys' countless requests for letters and support as they continued to have trouble settling into school. Nor did she mind Marion commencing her third year far from her, traipsing around Europe under the guise of learning about culture, art, and language.

Although not personally involved with the children, Edison still had to shoulder the financial burden. Edison's relationship with money was idiosyncratic at best. By June of the same year, Edison had fired those whom he thought were incompetent managers of his iron ore milling plant and had invested $1 million ($30 million in today's money) in the project at that point. The money paid for the property, the construction of the mill, and the cost of experiments. However, months prior, Edison received a letter to contribute to the endowment fund for the Orange Memorial Hospital. He responded that he regretted "very much that it is impractical for me to subscribe to this fund. I already have a very heavy drain on my resources. I need every cent I can spare in my experimental work. . . . I think the rich merchants and business men are the ones who should subscribe to the Hospital fund."[4]

Edison gave the final answer when it came to expenditures and used all sorts of methods to cut costs. In addition, all bills, even the ones for Mina's personal expenditures, had to go through the laboratory. In essence, Edison treated the household as if it were an extension of his laboratory. Mina would eventually learn to incorporate this idea into her own vision of her role in managing the household. The standard practice became that Mina would send a purchase request to the laboratory, and Edison's secretary would see it and pass it on to Edison for approval. Edison's availability determined the timetable. More often than not, Edison cut from the list or wrote an emphatic "NO" across the top of the paper. His staff saw Mina's intimate requests, and it was demeaning that Mina's opinion was of no consequence.[5]

He also maintained his Menlo Park property, which remained in his late wife's name. Eventually, he planned to pass it on to her three children when they came of age. In the meantime, Margaret Stilwell, his first wife's mother, was living there. Since his first wife's death, the Stilwell family corresponded with Edison regarding various financial needs. Edison paid for the schooling of Eugenia, his first wife's younger sister. Charles Stilwell, her brother, had been working for Edison for years. He was currently living in Hamilton, Ontario, and employed as the superintendent of Canada Lamp Works. Edison appreciated Margaret rearing his children after his first wife died. Allowing them to stay at home in Menlo Park and maintain the property in his absence was Edison's method of showing his appreciation. They accepted anything that Edison threw their way. Whether Edison's gratitude was genuine or simply a means to an end, it was clear to the Stilwells that he had no intention of spending one cent more than required. That year, he received a letter from the Improvement Society of Menlo Park secretary regarding "the plank walk" that remained at the property or "have it repaired." Either way, Edison did "not desire to spend any money on it." Edison even attempted to cut his insurance payment on the property by half until his attorney informed him there would be "legal liability" involved. Finally, Edison was overwhelmed with his considerable legal costs and decided to "let it go."[6]

There is no existing correspondence regarding Mina's feelings concerning Edison's interaction with his previous wife's family. She felt plagued daily by her poor mothering and lack of decent education. Edison hired a clipping service to retain articles about him covered in the press. Many of the newspaper articles clipped covered the courtship Edison had with his first wife. Thus, it is unlikely that Mina never read them. Lynn Given, Mina's assistant, in an interview after Mina's death, referred to Mina as "a very jealous woman—jealous of her children or anybody."[7]

Mina had ample reason to be resentful. If the iron milling business was not enough to steal her husband away, there was an even more significant, more sensational innovation in its infancy that would change the world to the same degree as the phonograph and electric lamp. The laboratory had designed a primitive motion-picture camera called the kinetograph and the eyehole movie viewer called the kinetoscope. Unfortunately, Edison was not as clear on his market for the new invention as he had been with his earlier creations. William Dickson, an employee of Edison, made further developments to the existing project.

After meeting English photographer Eadward Muybridge in 1888, Edison became interested in moving images. Muybridge was interested in understanding the movements of animals; as a result, he made a device called the zoopraxiscope, which displayed the moving pictures of various animals. When Muybridge visited Edison's laboratory in 1888, they talked about combining his zoopraxiscope with Edison's phonograph. Fascinated, Edison drafted a patent application for a device to record images, a device for viewing pictures, and an apparatus that merged viewing the photos and listening to sound at the exact moment. Edison thought one camera should produce a large number of images in quick succession. When Dickson took charge of the project, he tried to improve the picture quality and design a camera and film for recording many photos.[8]

At the Paris exhibition, Edison met Etienne Jules Marcy, who designed a camera capable of taking continuous exposures on a strip of film made of paper. Upon returning, Edison drafted another patent application for photography with a roll of paper with holes on opposite sides that fit on a small wheel. The film paper attached to the wheel and the wheel-turned holes would advance the film through the camera. That spring Dickson and others at the lab designed a horizontal-feed camera. Edison had used his knowledge from previous experiments, such as stock tickers and the telegraph, to help him develop the mechanism's movement. The public viewed the films through a wooden box. There were compartments for an electric lamp, a battery-powered motor, and a fifty-foot ribbon of film made of celluloid on rollers and pulleys. He, or rather Dickson, began to make short movies. There was still more research even though he showed some short films to the National Federation of Women's Clubs, hosted by Mina, on May 20th, 1891. Mina was overjoyed that her husband used and valued their home to show off his latest invention. But Edison recognized Glenmont as only an extension of his lab. Edison did not market it to the public until 1894.[9]

He built a makeshift movie studio on the property of his laboratory. A semi-retractable roof allowed for natural light for the film; electric light was not powerful enough to expose the film. Edison's workers named it the Black Maria because it resembled the nineteenth-century police wagon to transport prisoners. One of the first copyrighted motion pictures was *Edison's Kinetoscope Record of a Sneeze*. It was the film of one of Edison's workers sneezing.[10]

When the press asked Edison about the future of motion pictures, he was far from prescient. "This invention will not have any particular commercial value." And further validating his lack of emotion, he added, "It will be rather of sentimental worth." He believed people would use the invention in their home libraries to watch actors projected on their walls. But Edison's lack of empathy might be the reason he failed to understand how moving pictures created an emotional bond for audiences. He thought these "devices are of too sentimental a character to get the public to invest in" and was "doubtful there is any commercial future."[11]

The laboratory men were giddy with the new invention, and their first films reflected their excitement. The early films were made by, for, and about them. Early subjects included John Ott's *Sneeze*, work scenes such as a *Blacksmith Scene* and *Horse Shoeing*, *A Bar Room Scene*, a *Cock Fight*, *Dancing Bears*, *Boxing Cats*, and *The Wrestling Dog*. Other subjects included novelty acts from Vaudeville such as *Sandow* the strongman, female contortionists and dancers like *Carmencita*, and performing animals. *The Leonard-Cushing Fight* was the first of many boxing movies. Soon the movies became longer and had more actors. The interest and thrill grabbed the public's attention. Buffalo Bill and Annie Oakley came to the studio to create animated films. The Black Maria studio made seventy-five films in 1894.[12]

While Edison thrived in new environments, his sons were floundering. William's letters revealed that he continued to fail most of his classes. After he disclosed his grades, he repeatedly promised in vain he would do better next term. He also realized he could make extra money from his father's fame and requested his autograph to hawk to his classmates when his allowance fell short. Mina became further despondent that William could not rise to the standards St. Paul's had set for their students. On the other hand, her younger brothers continued to excel in all their activities. At that point, Mina hoped William would eventually adopt the guidance and structure of the school and come out more like a Miller boy.

Tom Jr. possessed a more delicate nature than his brother. His failures in sports and academics manifested themselves into physical ailments. He claimed it was "not his fault that his grades are so bad . . . he had been sick all term," and he "never feels like studying due to his horrible headaches." He surely thought both Mina and Edison would be concerned about his health issues. He further explained that "the work is too heavy. I don't want to go to the infirmary because I am afraid I bother them too much. . . . I have kept this from you and Papa because I am really sick . . . I can't stand keeping it from you anymore." Neither parent was alarmed by Tom Jr.'s complaints, and he had to remain in school. They had no intention of Tom Jr. returning home to see a local doctor for a more thorough examination.[13]

Unfortunately, at this point, a watershed moment occurred for the family. The Edison boys were now cementing their personalities in the ground. Likewise, Mina played her role as the wife who deferred her husband's desires regardless of cost. As a young boy of fifteen. Tom Jr. could not fathom that his father nor Mina would not be compassionate to his suffering. He now understood that his pain would not receive sympathy, not even from his own family. Like anyone calling out in pain and left unanswered, he would turn to any means to soothe himself.

His first idea was to bypass his father altogether to get his needs met. He started writing directly to Edison's secretary, John Randolph. This idea began well. Edison was not interested in hearing about his offspring and was pleased that his office staff ran interference. The bids ranged in frequency and need. The first request was a lamp to send to the rectors to give lectures to the students. Tom Jr. assumed currying favor with the administration would adjust poor academic reports sent home to the Edisons. The subsequent request was for an electric pen. Tom Jr. hoped the exciting new technology would build popularity and future friendships that he could not attain with his personality.

When the boys returned for the Christmas break, they received a reprimand about their grades. They had to work harder and do their best. However, Tom Jr. returned to school so distressed after the holiday that he counted out the "seventy-six" days until he returned home. He had counted the days on his calendar on the train back up to New Hampshire.

He hoped the act of tallying itself would display his affection or need to be with Mina. However, she disregarded what she construed as childish behavior and could not understand his cry for help. Ignoring their needs began the impending onslaught of dire complaints that would emanate from the boys and affect their relationship with her for the near future.[14]

"I will go crazy if I stay here much longer," Tom Jr. informed Mina. She was unaccustomed to this intense language. As a devout Methodist, Mina associated that word in sermons when discussing the evils of Satan. Tom tried to express his needs more directly: "It seems there are so many places that I could be happy, yet I have to go to a place where I am very unhappy, those are the things that bother me and worry me. I feel something weighing heavy on my heart, and I can't get it off in any way . . . it seems to grow heavier all the time. I can't go home because I promised to stay. . . . I feel like I would like to be shot because I have nothing to live for, nothing at all. . . . My hatred is increasing instead of decreasing, Mamma!!!"[15]

The very next day, he wrote directly to his father and begged and pleaded to come home. He promised to study all day if he could return, adding that studying was for his benefit. Further attempting to state his case and play each parent against the other, he wrote, "I hope you see what I am driving at because I don't think Mamma does at all."[16]

Tom Jr.'s hysteria and complaints were trickling down to William. They shared a room, and although William tried hard to fit in and study, he was privy to all his brother's emotions. To placate them, Edison sent them a new phonograph at school. William was grateful beyond measure. Even at a young age, he had a more keen understanding of his parents' nature and what pleased them. At times he defended his brother to his parents and reminded them of his strengths and accomplishments, even if few and far between. The phonograph pacified the boys. By year's end, the principal had written home to the Edisons about their progress: "Will has been difficult and self-willed."[17]

Mina rented a cottage affiliated with the Long Beach Hotel on Long Island to relax her nerves for July. The boys' constant disorder caused great uneasiness for Mina. She needed a change of venue. The tough decisions overwhelmed her, and she could only devote finite attention to them because she was fighting a battle on two fronts. Within the same month that Tom Jr. threatened to commit suicide in New Hampshire, Mrs. Earl wrote Mina that Marion had been spending time with a gentleman named Charles Levison. Their relationship had reached an advanced stage, and he had proposed marriage.

Mina attempted to enjoy the seaside resort. The luxury hotel had dining that could accommodate one thousand guests and catered to "the most fastidious taste." There were concerts and ballrooms for dancing, billiards rooms, and bowling alleys. Edison spent a few days at the cottage with Mina's children but spent most of the summer at his mine. The older boys spent the summer with their aunt Nellie, who looked forward to their arrival with anticipation; she had been lonely since Edison's brother died in January. The boys could spend time with their paternal grandfather, who, despite his advanced age, they described as "bright as a button." Mina, preoccupied with her children at the beach, neglected to send William and Tom Jr. any money. Still inundated with a barrage of family stresses, the seaside and its environs could not calm Mina's nerves.[18]

Marion had revealed the existence of Charles Levison the previous year, but she remained cagey at best about their relationship. Back then, Mina did not seem alarmed that a wedding was imminent. Marion described him as a friend of Mrs. Earl's and that she had met him and his brother the previous spring in Tangier. They continued to meet in Spain and kept on running into each other in the hotels they frequented. Marion put on the charade that they were merely acquaintances. Yet she whetted Mina's appetite for more gossip when she added that Charles and his friends had "the bluest of blood in their veins."[19]

The young couple continued many "gay times" together. Yet, Marion was reluctant to disclose their friendship earlier because Mina might have gotten the "wrong impression" about its trajectory. Nevertheless, Marion did want to vouch for her excellent judgment in attracting him and subsequently befriended him. She even claimed that Mrs. General McClellan, whom she saw in Tangier, and who lived in Llewelyn Park, was an "intimate friend" of Charles Levison.[20]

Marion continued to describe her flirtations from afar in great detail. Marion's letters read like a romance novel. Mina received weekly updates of their burgeoning romance. Mina had a front-row seat to Marion's courtship, living vicariously through her stepdaughter. Charles teased Marion and feigned unkindness because Marion would not promise to visit his home in Bilboa. At that point, Mina was unsure how to interpret Marion's new relationship. The distance precluded her from understanding the dynamic between the couple and compelled her to wait for more information in the following letter.

Charles Levison was not the only object of Marion's affection. Marion had a preexisting interest in Mina's older unmarried brother Edward. Marion mentioned to Mina that they often corresponded, passing on her dearest regards. However, Mina had no desire that Marion and Ed's relationship would manifest into anything more than step-uncle and -niece and yearned for her infatuation to dissipate. Nevertheless, Marion, still harboring unresolved anger toward her stepmother, continued to provoke her. Marion admitted she only purchased two Christmas gifts for her family—one for Mina's mother, whom she referred to as Grandma, and the other for Edward. She sent Edward's via New Jersey and hoped her father could pick up the customs tax rather than burden Edward with that exorbitant payment. In addition, she would like her parents to pay off the debts that she'd run up while traveling throughout Europe.

Mina tried to ignore the petty taunts and inquired about Marion's travel plans back home to New Jersey. Marion was swift to clarify her plans and noted how they directly contradicted the false press accounts circulating the globe. At that point, she wanted to remain in Europe because of her pocked face and not because she continued to learn European languages or was an accomplished pianist. She further added that she was "quite a different girl now than I was when I left home."[21]

After the holiday season, Marion considered it was time to return home, owing to her choice. Marion was confident that Mina had shared the information about Charles Levison with Edison. Thus, any immediate blowback by Edison had hit Mina, and the Atlantic Ocean's expanse had safely shielded Marion. However, Marion realized that she would again face her domineering father, whom she had not seen in more than three years. "I will only marry Mr. Levison if Papa is willing that I should do so. . . . I know that Papa would be happier if I married an American rather than an Englishman, and I have struggled with this fact" were her only conciliatory remarks before returning.[22]

Marion hoped to receive her father's blessing and shared that his family is "royalty," and she has to be presented at court because his family is "conventional." Furthermore, Charles had already told his closest friends of the "conditional engagement" and invited them to spend their honeymoon at the Madrid home of the Marquis of Villamajor. And finally, in her February letter, Marion added she "hopes to bring him home in two weeks."[23]

Mina still developed recurring "blue" periods over the winter and still required her mother to confirm her love and validate how challenging her life was, bringing up babies without support from a husband. Her sister Mame paid extended visits to boost her spirits throughout the season.

That spring, the Millers were pleased to announce a much-anticipated event. Finally, Jennie had decided to marry Richard Pratt Marvin. Mina was so delighted that her thirty-seven-year-old sister was to settle down after a courtship lasting a decade. This occasion should have altered Mina's aura. But instead, Mina could not shake the torment that Marion, Tom Jr., and William deposited on her fragile psyche. The wedding would now bring them all together under one roof. Jennie understood the discord Marion caused the family and attempted to be supportive. She offered Mina the option of excusing Marion from attending if she did not desire to do so. Mina thought she would participate despite her recent apology "for treating the boys atrociously, but it is the selfish side of me that I do not write the boys, and I just cannot bring myself to agree to something that I absolutely hate. So, I will not do what is not agreeable to me." Mina knew that Marion would want to get all dressed up and see her brother Edward and attempt to manage her interaction more maturely with her younger brothers.[24]

The Edison family, however, did rise to the occasion, at least for the public. The ceremony again took place at Oak Place, which the Millers adorned with a "profusion of floral decorations," so much so that the guests felt as though they were waking into a "magnificent conservatory." Lilies and roses of every kind covered any area that would accommodate them. The Millers intentionally darkened the surroundings but for the electric lights, which showed through flowers adorned from chandeliers. Mina's friend Helen Storer was honored to play the wedding march on the Miller baby grand. Jennie included Tom Jr. and William in the ceremony, having them be ribbon boys with her brothers Theodore and John while she and the bridal party walked toward the clergymen officiating the ceremony. Jennie wore a Venetian lace gown with a pendant of pearls and diamonds given to her by her groom. The press also took notice of Marion's magnificent green silk and black lace gown. George Vincent and his father attended the wedding, but Mrs. Vincent was noticeably absent. There is no record of Charles Levison as being in the company of Marion.[25]

The local society attended. Unfortunately, Richard's father had died three weeks prior, which made the ceremony bittersweet. The estate left a generous $1,000 check ($30,000 in today's money) as a wedding present for the bride. Richard had secured a position with the B. F. Goodrich Rubber Company and was permitted a luxurious six-week honeymoon to the south and west, including New Orleans, Denver, and other cities.[26]

The Edisons returned home. The boys continued to improve their outlook and behavior at St. Paul's, giving them additional opportunities to rise above their insecurities and fit in with the other boys. Mina practically held her breath in anticipation of any type of good news emanating from New Hampshire.

As fall returned, Mina sent the boys back to school despite their protests. Mina did not want to administer them at home. She hoped the summer had changed their outlook and that they would do better this term. What concerned her more than ever were the hints of bleak economic news sweeping across the nation. Mina worried her father's work could collapse due to the economic downturn and that he would lose everything he had worked hard for most of his life.

In the midst of her family's ordeal, Mina's one bright spot was looking forward to appearing in another magazine. This time it would be about both her and Edison. She knew it was her duty to preserve and elevate her husband's name, and she knew he was becoming a national treasure. William Dickson authored the article—the same employee who was working on the kinetoscope at the lab. Dickson wrote the piece because

Edison trusted him. If possible, all family accounts would be in the hands of friends or associates whose judgment and discretion he could trust and whose intimate knowledge of the facts would save him from any misrepresentation.

As the time approached for the interview, Mina staged her home for a multipage, fourteen-part series of articles titled THE LIFE AND INVENTIONS OF EDISON by Antonia and William Dickson. They appeared in *Cassier's* magazine between November 1892 and December 1893. The last article of the series was the one on Glenmont, Mina, and the family. These articles became the basis for their 1894 book, *The Life and Inventions of Thomas Alva Edison.* They mentioned the articles in their preface, along with their article on the kineto-phonograph in *Century* magazine and additions they made for the book. *Cassier's* magazine was primarily a magazine about engineering, but it had agreed to do a human-interest story on Mina and Edison. Mina knew the article would draw a larger readership than the previous writeup in *Ladies' Home Journal.* This one would also include photographs of the family and home.[27]

Dickson did not disappoint the public with his over-the-top, sappy, and sugary prose. Papers and magazines needed to sell their issues, and the Edison name helped them reach their bottom line. He described Glenmont as "refreshingly independent of architectural rules . . . yet present a wealth of fancy . . . and delicious surprises." He described Edison in his den not as a lion, but as having a "luminous face with good nature and kindly humor . . . and lovable personality," further adding that "we owe such immeasurable debt to this man."[28]

Further deceptions were couched in flowery language and spoon-fed to the public. A glaring misrepresentation was Mina's love for the French. While she and Edison attended the Paris exposition, she wrote home with heaps of disdain at their immodesty and racy behavior. In the article, Mina said, "I couldn't have anything but affection for the French. They are so enthusiastic, so kind, so appreciative." The tales continued to spin when they described Marion's room as having French knick-knacks because Mina liked to accommodate her stepdaughter's tastes. As they entered Tom Jr. and William's room, the author marveled at their neatness. The magazine portrayed Edison in a most optimistic way for their readership.[29]

However, Mina, who was not yet thirty, was not a seasoned actress. When asked if Tom Jr. "inherited any of his father's genius," she replied, "no." When further pressed and asked, "Upon whom do you think the father's mantle will descend?" she laughed. "I believe Charles will be the one." Although he was only a toddler, Mina revealed her bias.[30]

The interviewer continued to exalt Edison to the highest degree as the "greatest genius of this or any other age." Mina composed herself and went back into her role. "He is better than a genius . . . he is a gentle, patient, kindly man." Mina wanted the world to believe it, so she pushed her point: "People only know him exclusively as an inventor, but of his personal qualities, they know little. Discord does not live in his presence."[31]

The inconsecutive ten-day interview covered months of visits to Glenmont. The article came as a series, which caused its readership to be excited in anticipation of the next installment. The report-ending remarks lauded Mina as having the "admirable power of adaptation" concerning her husband's career. The Edison family being a "harmonious family," and the older boys never "burdened with obtrusive piety," Mina succeeded in turning every rumor that might have slipped out of the house through the staff or the older children.[32]

Mina fully cemented the Edison charade with a solid foundation. Edison's adoring fans were fully convinced of the happy household that existed at Glenmont. But it was all a sham. At the same time the article was published, the boys often wrote home asking for much-needed clothes or travel money. Additionally, they were doing poorly in school and reprimanded by teachers. Both boys were not raised to fit in with young boys at St. Paul. Life at school was miserable for the boys, who claimed the other boys turned against them, and even the rector disliked them. Mina, in turn, complained to her mother about their lack of effort. Mary Valinda, as usual, came to their rescue and told her daughter she should not expect so much from them, yet she was pleased that Marion enjoyed Mina's company and had acclimated to life at Glenmont while she was home.

But Mina finally reached a breaking point with Tom Jr. His incessant letters wore her down. He claimed he had constant headaches, no girt, and an inability to learn. Mina was at a loss with him. She had never encountered a child who felt so alienated, so sick, and lacked such motivation. She and Edison decided he would leave St. Paul without a diploma. Tom Jr. was sixteen years old and had no direction in life. Edison agreed to have him work at the Machine Works in New York and learn the various aspects of that business. Within a month of working, his eyes needed bandages because of a mishap with metal getting into them. Tom continued to be down on himself and continued to complain of his health problems.

Unfortunately, William felt abandoned without his brother by his side. Likewise, when one domino fell upon another, he began to complain incessantly. He wanted to cry his eyes out "because Tom is gone." Furthermore, William "hates it and has been apart from his mother for five months." Somehow his friends turned on him and were "being cruel to him." When he did do well enough in his classes, he wondered why he did "not receive fruit from his mother." When he realized his letters were not getting any response, they became even more intense.[33]

William needed support from either parent, and he declared that he would "rather be in prison than up here." He thought he could bargain with his father, who despised paying for boys who did not excel. William asked if he could "come home and go to public school or any school near home. I can't stand it up here. If you want to put me out of my misery, you will say yes if you don't, you will say no. I would give all I got money, clothes . . . and everything to get out of this place."[34]

Complete opposites of the Edison boys, Theodore and John were thriving. Their grades were high, and their classmates cheered on their successes. Mina was getting their letters as well as William's. The contrast was glaring in Mina's eyes. When her brothers shared their accomplishments, she rewarded them with gifts and accolades. Rather than having compassion or understanding for William's learning difficulties, Mina compared them to her younger brothers. William and Tom, for that matter, consistently failed in comparison. They could never compete, and Mina blamed the boys for their failure. They were an embarrassment to the Edison name, which she worked so hard to promote.

The stress of William and Tom Jr.'s inability to succeed had to be thrust aside for more urgent concerns, however. The economic downturn headed toward the Midwest. The Panic of 1893 was about to commence one of the most severe financial crises in the history of the United States. Lewis Miller did not foresee the crisis. In the past two years in Akron, Aultman, Miller & Co. had prospered. Lewis and Mary Valinda were so pleased with the business that they went on a second honeymoon. They traveled to California and stopped at the Chicago Exposition. However, they cut their trip short and feared that his company was in jeopardy when they learned of the news of the economic crisis.

The financial decline in the United States affected every sector of the nation, producing political upheaval. Frightened stockholders ran to the bank to withdraw their savings, which caused a run on banks. A credit crunch rippled through the economy. Businesses failed, and four million people lost their jobs in the United States. Trade magazines wrote, "Business is so dead that the mourners have not even the heart to hold a wake." Lewis's company went to court and asked for a receiver to option over the company because its assets were insufficient to cover its liabilities.[35]

The company's creditors called in their loans, which Miller personally had endorsed. Lewis Miller put his remaining stock into an escrow account. He quickly arranged a deal with his bankers for more time. Edison loaned the company tens of thousands of dollars to save them his impoverishment. The Akron plant survived, but the Canton plant could not withstand the depression. In April, Lewis Miller suffered a heart attack. Although the doctors could not conclusively connect it to his economic woes or general overexertion, these certainly contributed to his declining health.

In 1893, C. Aultman & Co. declared bankruptcy. New management took over the following year. The company's liabilities equaled $1 million ($30 million in today's money). Lewis agreed to personally guarantee the debt of Akron Iron Co. and Altman Miller & Co. Both companies owed money to their creditors and could not pay. Lewis was on the hook to those creditors for that money. He offered to turn over his own estate to revive those properties and pay the company's creditors. Two years later, the Canton plant and its assets sold at auction for $300,000 ($9 million in today's money). After a reorganization, the firm was renamed the Aultman Company and continued to make farm equipment.[36]

The pressure facing Mina did not end with her beloved father's failing health or his company woes. A further embarrassment assaulted the Edison name, which Mina needed to quash. Tom Jr. was now working at the mine with his father in a menial capacity. The work was tedious, and he spent his days wandering around the site aimlessly. Edison was compelled to interact with his directionless son and witnessed his lack of interest in iron ore technology. The embarrassment consumed Edison, and the tension between father and son added another layer of stress onto an already fragmented family.[37]

Still, there was even more for Mina to endure; Marion's beloved Charlie Levison had syphilis. He was "in search of health in the states." But Marion realized that "like all young bloods with plenty of money, he has been very fast and repents when it is too late." And soon, she found out, "Mr. Levison had the most dreadful diseases." Instead of admitting her terrible judgment of men, Marion turned on her trusted chaperone, Mrs. Earl. Marion claimed it was her fault, and she "wanted to push Marion into a danger." Although Marion broke the engagement with Charlie, she never received sympathy from her parents; Marion still felt unloved because she never received the compassion she hoped to get. At this point, her father was more focused on the economic downturn affecting his business. He doled out more money for her as an allowance, but he was not going to provide emotional comfort.[38]

Mina had no more room for warmth for her stepdaughter. She was still recovering from her father's suffering. Her parents' everyday lives and living standards had changed irreparably; it was brutal for her to bear. Her worry and concern was only focused on her parents' needs. Her only bliss was that her children were too young to comprehend what she had to endure.

Marion assessed the family situation and did what she believed she had to do for own self. She returned to Europe. That continent embraced her, and she desperately needed an embrace. But unfortunately, she left on bad terms with both Mina and her father. Mina could never be a street fighter like Marion, and she confessed to her mother, "Marion does not love me." Before her departure, Marion used her strength to attack Mina dramatically: "Please stop telling people that I am returning to Europe to marry Charles Levison because I have no more idea of marrying him than you have."[39]

10

Isolation

THE MILLER FAMILY, ONCE CONSIDERED AKIN TO OHIO ROYALTY, NOW maintained a lower profile on the streets of Akron. Some of Mina's brothers were despondent and rarely seen. Lewis Jr. wrote Mina often, claiming their father was always "blue," "life is bleak at the Millers," and there was nothing he could do to put "father in good spirits." Louise and Cora, her sisters-in-law, wrote of the discomfort for Robert and Ira, who were uncomfortable interacting with their local friends.[1]

Mina's father spent a considerable time at Glenmont, attempting to save and repair his company's insolvency from afar. Mina also made significant efforts to visit Akron and provide succor to her family. Edison, however, spent entire weeks at his mine in Ogden and came home on rare occasions. The situation was dire; for the first time, Mina's concern for Edison took a back seat to her parents' emotional well-being.

Between the visits, her siblings wrote to Mina frequently and shared their behavior to help them through their depression. The financial tornado ravaged the Midwest and left many families destitute. Many who were once friends looked at each other askance, thinking they were concealing money. Mina had become a caregiver of sorts and sent gifts to her siblings and their families to cheer them up.

Ohio and many other states—indeed, much of the country—were in financial shambles, with the unemployment rate as high as 30 percent. As a result, soup kitchens were opening everywhere to help feed the destitute—people who once had well-paying jobs now chopped wood and sewed clothing in exchange for food for their families.

Edison continued to focus on his iron ore mine throughout the collapse. Although he was obsessed with its success, he could not insulate himself from his financial difficulties. The bank panic caused him to fire many of his original employees and suspend many of his ongoing inventions at the lab. Edison had an intermediary on his staff to attend to the firings. When he returned home on weekends, he often went straight to his laboratory; Edison wanted to check on the status of the inventions.

Although Edison had to make significant cuts at his laboratory, he was not in a crisis like many other companies. On the contrary, the success of his electricity brought Edison fame and wealth when electricity spread around the world. He and the board members decided to combine his light company and his smaller affiliated companies for financial reasons, and the companies formed Edison General Electric. Despite the use of Edison's name, however, he did not control the company.

Recently, the company had acquired an electric railway and motor company and subsequently merged with the Thomson-Houston Electric Company, an Edison competitor. That company was now called the Edison General Electric Company. Finally, the company dropped Edison's name, becoming General Electric. With these changes, Edison worked as a consultant for the company and received stock when the companies merged. While the country was at its lowest point, Edison's stake was close to $2 million ($430 million in today's dollars).

While the country's citizens continued to struggle to put their lives in order, Edison financed his iron ore mine with the sale of General Electric stock. Edison was too involved in his narrative to be concerned about others' struggles. Instead, he was absorbed in his own thoughts, needs, and desires for the success of his iron ore plant. His mining operation took a lower-grade iron ore, crushed it, and magnetically separated it, turning a raw material from 20 percent iron to 68 percent iron. It was shipped down the old Ogden Railroad to the Morris Canal and made its way into area furnaces and other products.[2]

To Edison, the mine was more than an enormous landmass with machinery that crushed rocks; it was his ability to invent something new that would help the nation. He planned to automate the entire operation. In his mind, he believed he could work out a solution to all the challenges that arose there. If he did not have the funds to cover the new cost, he asked his assistants to sell more of his stock to fund the operation further.

Edison's fame was so widespread that hundreds of letters came into the laboratory daily. His admirers wanted answers. Some who knew he had hearing loss from his childhood begged him to invent an aid; others wanted employment or confirmation of their inventions and patents. The mine took him away from all those distractions. There, he could be with his own variety of people. He ate outside with his foreman and laborers, living without indoor plumbing, getting his hands dirty, and pushing his mind to work out myriad problems of separating iron ore.

Edison would happily roam around the village he had created, watching his colossal jaw-crushing machine and two miles of conveyors and steam shovels. Edison continued to finance the mine, and it began to resemble a town. The plant had a row of tiny houses on top of a small mountain for 250 workers. The "city" included a train station, two general stores, a post office, a blacksmith shop, and forty homes. Edison lived in a ramshackle clapboard house without indoor plumbing that he dubbed the "White House." Some of the industrial buildings housed many of Edison's inventions, on which he constantly improved during this operation. They also housed giant rock crushers, which transformed the ore into granules, and magnetic separators, which split the iron from the waste.[3]

He wanted the men and their families to live near their work. If families lived near their spouses, they would not complain about their twelve-hour shifts. Wives could see their spouses periodically during the day. The men at the plant appreciated that Edison lived and worked beside them. There was nothing Edison refused to do at the mine. His hands became as calloused as his employees. When Edison came in at the end of the day, he would drop his clothes on the floor beside his bed so they would be ready to jump into the following day to work. Edison loved working with the men at the mine. The freedom from interruption often punctuated his day; there were no administrative duties here. Edison worked with the men and ate with them. He later reminisced, "I never felt better in my life hard work, nothing to divert my thoughts, clean air, simple food."[4]

Mina, however, did not see life the same way. Her husband lived at the mine during the week for six years. He came home on Friday evenings and returned to the mine on Sundays. With enormous machines came frequent repairs, which forced Edison to shut the mine to make modifications. Those were the only respites that allowed Edison to return home for blocks of time. While home, he mainly spoke of returning to the mine and selling more stocks to finance the repairs. The children hardly saw him and rarely interacted with him in their early childhood years.

After leaving school, Tom Jr. continued to flounder and had difficulty finding a career path that he could grasp with enthusiasm. Finally, after much deliberation, Edison suggested that he work at the mine with his father. At the outset, it was tough to prove to his stepmother it was a good fit. But after an inordinate amount of pleading, he was relieved his stepmother rescued him from that competitive and upper-crust school in New Hampshire where John and Theodore Miller thrived. He had never had the stamina or grit to withstand St. Paul's methods to transform its young boys into future leaders.

During that winter, in mid-February, Tom Jr. admitted to his stepmother he could not tolerate the "two degrees below zero" temperatures at the mine. The work and new living conditions were a shock to his system. He preferred to warm up in cozy Glenmont a day before Friday, the Edison-sanctioned departure date for their return. He hoped his father wouldn't be too angry at his early departure. Early on, Tom Jr. understood that he and Edison did not have a synergetic relationship, so he latched on to Mina as the parent for support. Yet he knew to curry favor because he had dropped out of school. He always played to her religious side, tattling on his father and divulging that they worked on Sundays. He knew, however, to admit "it was wrong." He hoped his mother would "forgive him" because "they lost two days last week" due to chronic breakdowns in the machinery.[5]

As the months wore on, iron ore separation grew less intriguing to Tom Jr. and widened the divide between father and son. Instead of working, Tom Jr. began shooting red squirrels and using their tails as paintbrushes; he had long appreciated nature and informed Mina how he'd set up a painting area for himself to paint the colors of the natural images that "he lived in."[6]

Edison did not appreciate his son's new hobby and demanded he engage with his mammoth project rather than paint landscapes. Unfortunately, after their altercations, Tom Jr.'s headaches and other ailments returned. His letters turned negative, and he looked to Mina for pity and warmth. "I was not made for the world. I have a headache that is enough to drive me in the clutches of despair."[7]

Mina had mixed feelings about Tom Jr. She was frustrated that he could not find any successful path, but she also knew he was still a teenager and needed to be with his peers. Since he'd dropped out of school, his only companions were the laborers at the mine. When he returned to Glenmont, he only interacted with Madeleine and Charles; boys his age were still in school. However, Mina believed Chautauqua could cure all of life's ailments, and so she sent Tom Jr. to spend the summer there.

That atmosphere did wonders for his self-esteem. The countless teens there, not to mention the Miller boys, kept him happy and grounded. Tom Jr. wrote letters home regarding taking classes in French and painting. He met other young men and played sports, baseball, and football with them on the sprawling lawns. He no longer felt like an outcast, and his last name brought fame without disclosing the poor relationship he had with his famous father. He was embraced by many without hesitation. Peers finally accepted Tom Jr.; he felt like he belonged somewhere and informed Mina of his joy.

Edison did not care for the activities at Chautauqua. He did not understand that Tom Jr. needed a break and interpreted his behavior as analogous to that of an entitled son of a wealthy man. He had disdain for Tom Jr.'s visits to Glenmont with his new young friends; he only wanted him to work. Edison, who had started working as a boy, was never interested in playing sports and lounging around with his peers. He could not identify with the lifestyle of a college-age boy, and he never guided him and taught him what to do or how to behave. Edison wanted the world to instruct his son rather than be personally responsible for his upbringing.

After strangers spent considerable time with Tom Jr., they often realized his inelegance. It was that particular way about him that Mina detested. She could not contain her snide remarks about his lack of true friends or lousy judge of character. Other boys took advantage of his naivete, and Tom Jr. began to struggle to come to terms with his awkwardness and anxiety. Out of anger, he quarreled with Mina because she was an easier target than his father. Ultimately, though, he realized she was his only ally and apologized for "speaking out of turn" to his stepmother. Tom Jr. was embarrassing and clumsy and did not represent the Edison name well; it was another cross Mina had to bear.[8]

While Mina contended with Tom Jr.'s fluctuating moods, William informed her he would not continue school at St. Paul's. Mina no longer had the stamina to argue with William, and he transferred to Trinity Preparatory School on Staten Island. It was distant enough that Mina did not have to manage William's daily needs, but he could return on the weekends. William made better friends at that school, but soon became known as a troublemaker. He displayed his unruly behavior to any audience. Barely into his first term at the school, the headmaster asked William if he could meet with his father about his progress in school.

William informed the school that his father was too busy working and had placed his stepmother in charge of the children's schooling. The headmaster felt very distressed that Edison would not participate in his son's upbringing, and he believed it was an imposition to share his thoughts with Mina. He stressed that William needed more guidance, stating, "it is impossible for a teacher to effect any change in a boy's moral character unless he has the full sympathy and earnest support of his parents." Further, he stated that William "is careless about his person, his clothes, and in his preparation of work in school ... he is boisterous and rude and approached disrespect. . . . These are the child's faults, and he must repress them to cultivate dignity of character."[9]

Edison had not yet given up on William. During the school transfer, Edison expressed his strong beliefs on education and informed the headmaster he wanted William to go to the classical college at Cornell. But he insisted he did not want him to study Greek because Edison believed it was useless for training the mind. The headmaster continued to share his observation about William, that he was "inclined to procrastinate when there is amusement in view ... had a talent for spending money, whatever he had, got rid of immediately." What was most frustrating to the school was William's "bad temper which he displays often." Regardless of William's character problems, he had the propensity to study and excel. He had the grades to enter Cornell.[10]

The same hope was not present for Tom Jr. Edison only exhibited an interest in his family when they amused him or displayed some higher level of reasoning. No matter how hard he tried, Tom Jr. could never reach either bar. During Edison's short bursts of leisure, one could witness his interest in a small child understanding basic chemical properties. At another juncture, he would appreciate someone's ability to tell a captivating story. Tom Jr. had neither of those qualities. He was more of a fluid, emotional person. He was not motivated by cause and effect but by understanding the emotions and feelings behind his actions. Mina was too puritanical to sit and analyze the way of the universe. She left that up to the heads of the church, lazily accepting the spoon-fed methods to conduct herself.

Edison could not embrace others different from himself and could not rise to the occasion to mentor his son. Edison's lack of affection toward Tom Jr. caused irreparable long-term harm to his psyche. His son was even more disheartened when he worked within yards of his father at the mine. Edison's self-importance refused to break away from the plant's needs rather than attend to anything. Tom Jr. told Mina I can "love but [I am] Not loved."[11]

Edison's intense involvement in the mine accentuated his self-absorbed character. The utter length of time he spent living and working there perfecting the machines reached the level of obsessive-compulsive behavior. Nevertheless, no one could pull him away, and he continually poured additional money into his project. Hundreds of men worked alongside Edison, many of whom were skilled enough to fix the mechanical problems when Edison returned home. But when issues arose, Edison believed he was the sole person who could resolve them. His narcissism had reached new peaks.

Although Edison forced his son to return to the mine, Tom Jr. was not suited to his father's way of life. The relationship eventually became so contentious that neither side wanted to salvage it. Tom Jr. knew he could no longer please his father or work beside him. He wrote home to Mina, "My life is a burden now, and a disgrace to you all . . . such as the reward I get for trying to follow in the footsteps of a man who I thought was a model man. . . . Hereafter I shall walk in my way—And God, please help me."[12]

Mina was privy to Tom Jr.'s correspondence with his father. After all the love he professed to his stepmother and sharing his inner thoughts, he believed, "Mother and her folks do not understand me. . . . It makes me feel very severely." Further addressing his father directly, he wrote, "I feel that I have never pleased you in anything I have ever done—but I will never be satisfied until I do. I don't believe I will ever be able to talk to you the way I would like to—because you are so far superior in every way that when I am in your presence, I am perfectly hopeless—you have no doubt noticed this yourself. . . . All I ask of you is a chance to try."[13]

Edison, pleased with his new lifestyle and surroundings, wrote Mina to cajole her into visiting him at the mine. He recently had given her the nickname of "Billy." Unsure of its origin or effect on her, he called her that and tried to coax her to visit him. But unfortunately, there was no running water, and they lived on dirt roads. Mina was not about to rough it with a bunch of strange men—she'd done that on her honeymoon. Not to mention, there was the deafening sounds emanating from the machines. They did not affect Edison because of his lack of hearing.

Edison was well aware of his grimy surroundings, so he would continually ask her to come up and stay at his boardinghouse. He suggested she leave the toddlers at Glenmont and call them on the phone during the day and then again before they sleep. "If they get sick," he reminded her, "you can be home in three or four hours."[14]

Unfortunately, we do not have Edison's letters from Mina, but we can quickly fill in Mina's complaints about her husband's absence from his replies in which Edison defends himself: "I have thought about you 40 times since Monday."[15]

The fanatical need to remain there while he had a wife and children to attend to oddly strengthened Mina's resolve. At the outset, she might have yielded to his demands to work prolonged hours. But soon the days turned into weeks, months, and years. Each day Mina learned that her husband's persona had no space for mutual understanding. He was not open to accommodating others. Edison was unchangeable. During those years away, she realized she could no longer sit in Glenmont and mope. At some juncture, she would wither, but it is clear from Edison's letters to her at this period that he did everything he could to manipulate his wife, making her feel that she had abandoned him rather than the other way around. But now she had her sea legs under her and felt more confident stating her opinion to her husband than she had in previous years.

When Mina refused to visit, he would scribble, "Why don't you want to see me—no real love is the reason." Or "I don't expect to get much love when I return on Saturday, but? you are the sweetest Mama." From his notes to Mina, Edison seems to be amusing himself rather than trying to engage in the needs of his wife, signing his updates, "With all the love nature permits—the man who sleeps with his boots on and smokes 28 cent cigars."[16]

Mina did not need to deal with her husband's daily needs. The mine did that. She still had her family's concerns that needed her support. So, she spent a significant amount of time in Akron and the summers at Chautauqua to be with her family. However, when Edison felt ignored, he used his manipulative tactics to provoke his wife: "I didn't get a telegram from you from Chautauqua, but I guess you saw George and forgot about your lover." On other occasions, he signed his letters with fanfare: "With the kiss of a 13-inch cannon projectile" or "Your forlorn lover." Edison always preferred to work and did not require her letters; the jabs and jeers in his correspondence were more to entertain himself and provide a dose of taunting his wife.[17]

Despite Mina's aggravation about her altered marital condition, she could not show her feelings. Growing up as a daughter in the Miller house came with specific tenets. There was a sense of duty that stemmed from Victorian upbringing and Methodism. It was her duty to withstand the storm, which she did to the best of her ability.

Madeleine recalled in an interview that she rarely saw her father during his years at the mine. One day, Mina had gone up to the mine with Madeleine and Charles. They drove up, after having taken two days to get there, dressed in elegant summer dresses and beautiful hats. "A bedraggled man I had ever seen came got off the train at the station covered in soot was my father."[18]

The countless months went by, and Mina forced herself to occupy her days with family. But even when Mina designed a manageable life rhythm to survive, Edison interjected his voice from afar: "I realize how important it is to have a sister come back with you because I realize how lonely it is just now. I sometimes wonder if the darling Mama loves me, I don't see why she does; therefore, I am never sure. However, papa loves her to the ultima."[19]

The letters amused Edison more than they did Mina. He had a sense of humor that was often filled with self-deprecation for his appearance, and Mina could not tolerate slovenly dress. All her life, she had tried to have the children dress to represent the Edison family. She never wore a dress above her ankle—the Victorian ways imbued her spirit and psyche. Edison said, "What am I to do without a bath? Some smartweed seeds have commended to sprout out of the seams of my coat."[20]

Simultaneously entertaining himself and humiliating Mina's religious sensibilities, he once wrote, "You must tell Grace and Mame to have 1/2 dozen stories for me when I get there; they must be off a little, i.e., 'Frenchy.'" Mina had the children write to their father to remind him he was a family man, albeit distant. Yet Edison continued to disappoint Mina. He wrote, "Tell Madeleine and Charles that I can't answer their letters" because he had "dislocated his joint in his finger." That seemed like an empty excuse, and the children were so small they only needed a line or two and hardly needed a longer letter. After he penned his reason, he switched the onus to Mina about their distance and inquired, "When are you returning to the mine to visit me? I am always your lover."[21]

Edison's commitment to Ogden was more than financial. As soon as a bug developed in the system, Edison worked it out until he was satisfied; one worker reminisced that Edison once worked thirty-six hours without stopping. One time, Edison shut down the operation not because the machinery was shattering; the workers wanted a wage increase for the overtime and threatened to strike if Edison would not provide one. Before the upcoming meeting to strike, Edison shut down the plant. Many workers left and did not resume working until two months later.

Edison's continued enthusiasm for the project and desire to resolve the constant technical problems never ceased. But unfortunately, many of his trusted older engineers were approaching fifty years old and did not have the stamina or interest in contributing capital or working at the mine. He claimed, "My Wall Street friends think I cannot make another success, and I am a back number. I can not raise $1000 from them. But I am going to show them that they are very much mistaken."[22]

Edison spent his fiftieth birthday at the mine. Mina, trying to endear herself to her husband, sent him a birthday cake in the shape of the mine with figures of tiny miners and electric lights. As usual, Edison was busy and did not appreciate the interruption. He inquired, "has Christmas come again?" He did not want a cake or any festivity to distract him from his progress.[23]

The demeaning comments were piling up, and they were the only way he communicated with his family's needs. His snide remarks continued to erode his family's self-confidence and dismiss their feelings. Edison's arrogance prevented him from caring about others' boundaries, and he made sure no one would interfere with his own needs. His ability to humiliate others disguised as teasing was devastating to his family.

Unfortunately, the boys, Marion, and Mina never had the self-confidence to stand up to Edison. Instead of talking back, they would flee the scene, attempting to shut out the cruelty. Edison saw their insecurity and attacked; they could not protect themselves and suffered.

At the same time that Mina juggled William's foibles and her husband's taunts, she managed to enjoy herself with her younger brothers, Theodore and John. Both were attending Yale, and she entertained them during their school breaks, even paid for their travel to and from school during her father's hardship. Her welcome extended to her brothers' classmates, as well. Mina ensured that the holidays would mimic her childhood years at Oak Place, filled with family, lavish meals, and festive games. Edison was in attendance yet returned to work after a day or two. Her family members enjoyed Mina's graciousness and prolonged their time at Glenmont.

During the visits, Mina treated her younger brothers on trips to New York City. On one occasion, they went to see *Barnum* and *Twelfth Night* among other cultural events. Mina thoroughly enjoyed spending time with the well-mannered and culturally engaged boys. In addition, Mina attempted to find her peace and keep herself engaged during the vicissitudes of life that her husband hurled at her.[24]

Theodore was pleased with "how hard" the professors were, stating, "it makes a fellow feel so much better and makes him strong mentally and physically for I can study just about twice as well." Mary Valinda was so proud of her youngest son. He had it all: athletic ability, intellect, and good looks. Theodore was devoted to friends and family; everyone at Yale adored him.[25]

Easter also brought many Miller siblings back to Glenmont, where Mina had formal parties. She would decorate the house lavishly and offer many party games to engage all the guests. On all occasions, she would go over the top to compensate for her husband's lack of interest in family, friends, and festivities. Edison was home more than usual during that time, not from a desire to celebrate but because the machinery at the mine continually broke down. Mina entertained Edith Edison and her own family. Mary Valinda and Lewis remained in Akron with Robert, Louise, and their children. Lewis was slowly recovering from his ailments and began focusing on managing business post the financial depression.

Mina's family often visited. Her brother John, noticing what was simmering right under Mina's external surface to the world, implored his sisters: "Mina, I think, is the one that feels the loneliness than most, and you must arrange some way to stay with her when Mr. Edison is at the Mines."[26]

Meanwhile, Edison wanted repayment on a loan given to Mina's brother Ira. Ira hedged both the loan and the repayment. Never understanding his brother-in-law's disposition, Ira offered Edison a vacation from his overdetermined focus on the mine: "A while in Chautauqua would do you much good." Edison had no interest in spending leisure time. Instead, he remained focused on the much-needed loan repayment. Walter Mallory, his engineer and assistant at the mine, sent another letter to Ira and pressured him for payment. Walter's relationship with the Miller family predated his association with Edison. His sister Mary (Minnie) Mallory was a friend of Mina's, and his other sister Charlotte

Marie (Lottie) Mallory was a friend of Grace's. The families knew each other through their involvement in Chautauqua. Walter met Edison during the summer of 1885 at Chautauqua. They became friends, and he was asked to serve as one of the ushers at Edison's wedding in February 1886. In 1888, Edison established the Edison Iron Concentrating Co. in Michigan. The initial investors were Edison; Walter Mallory; Mallory's father, E. B. Mallory; and Lewis and Ira Miller. Unaccustomed to the intensity of Edison's demands, Ira promised, "$5000. Thursday or Friday of this week, we could send you $5000 or $10,000 more next week." He was "not positive where we can get the money . . . but think it more than likely we can raise this amount if you must have it . . . we don't want to go out and borrow money." Blood relations were insignificant to Edison, who never made exceptions for the family. Edison wanted his money back. It was not for creditors; he needed to strengthen his rock-crushing machines.[27]

While at home, Edison started working in the laboratory for prolonged periods. When he remained at the laboratory until 10:30 p.m. and asked for supper to be sent down (a frequent request), he added, "Don't growl too much." As the years moved on, Mina learned to state her needs more forcefully. During a lengthy mine closing for repairs, Edison returned home and wrote a colleague, "My wife will not allow me to go to work to the Laboratory nights for a month. I will be here every day except Sundays until six o'clock." Based on her positive results, she outlined further rules for her husband: "My wife has made it a rule to have no visitors call at the house on Sunday." Finally, she had started to find her voice, and either out of guilt or exhaustion, Edison complied with her demands.[28]

Besides the mental games, Edison's letters were filled with the dire need to sell more stocks to fund what seemed like never-ending repairs. Finally, Edison, acting more like a needy child, wrote to Mina: "without [the stocks], the works will have to shut down." Mina was in Akron and no longer sat at home awaiting his arrival. Edison's need for the money superseded anyone else's schedule and added, "I shall want them by the fifteenth . . . and you must come home even you have had to return to Akron. . . . I guess you better make a flying trip home and return or come home with the children." Finally, further emphasizing his desire and bribing Mina, he conveyed that once he sold his much-needed stocks, "Christmas will be a happy one for you."[29]

Mina did return home to address her husband. Yet her compliant mood turned cold and distant. Edison attempted to warm Mina with expressions of fictitious heartache: "I don't expect to get much love when I return Saturday," or by addressing his letter to "To the 648th grandchild of Eve." Both attempts fell flat. Mina's new remoteness toward Edison leaked out of Glenmont, probably by the staff witnessing the couple's interactions, and a newspaper dramatized the marital situation: "Mrs. Edison left her husband in Orange N.J. in his 'den' two weeks ago." When she returned, he was still there, unaware she had left. In another account, a newspaper reported Mrs. Edison, in a conversation with a friend, had stated, "Mr. Edison never takes a holiday. I fear for his health. There are days at a time when we never see him at our home, so steadily does he confine himself in his den." Not much would draw Edison out of his den, away from his laboratory, or far from his iron ore mine.[30]

Meanwhile, Marion had found her true love and decided to marry. This time, it was not an Englishman or an American traveling in Europe, but a German lieutenant named Oscar Oeser stationed in Chemnitz south of Dresden.

Before her departure, Marion had spent some time alone at Glenmont while Mina was in Akron. She'd had her father's undivided attention, except for his laboratory, but Marion expected that. Upon Mina's return, however, her stepmother usurped Marion's position as "most loved." Marion would never be able to recoup the love she had before Edison's marriage to Mina, and she did not want to wait around Glenmont, argue with Mina, and vie for her father's attention. Furthermore, Marion had come of age and could now inherit what her mother had left her—the deed to Menlo Park. She and her two brothers and, of course, Edison could divide the property, worth $74,000 ($2 million in today's money).[31]

After Marion's dramatic departure, her relationship with Mina changed forever. Marion no longer referred to Mina as "Mama." Instead, she addressed all letters to "Mina." In Marion's eyes, Mina was no longer her mother or even a stepmother; she was her father's wife, and they would now be on a first-name basis.[32]

To the wonder of her family, Marion spent her first months in Germany. Then, after spending just a few weeks in Italy, she decided to live in a children's institution and learn German. Marion immediately thanked her father for their agreed-upon allowance, ensuring he knew it was more than sufficient because the food was not expensive. She kept her demure tone, however, stating, "Let me hear from you once in a while. A few words from you would make me happier than you believe."[33]

In the following letter, Marion asked her father for "one more favor, and that is let me marry the man I love." Knowing full well that Edison would scoff at that letter, she begged her father to "answer this letter at once as well-bred people in this country are very particular about such matters." Marion knew Mina would see the letter and was well-aware that nothing was more important to Mina than appearing "well-bred." Furthermore, Mina would want to reverse the last impression many Germans had of Edison, since Edison never wrote to his daughter while she was in the hospital.[34]

Another letter came from Sister Louise, an Albertine nun who had cared for Marion Edison when she returned to Europe in 1894. Sister Louise had introduced Marion to the Oeser family. Oscar spoke little English and would undoubtedly need help writing a letter to Edison formally asking for his daughter's hand in marriage. Sister Louise wrote Edison vouching Oscar was a "good man and loves her." Marion continued to explain Germany's bureaucratic process for a marriage to occur along with a baptismal.[35]

Oscar's letter followed the next week, stating he "loves" Marion and "wishes to have her for my wife." It was not just Edison's consent that he needed. In addition, German law required that the King of Saxony grant officers permission to marry foreigners.[36]

Marion desperately pleaded with her father that she "would do anything in the world to marry Oscar for, at last, I love someone better than myself." Marion hoped her father would "make a trip to see her married." She was concerned many Germans would think she was "an imposter" because she did not go around flaunting and spending money. Edison's presence would confirm the truth that she was, indeed, his daughter.[37]

There is no letter explaining what precipitated Edison to respond promptly; it was not his nature. From past experiences, Marion did not "believe that her father" cared enough about her affairs to write back. She even cautioned Oscar that her father would not write back or consent. However, Oscar was utterly unaware of Edison's personality at that time. He assured Marion that her concerns were baseless, and that Edison indeed had "a father's heart."[38]

Marion was pleased with the outcome, and out of sheer guilt, she felt obligated to apologize to Edison for thinking him to be "unjust." Then, hoping for a wedding before Christmas, Marion added, "I cannot give up the idea of you coming over for my wedding. I want you to see and know Oscar."[39]

Further, Marion hoped her $200 ($6,000 in today's money) monthly allowance would remain in place even after her marriage, and she claimed to her father that people charged her more for things because of her last name. Also, she told her father that any dividend she received from bonds in the United States, she would now like to invest in Germany in good faith. Finally, again hoping her father would visit, she told him to "practice his French" because the Oesers only spoke French and German.[40]

Edison did not need to practice any languages because he had no intention of going to Europe. Sending money was the limit of his affection toward his daughter. Instead, he sent his uncle to Europe to "look after Marion's affairs." Simeon reported back to Edison that Oscar was "very popular with the officers and men," and he had spent a "good deal of time" with Oscar and believed it was a "love match." Simeon also met Oscar's parents and younger brother and thought them to be "very nice people."[41]

In November, Edison had his secretary send formal permission for the marriage. Edison also sent $10,000 ($300,000 in today's money) to the couple, covering their legal expenses to marry in Germany. Marion revealed to her father, "If anything could add to my happiness, it would be to have a son as near as Oscar's character." She told Edison she was happy his work at the lab and the mine was "getting on so well" because she knew he "desires that above all things." Although Marion had finally found a mate, there remained an emptiness in her heart. Once again baring her soul to her father, she begged for his love, beseeching, "it hurts me to see you send me none."[42]

After significant discussion, Edison agreed to give her an additional $1,500 ($48,000 in today's money) for her trousseau, finally paving the way for a wedding date. Never intending to go to Europe himself, however, Edison instead sent his oldest son on what he deemed an errand—to give away his daughter in marriage. Tom Jr. and Marion were more strangers than siblings, having lived away from each other for close to a decade. Uncomfortable with his position, Tom Jr. returned the day after the wedding.[43]

Edison's older sister Marion Wallace wrote Mina frequently, sharing that she wished her brother would "write to me or notice me in any way." Dutiful Mina often invited her to Glenmont and trips to the seashore. Always concerned about gathering artifacts to preserve her husband's legacy, Mina asked her to send Edison's baby cradle to Glenmont.[44]

Within months after Marion's wedding, Edison received word of his father's passing. He telegrammed the authorities to deal with the funeral arrangements. Unfortunately, the obituaries omitted Mary Sharlow, his father's second wife, and their children. The papers had deleted them from the Edison narrative. Instead, Edison's mother, who had died twenty years before, was prominent in the article. Edison agreed to a newspaper interview, admitting that when he heard of his father's death, he immediately left his laboratory, changed, and took the train directly. The reporters fawned over Edison, and in his typical fashion, he disclosed he did not mind: "The newspaperman must have something to give to his readers."[45]

Despite his father's death and his daughter marrying and remaining in Europe indefinitely, Edison remained focused on the mine. When Mina could not shut out the agonies of the world, Edison made a formal diagnosis of her condition: "Blues are from a disorder liver or come from long sinuous intestine that blushes from inflammation." Mina, not tough enough to push back against her overpowering husband, continued to endure a pummeling of bullying and humiliating comments. She still could not fathom why he could not display a modicum of empathy or compassion. Then Edison contemplated his return home: "I wonder if you will be cold artic like," thinking of extending his absence, "should I come out in 3 or 4 weeks."[46]

Thomas Edison's Phrenology Chart, 1885

Mina Miller Edison, circa 1880

Mina Miller Edison (center) with friends and brothers at Oak Place, circa 1883
THE CHAUTAUQUA INSTITUTION AND ARCHIVES

The Miller Family: (top row from left) Lewis Miller, Mary Valinda Miller, Ira and Lewis Miller Jr., Mina Miller Edison, (middle row) Theodore, Mary and Jane, (bottom row) Grace, Edward, Robert, and John THE CHAUTAUQUA INSTITUTION AND ARCHIVES

Oak Place, the Miller home, Akron, Ohio THE CHAUTAUQUA INSTITUTION AND ARCHIVES

Glenmont, the Edison home, Lewellyn Park, West Orange, New Jersey THOMAS
EDISON NATIONAL HISTORICAL PARK

Seminole Lodge, the Edison winter home, Fort Myers, Florida EDISON FORD WINTER
ESTATES

Marion Estelle Edison,
circa 1885 THOMAS EDISON
NATIONAL HISTORICAL PARK

Thomas Edison Jr. and William Leslie
Edison, circa 1883 THOMAS EDISON
NATIONAL HISTORICAL PARK

Thomas Edison, Mina
Miller Edison, Gus-
tave Eiffel, and various
business associates
on the Eiffel Tower,
1889 THOMAS EDISON
NATIONAL HISTORICAL PARK

(From left) Thomas Edison, John Miller, Ira Miller, Cora Miller, Grace Miller, Lewis Miller Jr., Marion Edison, Richard Marvin, Jane Miller, Louise Igoe Miller, Robert Miller, (second row standing) Theodore Miller, Thomas Edison Jr., Lewis Miller, (on lap) Rachel Miller, Mary Valinda, (front row seated) Madeleine Edison Sloane, Mina Miller Edison, (on lap) Charles Edison, Mary Miller, Edward Miller, (on lap) Robert Miller Jr., (standing) Margaret Miller, Prince (St. Bernard dog), and William Edison, on porch of Oak Place THE CHAUTAUQUA INSTITUTION AND ARCHIVES

Mina Miller Edison, Madeleine Edison Sloane, and Charles Edison at Glenmont, circa 1897 THOMAS EDISON NATIONAL HISTORICAL PARK

Mina Miller Edison, Madeleine Edison Sloane, Charles Edison, and Theodore, circa 1902 THOMAS EDISON NATIONAL HISTORICAL PARK

Thomas Edison, Mina Miller Edison, Madeleine Edison Sloane, Charles Edison, and Theodore, at back porch of Glenmont, circa 1906 THOMAS EDISON NATIONAL HISTORICAL PARK

Mina Miller Edison, circa 1905 THOMAS EDISON NATIONAL HISTORICAL PARK

Marion Edison Oeser, Oscar Oeser, Theodore Edison, Mina Miller Edison, Thomas Edison, and Madeleine Edison Sloane, 1911 Europe THOMAS EDISON NATIONAL HISTORICAL PARK

(Foreground) Madeleine and John Eyre Sloane wedding, (seated) Thomas Edison and Mina Edison, June 1914 at Glenmont THOMAS EDISON NATIONAL HISTORICAL PARK

Mina Miller Edison at Greenhouse in Glenmont, circa 1920 THOMAS EDISON NATIONAL HISTORICAL PARK

Thomas Edison and Mina Miller Edison, circa 1920 THOMAS EDISON NATIONAL
HISTORICAL PARK

Mina Miller Edison at desk at Glenmont, circa 1925 THOMAS EDISON NATIONAL
HISTORICAL PARK

Edison taking a bow, (standing in background) Charles Edison, Carolyn Edison, Mina Miller Edison, and Thomas Edison Jr., circa 1925 THOMAS EDISON NATIONAL HISTORICAL PARK

Henry Ford, Clara Ford, Thomas Edison, and Mina Edison in Fort Myers, circa 1925 EDISON FORD WINTER ESTATES

Thomas Edison and Mina Miller Edison, circa 1930 EDISON FORD WINTER ESTATES

11

Bury Thy Sorrow

MINA RETURNED FROM HER DOCTOR'S VISIT EUPHORIC. HER FIRST instinct was to write her mother and share the exciting news about the early stages of her pregnancy. Mary Valinda "delighted in learning the secret." The past years had been grueling for Mina. She longed for her husband's work at the Ogden mine to wind down, reaching its ability for complete automation. She prayed the birth of their third child would bring her husband home permanently.[1]

The Millers gradually returned to a calmer financial state at Oak Place, not short of other unintended hurdles. Although Chautauqua was flourishing and summer sessions drew two months of cultural expansion for its visitors, a recently published article had credited its entire inception and success to Rev. Vincent. The piece excluded Lewis Miller from taking any part in the founding of the movement. Instead, Rev. Vincent received all the glory for the institution's accomplishments. Lewis Miller and his family were demoralized. The institution, besides his family, was all he had clung to during his financial woes.

After reading the widely circulated article, Mame was incensed. She directly asked the Vincents, whom the Millers believed were lifelong friends, if they approved of the published article. The Reverend feigned ignorance but wrote his son George that Lewis Miller is "sure to be on the warpath." Lewis realized this was more than an innocent error; there was evidence of duplicity. Although Lewis was known to have faith in human nature and avoid conflict, he contacted the journalist, Dr. Harper, a protégé of the Vincents, who had interviewed Lewis for the article. Lewis questioned why he decided to "give the credit for the origin of Chautauqua to Bishop Vincent." The article caused a schism among many prominent members of the institution after considerable pressure from lay leaders of the movement. The magazine published a correction weeks later, but Lewis Miller was not quick to mend the rift between him and Rev. Vincent. Since Jennie's marriage, the two families did not have reason to engage as they had in the past. As a result of this article, the Vincents lost their position as trusted friends of the Millers, and the interactions at Chautauqua became pro forma.[2]

Despite the recent latent hostility during the summers at Chautauqua, there still was much pleasure in life for the Miller family. Theodore and John excelled at Yale and graduated with honors; the Millers were proud of their varied achievements. Theodore excelled among his peers. He was the president of the debating society, sang in the glee club, and made the crew team. After Theodore showed athletic prowess, he spent the summers at Chautauqua coaching younger men and women to excel as well. John showed his strengths in engineering.

Both boys showed signs of initiative and leadership. Although Theodore was less than two years younger than John, the brothers were so close in all their endeavors that friends and family rarely mentioned them individually. Throughout their childhood, they played and sledded on the snowy rolling hills of Oak Place. In the summers, they were sailing the Miller yacht, the *Olivia*, on Lake Chautauqua. As they entered Yale, their classmates realized Theodore and John were inseparable. Although John's interests were in science and Theodore's were in the law, they were roommates and scarcely ever apart. Theodore's bubbling personality filled every letter home to his family, and while visiting Mina, the brothers enhanced the holidays with their enthusiasm.

John was heading off to Cornell to further his studies in engineering, and Theodore had been accepted to New York University Law School and was looking forward to the beginning of his path to a legal career. It would be the first time the brothers would be separated. Theodore revealed his fun-loving personality when he invited his family to his graduation and wrote, "This is your last chance and positively last appearance of the

Miller Bros. in their famous melodrama 'College Life at Yale.' Come early and avoid the rush."[3]

Unexpectedly, William also managed to pass the entrance exam and entered Yale. Although his grades were decent, when he wrote home, his father was so embarrassed by his poor writing ability that he underlined his errors and wrote across the top of the page, "William, your spelling makes me faint see marks." If the admissions office knew of the spelling errors in his writings, they chose to ignore them and accepted William based on his surname.[4]

Mina's relationship with Marion had no real chance of reconciliation during this time. However, it did not distress her. On the contrary, Mina was calmer, knowing Marion would not show up on her doorstep. She had sent her a gift as a superficial truce and added pictures of Madeleine and Charles. Oscar seemed to be keeping Marion happy in Dresden, and with her father's monthly allowance, she was content in her new life.

What still poked at Mina was Tom Jr.'s complaints of physical ailments. Moreover, his relationship with Mina depended on his obsessive need to declare his love while he could not seem to find any gainful employment. Unfortunately, before Mina could genuinely enjoy the happiness of her pregnancy, Tom Jr. became exceedingly ill, and he hoped to travel to Fort Myers to recuperate. Attempting to solicit sympathy, he declared that his sickness was so debilitating that "he did not have the strength to walk." Tom Jr. asked Edison's permission to reside at his winter home while he recuperated. With his flair for the dramatic as strong as ever, he stated, "If I don't come back to you alive . . . you have not lost much, for I know I have not been the son to you as I should have been." Tom Jr. knew he could never meet the expectations that his father had set for him. Although he wrote Mina that his ill health was improving, he had no intention of recuperating at Glenmont. He was in constant fear of his father and no longer felt welcome.[5]

Edison was disgusted by Tom Jr.'s floundering and never took a genuine interest in him. However, when Tom Jr. ran out of his allowance, he had no choice but to return home and work at the mine. Days later, he complained to Mina that his father "has not even looked at me." Their strained relationship caused Tom Jr. to make poor decisions. His last name and naivete allowed strangers with more experience and unpleasant approaches to take advantage of him and line their own pockets.[6]

The machines at the mine needed constant repair, and Edison was obsessed with pouring money into fixing them. In addition, he was obsessed with supporting his project even though his colleagues informed him it would not achieve the success he'd initially anticipated. Edison's dislike and disdain for his son had also reached a new low. Although Edison had already mortgaged his phonograph works for $300,000 ($10 million in today's money) to put into his mine, he wanted an additional $11,175 ($350,000 in today's money) from Tom Jr. The request was insulting because Edison was borrowing money from what his son had inherited from his mother's estate. Tom Jr. did not have much savings, but that did not stop his father from pressuring him for money. Edison treated his son like a stranger and offered him 6 percent on the loan. Edison had already borrowed $4,500 ($150,000 today's money) from Tom Jr. in a prior financial agreement. After both transactions, Tom Jr. had little money left. Powerless in his father's presence, Tom Jr. could not speak up for himself.[7]

So distressed about the recent events, Tom Jr. decided to leave work at Ogden and never return. The stress and interactions with his father caused him to feel ill once again. "The treatment I have received at the hands of my family" caused his illness, according to Tom Jr., and he felt so sick he "might not survive."[8]

In his mind, Tom Jr. had hit his lowest point. He knew he had to leave his family and decided to make money independently. But with the same name as the most famous man in the nation, Tom Jr. could never be fully independent. Moreover, his inexperience in business and lack of sophistication always paved the way for more trouble.

Nevertheless, in an incautious letter to Mina, he was unusually upbeat while spending his summer at Chautauqua. He was surrounded by friends again. Regardless, Mina was concerned; she was dubious of his motives. As the summer ended, he moved to Manhattan. Once again, he checked in with Mina, ever seeking her approval.

Tom Jr. wrote Mina with hopeful pride that he was finally working in New York City, and he was not associated with "scoundrels." Nevertheless, he believed it was a "great insult" that his father thought he associated with men with malicious intent: "On the contrary, I have some of the best men in-country by my side." Tom Jr. believed that he actually "invented of the finest incandescent lamps in the world." Furthermore, he called his new invention the "Edison Junior Improved," and he anticipated having "ten thousand agents on commission and control the market of the world."[9]

But the lamp Tom Jr. was using in his company was one of his father's own inventions. The newspapers got word of his business and were printing giant advertisements. Over the years, Tom Jr. had learned to mimic Edison's famous stylized handwriting and signed his name in a similar style. Unfortunately, it could be confused as part of Edison's company to the uninformed reader, which caused unbearable embarrassment to both Mina and Edison.

Months later, Tom Jr. formed the Edison Junior Steel and Iron Company, which he claimed was backed by investors. As a result, Tom Jr. received great publicity for his companies. However, Edison was disgusted with Tom Jr. for creating a false business that amounted to nothing but using his name.[10]

Edison never understood what a husband or parent required of him. He did not see that it was something with which he needed to be concerned. He did not want to deal with emotional issues and, almost invariably, he tried to avoid any emotional contact. He had an intermediary address his dirty work, as he had done with his daughter Marion. However, in this case, Edison played one son off the other. He asked William to send Tom Jr., demanding he close down his sham companies. William was pleased to be his father's chosen errand boy, even if it was just for a day or two, and he wrote his brother, informing him that their father "says he is through with you and that you have disgraced him enough." William further warned Tom Jr. that their father and Mina did not want him dabbling in all different schemes and wanted him to assert better self-control.[11]

Tom Jr. had no intention of heeding his brother's advice. Despite his failure in those companies, the experience fueled him with bravado, and he attacked his father's ability to parent: "I worked for you faithfully and obediently . . . but now I look back on upon those days—what an ass— what a fool I was to devote my time to a man whose domestic attentions are foreign things to him and no right in this world to be a father—then a youth of six." Tom Jr. was full of venom: "Your name has been detrimental to me from the day I started. . . . If my name were Smith, I would be a rich man today. . . . I don't care to have anything to do with you in any way."[12]

After that letter, Tom Jr. and his father ended contact. Although he attacked his father with bitterness, it was a momentary flash of inner strength. In reality, he was a sensitive boy at heart and needed love. Mina always sided with her husband regardless of how sad and dejected the boys were. She had no choice but to cut ties with Tom Jr. when he cut ties with his father. Her task was to shine the Edison name, which the press had temporarily tarnished. The family members firmed up their stances. William abandoned his brother and sided with his father. Marion, so engrossed in her marital bliss, was unaware of the situation; Oscar was filling the void of love for which she desperately craved so long. Tom Jr. needed to find someone to lick his wounds and make him feel whole.

While William was at Yale, he enjoyed playing sports but did not put enough effort into his studies. Mina and Edison warned him that his grades were slipping, and he would need to leave the University. William revealed his argumentative side and pushed back: "Do you think I am up here to have fun? Do you think I want to be sent home because I did not study?" William's inability to take constructive criticism was his downfall. Instead of working harder, he claimed, "it was foolish of me to enter college knowing I had some conditions." He entered Yale because he thought Mina and Edison would consider him "the better of him . . . but let me remind you that my conditions are one of the greatest drawbacks one can have." The "conditions" William spoke of were never his fault. When he could not join the glee club, it was because of his ailments. Likewise, this excuse precluded studying enough. He never had the grit to work hard and instead let his conditions receive the blame. Furthermore, he never learned that claiming he had an illness was something neither Mina nor Edison would pity.[13]

Weeks later, William was injured playing sports and therefore was unable to get to a necessary exam. In addition, he had received a warning that he might have to leave college because of his poor grades. Despite William's pain, he was sure to remind Mina "not to forget to send me the check as soon as possible as I have outstanding bills which are due." Mina began to see the writing on the wall and knew it was a matter of time before he dropped out of school. William had reverted to his old self, spending more money than he owned. Mina grew concerned the press would get wind of the event and muddy the Edison name once more. His money problems became more dire, and William had to admit that he did not have "a cent to his name."[14]

Furthermore, he had to borrow money for crutches and medicine. Mina was mortified that Edison's son was penniless. Concerned about his arrival home, William asked Mina "not to put on the expression of disgust when I come home." That summer, he spent time in Chautauqua and asked for money, "promising not to squander it."[15]

William returned to school barely passing and still concerned about his upcoming grades. He continued to get hurt on the athletic fields, fall behind, and burn through his allowance. Sheepishly he wrote to Mina in his defense, "The trouble is that I never stop to think about those things which you told me repeatedly and that has caused all the trouble." He finally admitted he "is not enjoying college life," adding regarding his lack of tenacity, "I want to get out of it."[16]

Unfortunately, the countless injuries he received on the field became his excuse for not dealing with his studies. It was all over by March, but Mina had no intention of witnessing the academic failure of her second stepson. William was thoroughly embarrassed and admitted, "I don't dare to come home as I don't know what you and father think of me. I tried my best, but I failed." He assured Mina he would approach his father and "see what he wants me to do." William desperately needed direction and admitted, "I can only say, whatever he wishes I can try to do, I may not succeed, but I can try."[17]

While there was heightened conflict among Mina, Edison, and his two sons, another battle was beginning to erupt in the United States. The nation had just recovered from a financial depression and was not in a solid position to fund a war. Moreover, a war would reverse any possible gains the financial sector had made. Not far from the United States, many citizens of Cuba were fighting for independence from Spain. Some Americans supported the Cuban rebels and their need for autonomy, wanting the United States to intervene in the conflict.

President McKinley sent the battleship *Maine* to Cuba to protect American interests there, but it mysteriously exploded and sank in Havana Harbor. There was no concrete proof of who caused the explosion; warmongering Americans blamed Spain.

With just a year under his belt at the White House, McKinley was alarmed about the explosion but wanted to resolve the conflict peacefully. Unfortunately, he received political pressure from the Democratic Party to enter into war. McKinley signed a joint Congressional resolution demanding Spanish withdrawal and authorizing military force to help Cuba gain its independence. McKinley's first strategy was to retaliate by attacking Spanish battleships in the Philippines to prevent them from going to Cuba. First, however, the United States needed to recruit soldiers to help fight in the war. Theodore Roosevelt, who had recently resigned as the secretary of the navy, led a group of volunteers called the Rough Riders, consisting of cowboy ranchers. In the subsequent month, at the Battle of Manila, the United States Navy defeated the Spanish Navy and took control of the Philippines.

The news of the war proved exciting to numerous young men. Countless males decided to enlist and demonstrate their patriotism. After the press reported that William had dropped out of Yale because he had trouble with "eye difficulty," subsequent articles said he had joined the army to fight in the war. So, William took leave of cozy Glenmont and the fury of his father and enlisted. First, he wrote his half-sister and brother and wished them good-bye. Knowing full well that Mina would also be reading the letter he wrote to them, he included the line, "I hope when you both grow up, you will not be a burden like myself but an honor to your father and mother." Then, imitating a philosopher, he informed them to be kind and truthful and "never regret the past as I have." Then directly to Madeleine, he admonished, "Never do anything so foolish as your sister Marion did, for, in the end, you will regret it." If Mina had read this aloud to them, she might have excluded this portion, knowing it was more than a ten- and eight-year-old could comprehend. But William, true to character, sought out sympathy whenever he was able.[18]

Within six weeks, and without a drop of shame, William reversed what he initially thought was a glamorous view of being in the army. He wrote from Puerto Rico that the "suffering is terrible. . . . [I am] so weak, [I] can hardly stand up." William begged his father "to use his influence" and "get him discharged." Then, letting his father off the hook, he suggested that his grandfather Lewis Miller could get him sent home, yet he also requested cigarettes while the paperwork went through.[19]

William returned safely to New Jersey. But according to Edison, it was more due to the kindness of Mina's family writing to McKinley's people. Edison told Mina he believed "William deliberately walked into a yellow fever cemetery."

It seemed that William was recovering, although he claimed he was sometimes "coughing up blood" from his lungs. The entire ordeal did not teach him any basic life lessons, and he was still asking for his allowance to be the same amount it was while he was in college and did not understand why it should not be. Finally, William decided to move in with his brother Tom Jr. to save some money.[20]

Edison was still at the mine, hoping to succeed regardless of how irrational it was becoming. Mina could no longer give her attention to William and his escapades. In the last trimester of her pregnancy, she could not afford to be upset by his repetitive refrain for money or his need for attention. Instead, she concentrated on her two young children, enrolling Madeleine and Charles in the prestigious Dearborn Morgan school in West Orange. After witnessing the catastrophic academic reports of the older Edison children, Mina was going to take the opposite tactic with her own. She kept a remarkably close eye on both her children. As early as kindergarten, the school followed the Froebel system of teaching, a progressive teaching method made popular in the nineteenth century. Its founder, Froebel, called his approach to education "self-activity." It allowed children to let their interests guide them through learning and play and explore them as they wished. At school, "each pupil receives individual attention." They had "daily recitations and conversations in French." The school also allowed for "any special study or exercise" at the parent's request. Along with her children's schooling, Mina taught them piano and drilled them daily to ensure they mastered their schoolwork.

Once she identified their strengths, perversely, she believed she could mold them into the adults she wanted them to be.[21]

A month after William enlisted in the army, John and Theodore followed suit. Lewis preferred that the boys get an office job rather than risk going into combat, but the boys persisted. Theodore "wanted to do something worth doing." John joined the navy and started on the USS *Marblehead*. He then was transferred to the USS *Vulcan*, which "lay in Guantanamo Bay" throughout the battle. When Lewis Miller finally agreed to the boys enlisting, Theodore wrote he was "mighty glad to get Father expressing his approval . . . and I hope I may have some active service somewhere."[22]

Theodore was an ambitious person; he did what was required in the classroom and on the athletic field at Yale. So, when he heard about Theodore Roosevelt's Rough Riders, he believed it was his calling. The Rough Riders regiment drew considerable attention; his childhood friend Dade Goodrich of Goodrich tire fame had enlisted, along with many other Harvard and Yale men. Once Theodore heard there was a place in the unit, he would "have to go at once to secure the vacancy." He was thrilled and told his mother, "The regiment is made up of the finest fellows in the country."[23]

On May 4th, Theodore was sworn in. Within two months, he was in active combat in Cuba with other soldiers who did not have enough training or understanding of the complexity of battle. On July 1st, the regiment found themselves on the island of Cuba in water up to their knees, attempting to take further possession of the island. All the while, bullets were flying over their heads. The troop moved forward, believing they had made some territorial advancements. However, shells hit the brigade out of nowhere, and the after-action report read that "five men dropped at the same instant, among them was Theodore." After members of the battalion reached the wounded, they noticed a bullet had entered Theodore's left shoulder; initially, the men did not consider it serious, but the lieutenant soon realized there was a second wound in the right shoulder blade that had injured his spinal cord. Theodore was left paralyzed below his shoulders. As six privates carried him to the hospital, despite his pain, Theodore thanked his fellow soldiers: "Boys, this is mighty good of you. I'm afraid I'm tiring you out." At the hospital, six days later, on July 7th, he dictated a letter home to his mother: "A rather narrow escape, but I feel sure I will pull through all right . . . you must not worry about a thing . . . the head of the Red Cross is here . . . they are doing everything that they can for me. I remain your most loving son and will be with you soon. Good-bye."[24]

That night Theodore fell into a coma and never regained consciousness. He was buried the next day, on July 8th, in a grave on a hilltop behind the hospital overlooking the Bay of Siboney. His friend Dade Goodrich suggested they bury a bottle with him containing his name and home address in case someone needed to identify his body in the future.

Two days before, Mina had celebrated her thirty-third birthday at Glenmont. She was nine months' pregnant. Mary Valinda, Mame, and Grace were there to celebrate with her. They had arrived a week prior in anticipation of the birth of the new baby. The two birthdays were a thing of delight for the Miller women. On the morning of July 11th, Mina went into labor. No one was yet aware of what had occurred to Theodore, but that afternoon a telegram arrived at Glenmont from John Miller in Santiago: "Theodore died on the eighth."[25]

Fate ensued. Edison was in an unusual position. A man who was not comfortable with emotions or doling out sympathy would have to inform his wife, who was in labor, his mother-in-law, and her two sisters that their youngest brother was dead. So, Edison made a calculated decision and told Mame first. At that point, he sent a telegram to his father-in-law in Akron, adding: "Do not telegraph back as I am breaking the news gradually to the folks at the house."[26]

Mame, dutiful as ever, began sending telegrams to her brothers. Within a minute of Edison's telegram, Ira was next to hear the news. Because the Millers were concerned about the state of both John and Theodore, Mame was sure to inform the family that "John was well." Next, Mame sent word to Richard, Jennie's husband. Richard had been employed at the Goodrich company and was privy to the Goodrich family's concern for their son Dade, a battalion member. Only later would the family learn of his kindheartedness at Theodore's initial burial.[27]

Another concern of Mame, as well as Richard's, was Jennie's health. She had taken ill with numerous maladies concerning her heart in the past year. In the past few months, when Mina shared her concern with Edison about her sister's health, he responded, "I can put Jane on the right track; one remedy is to have a baby—the second is to try hard to get one." But Mina never appreciated his sense of humor. Unfortunately, Jennie was unable to have a baby. It might have been due to her advanced age or a medical reason—either way, she often was weak and confined to her bed.[28]

Lewis Jr. was still in Honolulu and was in disbelief when his father informed him of Theodore's death. He wished to return home on the next steamer to comfort his family with his siblings. His brother's death put his life in perspective, and he realized the money he made in Hawaii could be earned in the United States. He was considering going to Georgia with his brother Robert to start a new business venture. Unfortunately, since the reorganization of the family business, it could no longer support a large family.

At this point, Robert and Louise had two children of their own, Robert Jr. and Rachel Alice. Robert was bright and quite capable in business and had strong people skills. He had studied at Eastman's Commercial College, a business school in Poughkeepsie, New York, and graduated from Ohio Wesleyan University. After school, he'd moved to Canton and become the assistant superintendent of the Buckeye Reaper and Mower Works of C. Aultman & Co. After his uncle died, Robert replaced him as superintendent and general manager. Since the financial downturn, Robert began jumping around and was associated with several other companies as an officer or stockholder. Nothing was permanent. At this point, he needed to find a new career, and he was solicitous about inviting his brother Lewis Jr. to join him.

Robert and Louise had sent word from Chautauqua congratulating Mina on the birth of the new baby. They knew the delivery was imminent and were waiting to hear. Blissfully unaware of Theodore's death, they added, "We are well indeed and looking for a fine summer."[29]

Lewis used his relationship with President McKinley to allow John to leave his position in the navy to retrieve Theodore's body and inter it into the family plot in Akron. The trip to reclaim the body was grueling for John, yet he kept the "Akron branch of the Miller family" updated on his heartbreaking mission. However, the Methodist family clung to their faith and followed their father's appeal: "[We] must not grieve too much and believe that it is all for the best and according to the will of God." The following day, Mame, who remained at Glenmont, told Mina about Theodore. Devasted by the news, Mina named her newborn baby Theodore Miller Edison. Her sisters hoped the baby could help fill a "dreadful void" in her heart.[30]

It took thirty days for John Miller to retrieve his younger brother's body. When John arrived in Santiago, a casket was waiting there that Lewis Miller had shipped from New York. That same afternoon, Theodore's body was transferred to the casket for the long journey home. Three days later, men moved the coffin to a barge. When the ship passed the place of Theodore's battle, the twelve hundred men aboard sang "The Star-Spangled Banner."

When the ship reached the Long Island shore, the soldiers could not disembark because yellow fever had broken out on the vessel. They needed to quarantine for an additional three days. Those aboard were somber about the effects of war, and many were sick.

John's second-oldest brother, Edward, recovered John and the casket at Montauk and escorted them back to Akron. Lewis Miller, Ira, Robert, Lewis Jr., and Jennie's husband, Richard, immediately cared for the casket. Finally, after eight months, Theodore's body returned home.

Crowds of Theodore's friends came to pay tribute to his life. The papers reported that "thousands of people" filled the First Methodist Church as Rev. Vincent glorified his memory with an emotional eulogy. Lewis Miller supported his weakened and distraught wife as she buried her youngest son next to her oldest daughter. Consumed with grief, the Miller children and their spouses stood speechless beside the grave. Jennie was pale as she watched from her carriage. She had been ill and was unable to stand and join the others. Edison remained at work and did not attend the funeral.[31]

Life resumed, yet the Miller children had difficulty moving on with their lives. Eventually, Jennie and John placed wreaths on Eva and Theodore's graves. John had to return to Cornell for classes but was not yet ready to revert to his life before the war and his brother's death. Mary Valinda struggled through the winter months, looking to her faith for comfort. She could not accept that the bright future of her baby boy had been cut short.

Within months, Mame informed Mina that "Jane is in severe condition" and Mina "must write the cheerful letters she is very much discouraged." When Jennie became so frail, Mame moved into her home and helped attend to her personal needs while Richard was at work. Her doctor was concerned about her poor health and had been altering her medications to achieve the optimum results. Grace had received a teaching job in Atlanta and lived there for a short time.[32]

Mame was slowly watching Jennie decline. Mame was reticent in sharing Jennie's state with Mina but decided she wanted her to feel that she "kept nothing back." Jennie's lungs were so weak that she had trouble walking across the room. Jennie constantly repeated to anyone who would listen that her "sickness is a punishment that she did not have children." However, Jennie's demeanor changed within a week of Mame's update. She had become "indifferent to everything and everyone," and Mame was afraid "we can't save her."[33]

Less than three months after burying Theodore, Jennie died at the age of forty-three. Lewis and Mary Valinda were emotionally devastated as they buried their third child. The papers claimed that the death of Theodore "hastened her death"; however, she had suffered from valvular heart trouble for two years. When Mina heard the news, she scooped up her three children and a nurse and boarded the next train to Akron, Ohio. Jennie's funeral was more subdued than Theodore's. The Millers could not endure countless visitors. Although Mina wrote to Edison about Jennie's passing, Edison responded three days later, half-apologizing that this was the first chance he'd had "to answer it" and that he "scarcely gets any sleep as everything has to be attended to by me." He wrote about the snow at the mine and how difficult it was to accomplish anything. The Millers were tired of Edison putting work before family. Lewis Miller took the matter into his own hands and telegraphed Edison directly to come to the funeral and be a pallbearer. Edison responded he could not come, and the "400 men depend" on only him to run the entire operation.[34]

Disinterested in Mina's needs, he wrote that she could remain in Akron for three or more weeks through Christmas and the New Year. He was not returning for "2 or three Sundays more." But two days after Jennie's funeral, Edison required Mina to attend to his demands. He was having financial issues that he believed were dire to the point of sending a telegram and letter inspiring her return. He exclaimed to Mina that he was worried about funding the mine and "you must certainly be here by the 15th even if you go back," so Mina returned to Edison's side for Christmas and the New Year as the family celebrated the end of the nineteenth century.[35]

Before Jennie's death, Mina was still contending with Tom Jr.'s constant business debacles. Mina had been too preoccupied with her family's tragedies to keep a close eye on his movements. He had moved to midtown Manhattan while jumping from one business scheme to another. Mina and Edison warned him to keep from using his last name to "earn an easy buck." Edison once again sent William to tell his brother, "Father does not want you to go around the country using his name as a drawing card, and if you attempt to do so, he will send a lawyer to stop it."[36]

Turning to alcohol after sustaining another round of his father's insults, Tom Jr. began frequenting local nightclubs and theatres. There he met Marie Louise Toohey, a local evening stage performer. The press referred to her as a "Casino Girl." Marie was nineteen years old with massive "wavy golden hair" and blue eyes. Although she was young, Marie was more shrewd than Tom Jr. She realized who his father was and instantly fell in love. Desperate for affection and naïve about romance, Tom Jr. would do anything for attention from a female. He believed Marie was devoted to him, and they secretly married.[37]

Marie Toohey, originally from Chicago, had made her first appearance onstage at the 1893 World's Fair. She then appeared with Eddy Foy in *Robinson Crusoe* and acted with famed Lillian Russel in *La Belle Helene*. One evening, Marie giggled during a routine, angering the manager. She and the manager argued often; he finally told her, "You leave Saturday night." The self-assured Marie responded, "You need not tell me when I am to leave; I'll leave when I am good and ready; In fact, I'll leave now." The manager responded, "You can give [in] your costumes," to which

Marie announced, "I have a name, and it's Mrs. Thomas Edison Jr.," and she walked out of the theatre. The next day, a reporter interviewed Tom Jr. and Marie at their apartment on 214 West 50th Street in Manhattan, where they admitted they had been married since November 23rd.[38]

Upon learning about the secret wedding, Edison was livid. Soon newspapers across the country were spreading the news of Tom Jr's. secret marriage to a "casino girl." Edison would not allow his son's fraudulent businesses to tarnish his image. He officially announced that they were estranged, had nothing to do with his son's schemes, and gave him "no financial encouragement."[39]

Tom Jr. adored his new wife and shared his happiness with Mina regardless of his father's taunts and insults. They enjoyed their "little home," where Marie waited and attended to all Tom Jr.'s domestic needs. However, Tom Jr. could not remain happy for long. William informed Mina that his brother "has gone to the dogs." He had to leave New York and run to Pittsburgh to escape the sheriff chasing after him. In addition, he had been passing bad checks at hotels and saloons.[40]

Mina was mortified about the news of Tom Jr., yet she did not have the emotional capacity to give energy to this new crisis. Her brother Robert had been unsuccessful in starting a lucrative business in Akron. Sympathetic to his need for employment, President McKinley appointed him as the postmaster general of Puerto Rico. As a result, he and Louise, her dearest friend, would be moving far away. It was another devastating blow for Mina, but she put on a supportive face for her brother, happy he was now gainfully employed.

After burying two siblings and tending to a newborn, Mina had experienced enough. Yet more devasting news was about to befall the family. Two months after Jennie's funeral, Lewis Miller suddenly was confined to bed with abdominal trouble. Mina intervened and believed that he should go to New York for an operation.

Robert wrote from Puerto Rico with profound existential questions that he shared with Mina: "We certainly have been having our share of anxiety these days. What does it mean? Is there a lesson to learn as a family or as an individual? Are we doing our duty and all we can? Father and mother lived in many happy years in faith and taught us all to have lived up to that faith, and are we continuing in it? May God help us to learn the lesson and gain the happiness that is in store for us all if we accept it."[41]

Robert's words were prescient. The Miller family would have to endure tragedy again. On the way to New York, the sleeping car on the train carrying Lewis Miller to the hospital broke down, leaving its passengers on the train without heat the entire night. The lack of warmth exacerbated his suffering, and a deep chill permeated his whole body. The following day, he was taken by ambulance to the hospital and underwent surgery. However, Lewis Miller would not see the seventieth year of his life; his body did not survive the operation.[42]

Hiding from the Press

WHEN LEWIS MILLER TOOK HIS LAST BREATH OF LIFE, MINA WAS AT his bedside. The previous two years had been devastating for her mother. Mina now had the loathsome task of sharing the news with their mother in Akron. Mary Valinda was anxiously awaiting a telegram to hear about her beloved husband's recovery. She was planning for his imminent return to Oak Place. They needed each other now more than ever, as they were helping each other cope with the loss of two children in the past year; Mary Valinda could not withstand another death. When the news reached Oak Place, her body involuntarily collapsed onto the floor in anguish.

Newspapers across the country paid tribute to the man whom all believed made "inestimable contributions to education, the farming industry and nation." He was "true to his faith." He taught by "example and taught courage." His "boundless enthusiasm" affected all around him. Ministers from all over the Midwest eulogized this man who touched so many lives. Reverend Vincent also gave a eulogy; it was lengthy and personal—penance for sins against the Miller family.[1]

After the public mourning and numerous memorials ended, the family needed a source of income. Mary Valinda and the unmarried daughters were in desperate straits concerning a source of revenue. So, the family made a difficult decision to sell off much of the property around Oak Place. Mary Valinda and her unmarried children would live off the income from the sale of the property and any savings. It was inevitable that the family would need to make other tough decisions.

Edison had no choice but to travel to Akron to pay his respects to his well-known father-in-law. After missing Theodore and Jennie's funerals, the Miller family and Mina would never pardon his behavior. Upon Mina and Edison's return to New Jersey, William inundated his father with his latest personal and business escapades.

Mina struggled to shield the Edison name from random gossip in the papers. After the Tom Jr. debacle, it was more challenging than ever. Even though William witnessed the tension and ire created by his brother's marriage, William decided to follow suit.

William had met Blanche Travers in Baltimore more than two years before, and an immediate attachment grew between the couple. Both Edison and Mina thought William was too young to get married and forbade the engagement. William was only twenty years old and had dropped out of college. Moreover, he had no work prospects in his future. When William went to fight in the Spanish-American War, Edison thought the engagement would be forgotten. Instead, when he returned, the attachment was as strong as ever. The two publicly announced their engagement a year later.

Blanche Travers was not a showgirl. She was born in Scranton, Pennsylvania; her father was Dr. Edward Travers, a surgeon. He had died eight years before the wedding, and her mother, Mary Travers, had remarried. Her uncle was Senator John Daniel of Virginia. They had married four months before Lewis Miller died, in Elizabeth, New Jersey, at an Episcopal church. Even with these credentials, Edison and Mina refused to attend the wedding.

The press saw this final wedding as an opportunity to inform the public that Edison had a poor relationship with all three of his children from his first wife—as evidenced by each of their weddings. His eldest, Marion, had been in Germany and married without the presence of her father. The recent marriage of Tom Jr. to an actress was still current gossip. Now it was the talk of the neighborhood that by marrying Miss Blanche Travers, the youngest son of the inventor by his first wife, had also cut him off from the family circle. William was the third to oppose his father's wishes in selecting a life companion. Mina and Edison, mortified, refused to discuss the subject with the press. Thus, William's marriage to Blanche

Travers practically estranged the great inventor from all three of his children by his first wife.[2]

Marion seldom wrote to Edison or Mina directly. Her letters arrived around the holidays and included a perfunctory thank-you for gifts or condolences on the recent Miller deaths. She did add she wanted "a picture of the new baby ... and I regret not having any of my own." The more time she spent away from her father, the more emboldened she was with her comments, and she stated to him, "Having no letter from you to answer, I suppose the one side correspondence with you has to do." It had been eight years since they had seen each other. Marion did ask in vain if her father could visit. "Oscar is worth the journey over." At other moments, after receiving a letter from Tom Jr. and learning about his latest incidents, she shared her opinion that "His letter to me could not possibly have been written by a sane person." Furthermore, she added, "I cannot think Tom is in his right mind." In a moment of sorrow, she admitted to Mina that "I pity him."[3]

Sigmund Bergman, a longtime colleague of Edison's of German descent, visited Marion during his travels to Germany. He wanted to give Marion and Oscar some extra money and have Edison reimburse him when he returned, but Marion discouraged him. The father-daughter relationship was distant yet uneventful. Even though the gesture was thoughtful, there was no need to wake the sleeping giant. She was too fearful that Edison would be angry that she'd made a financial decision without her father's prior consent. Although she told Edison of Bergman's offer, it was more to show her father that men of different natures could exude kindness. Edison learned nothing from his daughter's anecdote and continued his financial transactions with his daughter through an intermediary.

Although William began to work on his own somehow, he did not grow out of his habit of spending money faster than he earned it. Edison, just recovered from spending more money on his iron ore mine than he owned, was riled when his son asked for help with his cash flow. Edison was eager to rebuke William for his mistakes but rarely gave him praise. Edison could not admit that providing advice or instruction might have benefited his sons when they started their own businesses. Instead, Edison was annoyed with William's lack of financial prudence. He explicitly told his assistant, "Do not deliver anything to William unless he pays."[4]

Regardless of his father's comments, William believed he was maturing and informed Mina that "I have outgrown my previous foolishness" and "having wiped the past from my mind. A lie is like candy to me now. I had too much of that stuff in the past and don't want any more." He also admitted he now had a considerable number of friends, "more than his brother could make in a lifetime."[5]

But Edison did not back down and refused to engage with his son. William was quite angry with his father, yet he ultimately blamed his stepmother and told Edison's assistant, "Mina Miller cannot run the whole ranch one handed." He wanted to have a caring father and exclaimed that if "My father was a true father [he] would look after my welfare." Now that William no longer lived at home, he realized he was treated much like Marion and stated, "my father never takes the trouble to find out if I am dead or alive."[6]

Blanche realized her husband's aggressive tone did not affect her father-in-law. Desperate, she decided to take the matters into her own hand and write him herself. New to the family, Blanche did not understand how her father-in-law functioned. She beseeched him that they needed more money and tried to play to his ego: "do you know that the children of the Greatest Man of the Century and for them to live as they should on forty dollars per week takes much more ability than I can display." It took three years after they were married before Edison prepared to accept Blanche as an Edison.[7]

But there would never be a question of accepting Marie Toohey into the Edison family. Edison opposed the marriage bitterly. Tom Jr. told his father and the public through interviews with the press that he could be an "electrical genius" like his father, and that he had gone out and "patented several devices." He claimed he had $60,000 in the bank. He began selling his patents for a tenth of their value to buy jewelry and clothing for himself and his new wife. He began selling his name to various companies that were often fraudulent. This incensed Edison, who was highly protective of his name and did not want it associated with these companies. Tom Jr. understood what his last name was worth and was willing to sell it to the highest bidder. But he gullibly believed what purchasers told him it was worth, and they paid much less than its actual value. So, he sold it for $100,000 and went to Lake George with the earnings.[8]

But Marie was not attracted to a life of earning quick money and spending it all. By that time, she realized she would never be invited over to Glenmont for tea. So, that summer, Marie Toohey, a veteran of the stage, left Tom Jr. with a flourish, giving interviews to anyone who would listen. She claimed he spent all his money on himself and drank terribly at times. In addition, he spent all of his money on many collars, ties, shoes, and suits. She exclaimed, "our married life was not a merry one," and she had "got enough of it very soon."[9]

Timorous at heart, Tom Jr. could not keep up with his exhibitionist wife. He hit bottom when he was spotted on the street of New York City, "bedraggled and dirty and unshaven without a penny to his name. And sobbing a whole lot." He drifted into the bar to sit because he thought he would get better treatment there than at home or with his family. He claimed he had walked there from Yonkers, having been thrown off the train because he had no money. He admitted his wife had deserted him after they'd spent time at Lake George.[10]

Over the following month, press reports claimed that Edison was trying to locate his son and give him a chance to reform. Instead, Edison had placed William in charge of finding him after he had been missing six weeks. Edison also used the police and the Pinkerton private detective agency to locate him. William was distressed about his brother's state, telling reporters "he is penniless, so he is leading a precarious life in 'the wilds of New York City.'" In his effort to help locate him, he had the papers print his address so Tom Jr. could find him.[11]

Mina and Edison needed to stop the daily stories in the papers about his behavior, so they spun a tale for the press. The family claimed Edison had never lost faith in his son despite his erratic career, and now they wanted to allow him "to brace up and be a man." They would welcome him back on the condition that he divorced his wife. Attempting further to salvage the integrity of the Edison name, they told the press it was "infatuation for her which ruined Tom and that life with her or interest in her would prevent his reformation."[12]

Tom Jr. followed his father's instructions and retained a divorce law-yer. Within months, he publicly sought a divorce with his head tucked under his tail. The entire marriage had lasted nineteen months. Lost and dejected, he moved to Newark, to his mother's brother's home, where he announced to the press that followed him there that his wife "did not desire to begin divorce proceedings, so he had to do it himself."[13]

After a few weeks in a warm bed with some nourishment, he and his uncle tried to start a steel company together to manufacture hard steel into iron. They began advertising in the paper. Not learning his lesson from his previous financial disasters, Tom Jr. had the ad state, "vast for-tunes will be made." He and his uncle hired William McMahon to create the company, put up some money, and seek other financings. Unfortu-nately, the invention was never adopted. Instead, McMahon sued Tom Jr., breaking the contract by refusing to pay him his share of stock. Rather than helping his nephew out of the jam, his uncle traveled to England, leaving Tom Jr. to fend for himself.[14]

Still hoping to succeed in other ways, Tom Jr. started other businesses. One of these was to sell "Wizard Ink Tablets." From the outset of the venture, he was involved with shady businesspeople who just wanted to use his name. They paid Tom Jr. $5,000 for his name and a $25 monthly salary. Another was the "Magneto-Electric Vitalizer," for which he was to receive royalties. But this proved to be a phony medical device, and Edi-son shut it down once he found out about it. Tom, thinking these ventures would make him rich, met his brother in Maryland and chartered a boat down to Florida with his friends.[15]

After the trip, during which he passed more fraudulent checks, he returned to Newark to live with his mother's brother, Charles Stilwell. After all the negative publicity that Tom Jr. had created for the family, Edison expressed his anger when asked about his son: "I could never get Tom Jr. to go to school or work in the Laboratory. He is illiterate scien-tifically or otherwise." He also refused to send him a dime to cover his fraudulent checks and found himself contending with a barrage of letters from men who had lost money because of his son.[16]

Lacking the energy to contest his father, Tom Jr. eventually gave up. Edison was unsure of his whereabouts. He wrote to Tom Jr.'s lawyer with the intent that his frustration would be passed on to his son: "I don't see what the public had to do with your affairs." Edison implored his son to keep his business out of the press. But at that point, Tom Jr. had worn himself ragged. Company after the company had failed, as did his marriage. He needed money, and his father refused to send a cent after the harmful exposure that Tom Jr. created for himself.[17]

Finally, in June, Tom Jr. formally agreed to "no longer use the Edison name commercially." This prompted Edison to write his son: "Tom, you must know with your record of passing bad checks and use of liquor, all of which is known to Everyone who has business connections with my concerns that it would be impossible to connect you with any of the business prospects of mine. However, you can go into something small business there are more than 10,000 such businesses; William seems to be doing well."[18]

Crestfallen, Tom Jr. decided his health was so poor that he would enter a St. James hospital sanitarium under the care of Dr. Welshman for two months. His uncle dropped him there and shared his condition with Edison's secretary, Johnny Randolph, who handled all the children's allowances and interactions. Although his uncle felt terrible for Tom Jr., "the poor fellow was so friendless, I had to give some moral guidance." Charles added that he understood if Randolph might want to share the news with Edison, but "I hope we can keep quite the latest disgrace to the name of Edison."[19]

William, still causing friction in the family, was more settled than his older brother. He lived in New York City and became involved in two short-lived companies: "W. L. Edison, Dealer in Phonographs, Records & Supplies" and the "Edison Vehicle Supply Co." It was astonishing to Edison that William was utterly oblivious to what had just transpired with his brother. He did not heed the countless warnings of his father and used his last name when he created a business. Edison, furious, exclaimed, "You copied what your brother Tom did, and after I give the seed money that I promised, I am through with you." Edison, further making his son feel inadequate, added, "I hope you will learn from this experience, but the hope is pretty weak."[20]

Afterward, William shared his father's sentiments with his wife. Blanche was still getting accustomed to the gruffness of her father-in-law and decided that if she begged, it might change his mind. She wrote a long-winded letter to his secretary about how they "barely make ends meet" and needed food for rent. Unfortunately, regardless of her pleadings, Edison told his secretary, "Not to send another cent." So, William and Blanche left New York and attempted to start over. He and Blanche moved in with her aunt in Salisbury, Maryland. William eventually opened an automobile garage in Washington, DC, and subsequently worked as an agent and factory superintendent for several automobile companies.[21]

As problematic as Tom Jr. and William were for Mina and Edison, they learned to use the press to manage publicity about them. Tom Jr. made a scripted public statement directed at his father: "It is hard for me to realize now how I have been so weak as to yield to the persuasion of these men, who have been trading on our family name and your reputation." While William had moved away, Tom Jr. was sobering up in the sanitarium, and the dreadful years of iron ore milling were behind them. The episode was arduous for Mina, and she needed to recuperate away from the debacle caused by the boys. Mina checked herself into Battle Creek Sanitarium under the care of two nurses. The sanitarium was a world-renowned health resort in Michigan based on health principles advocated by the Seventh-day Adventist Church. The famed Dr. John Harvey Kellogg managed it. Kellogg explored various treatments for his patients, including diet reform and frequent enemas. He described the sanitarium system as "a composite physiologic method." The many doctors on staff treated the patients with hydrotherapy, phototherapy, electrotherapy, cold air cure, and other remedies. Mina shared her visit with her sister Mame in confidence that she was "seriously ill." Upon returning to Glenmont, Mina was relieved that her trip there did not "make it into the papers."[22]

Mina focused on her three children and was frailer than a healthy mother. With Edison's help, Mina began to work on the wording of her will. After the family's sudden deaths, they wanted all the remaining property to end up in the rightful hands of specific family members. All the family issues took a toll on Mina. She freely admitted to her mother that "she is getting fussy in her middle life and inclined to be a little nervous for some reason," and she found solace in rearing Madeleine and Charles. Their growth and development were her constant comfort. As they continued their local schooling, she ensured they were exposed to as many cultural events as she could cram into their schedules. Mina hired a French governess to speak to the children in French. By the time they reached their teenage years, Madeleine and Charles were fluent.[23]

Mina was cautious to ensure their friends were children of other families in Llewellyn Park or families she deemed fit. Mina hoped her children would bring Edison's reputation to its rightful place in the nation. Llewelyn Park, eight hundred acres, had sprawling estates, yet it was a gated community that allowed the children to roam outside their homes. Charles would often play with Henry Colgate, heir to the soap fortune. His family lived directly opposite the Edisons and had a playhouse where the boys would go after school. Other boys of whom Mina approved were Jerome Franks, the son of Andrew Carnegie's "confidential financial man," and Lloyd Fulton of the Fulton Iron Works. Further safeguarding the children's social network, Mina rented a home in Deal one summer on the New Jersey shore. At the time, there were only three homes on the beach, and Mina rented the house next to Robert Lincoln, Abraham Lincoln's son.

The family savored the Christmas holiday as a much-needed respite from the pressure of living in the "Edison fishbowl." In a personal composition Madeleine wrote describing Glenmont on Christmas Day, we see how Mina would do everything in her power to create a fairy-tale life for her family. Madeleine and Charles would wake up early, as other children across the world did, "rather disappointed" not to see the grounds covered in snow. As a consolation, they eyed their stockings, guessing what their mother had placed inside.[24]

The children knew they had to sing carols outside their room before opening presents. Once Madeleine and Charles finished breakfast and emptied their stockings, they were permitted to enter the parlor to view the family tree. The chains of gold and silver balls glistened amongst the miniature-colored electric lights and tinsel. For that moment in time, the Edison children grasped the melding of their father's sparkling invention with their mother's aesthetic sense and admired their most beautiful tree.

While Mina shielded her children from the harmful influences of the lower classes, Edison had to face life's harsh realities head-on. His last remaining sibling, Marion Wallace, died after battling poor health for several years. He and Mina traveled to Milan, Ohio, for the funeral and then made a short stopover at Akron to visit Mina's mother and siblings. Unfortunately, he was so sick that the visit turned even more miserable, as he could not return home to Glenmont. The continuous lack of sleep, overwork, and poor eating habits had brought about influenza and acute laryngitis. Edison's poor health compelled him to remain at Oak Place to recuperate instead of returning to work.

The enormous stresses upon the family were unrelenting. Mina and the family craved a respite. Florida's warm weather and distance would help Edison and Mina return to a calmer state. Edison had avoided his winter home for fourteen years. Fort Myers entered into the new future without Edison fulfilling his original promise to bring electric light a year prior. However, Edison had not entirely dissociated himself from the town or his property. Besides visits from his father and a companion, he had a caretaker looking after the property. After multiple warnings, Edison finally paid overdue property taxes. And they added indoor plumbing and mesh screens on all the doors and windows to protect against mosquitoes. Mina also had the outside repainted, so it looked updated and clean for the many onlookers.

While the citizens of Fort Myers had given up on the return of their famous resident, another renowned family replaced him. Ambrose McGregor, a Standard Oil executive, had arrived ten years prior, bringing his gregarious wife, Tootie, and their son. They loved the area so much that they purchased the empty Gilliland house and became Edison's new neighbors. Tootie refurbished the house and hired a caretaker to watch the home in the off season. They bought a yacht and fished for tarpons. The townspeople were enamored with the family when they returned from their excursions, revealing their catch. Ambrose invested vast sums of money in Fort Myers. The land was called the McGregor Plantation, in which he planted citrus trees and rice and tobacco. There was a new hero in town. Edison and his unkempt house were not often in the news. Instead, the townspeople had hopes that MacGregor, who succeeded

John Rockefeller as president of Standard Oil, would lead a rebuilding of the town. These hopes evaporated when he died of cancer as the new century dawned.

That same year, Edison decided to return, but the Edisons never made it to Fort Myers. Instead, the family traveled only as far as Tampa, where they resided at the posh Tampa Hotel. The hotel was owned by Henry Plant, the famous Florida businessman and entrepreneur who ensured that its opulence met the needs of the wealthy leisure class of the Gilded Age. In contrast to her first Florida trip, Mina greatly enjoyed her stay.

After his arrival, Edison, swarmed by the press, gave regular rounds of interviews. Likely for Mina's benefit, he clearly stated that he is "'not in Florida on business but merely for the health of myself and family.' He fully admits that he needed to break away from the winter in the north." During the family's stay, they made public excursions. Edison toured a cigar factory and the surrounding city. The family went back to Glenmont without ever visiting Fort Myers. Their initial intention was only to go down south for three weeks.[25]

Edison returned well-rested. Although he did not visit his Florida home, his love for Fort Myers did not falter. He realized that the weather had done wonders for his recuperation. George Stadler, a fellow business-man and member of the New York State Senate, was aware that Edison had not returned to his Fort Myers home for many years and offered to buy his home. Edison replied to the advance, "I know no finer place in the U.S. for a short winter stay than Myers, and as I am getting old and intend going there more to spend the winter."[26]

Edison was true to his word, and the following winter, he and his family returned to Fort Myers at long last. A nurse accompanied the children. Mina's sister Mame and Edison's cousin Edith Edison also joined them. Her father, Simeon Edison, had moved to Orange, and she often spent significant time with Mina and the children in the years when Edi-son lived at the mine. She was six years younger than Mina and an excel-lent companion to her.

The large group of eight was cramped in the Edison home. Mina had neglected to make reservations in advance so that some of their party could stay at the Fort Myers Hotel. When they arrived at their home, they also realized that the kitchen was inoperative for themselves or guests and took their meals at the Fort Myers Hotel. They realized that since their last visit, many other wealthy families had made Fort Myers their home and built large houses for themselves. Mina and Edison were pleased to see the town's progress. Mina knew she had to make up for lost time and made sure that Edison mingled with others in their class and perhaps shared his interests.

Every year, Edison used the press to announce his return for the winter to Fort Myers, where he would remain for a month. During his visits, the manager of the Fort Myers Hotel, knowing the famous inventor's presence would enhance his business, invited the well-known lover of fishing out on the river for his daily catch. While on the river, Edison basked in the tropical flora and fauna. The alligators, orange groves, and other tropical fruit made the environs so distinct from his life in West Orange.

The rest of the family also enjoyed their time in Fort Myers, where Edison was always more relaxed. Madeleine recalled, "we were allowed to do more [in] Ft. Myers than any other place." Mina would enjoy luncheons with the wives of other industrialists who spent winters there. She and Madeleine built relationships with these women, including Tootie McGregor, who returned as a widow with her son to live next door in the former Gilliland house she'd renamed "Poinciana." The two families spent significant time together at the Hotel and fishing on the river.[27]

After their return to Fort Myers, Mina decided to improve the house, adding a second bathroom and updating the kitchen so they could have more meals at home. In addition, she enlarged the porches for more seating and painted the inside. When her mother and sister accompanied her to Fort Meyers the following winter, she could show off these improvements.

Mina hoped the easygoing state that encompassed the Edisons in Fort Myers would pervade the family dynamic after they returned to New Jersey. One event suggested it might. The Edisons hosted Signor Guglielmo Giovanni Marconi, the Italian inventor and electrical engineer who created the system of radio wireless telegraphy. Marconi was accompanied by Sir William Thompson, known as Lord Kelvin, the British mathematician, physicist, and engineer who formulated the emerging discipline of physics. In addition, they were joined by heads of the railroad industry. The men received a tour of the Laboratory before having a formal dinner at Glenmont. Weeks before this event, Mina wrote her mother and fretted about the details surrounding the evening for Edison and all those involved. She desperately needed to be the consummate hostess. These men meant so much to her husband, and the evening needed to be perfect. The event, which was covered by the press, went off flawlessly. Readers relished the meeting of all these significant minds in one place.[28]

But trouble seemed to creep into the crevices of the Edison home. A force of men with rifles now guarded the once-bucolic Glenmont. Edison had received a letter threatening that Madeleine would be kidnapped if he did not leave $25,000 at a designated place on Orange Mountain. Moreover, if he did not provide the money at once, the ransom would be three times the initial demand.[29]

Mina was beside herself with nervousness and anxiety. Many of his colleagues noticed that even Edison was anxious. Charles remembered in his memoirs that "somebody came down for us at school and I couldn't understand why we couldn't ride our bicycles home and stop for our soda and we were bundled into a closed carriage and the bicycles were put on top of the carriage and we were taken home in great secrecy." When the regular local reporters approached the home, they were no longer allowed to walk within 150 yards of the front entrance, and no one was allowed to come near the door. Within days, other reporters flocked to the laboratory to inquire about the noticeable police presence and ensuing commotion. Edison's secretary, John Randolph, was instructed to deny the family had received any letter. However, in subsequent days, the Edisons had to retract this initial denial and admit to the threat on his daughter. Edison hired a private detective from the Pinkerton Agency who worked with the police and interviewed all names involved brought up by the local police. It was common at that time for those in the wealthy or upper classes to hire a company to handle their personal safety needs. After three months of investigation and an advertisement in the New York newspaper, the police located the culprit and obtained a confession. The perpetrator had become desperate due to financial difficulties and had written threatening letters to Edison and others in an effort to obtain cash. Because he had inflicted no physical harm on the Edisons or other families he had threatened, he was given immunity once he admitted guilt and wrote an apology, thus closing the matter. Edison did not want the case discussed in the press. At that time, the subject was closed because the bourgeois had banded together in unity.[30]

Edison was cognizant that the press had affected his business and reputation within the past few years. Although parsimonious with money in many parts of his business, he maintained a longtime engagement with a clipping service to send him articles written about him. They were primarily taken from newspapers and popular magazines, although some were from trade publications, technical journals, and other printed sources. The articles and interviews pertained to a variety of subjects, including the development and promotion of Edison's inventions and the personal affairs of Edison and his family. In addition, Edison wanted to keep abreast of all aspects of his business, and at times clippings were included relating to the personnel, activities, and legal affairs of Edison's various companies and articles about phonographs and phonograph records, motion pictures, and storage batteries.

Now that Edison was through with ore milling, he had to focus his overactive interests elsewhere. While trying to develop his low-grade iron ore milling process, Edison found that he could sell the waste sand to cement manufacturers. So, in 1899, he decided to investigate how he might transfer his rock-crushing technology to the production of Portland cement. During the next few years, Edison made other improvements in cement manufacture. The most important was a long kiln, which he licensed to other manufacturers. He also built a large plant in Stewartsville, New Jersey. Edison Portland cement was used extensively for buildings, roads, dams, and other structures, including Yankee Stadium. In addition, Edison designed a system for building inexpensive cement houses, which he licensed to other manufacturers, but few were ever constructed.

As with the iron mine, Edison stayed there for extended periods working on his new invention. But Mina, now thirty years old, was able to coax her husband back home on a more regular basis. His more-frequent visits home might have been due to frequent and chronic stomach pains as Edison frequently worked till near exhaustion and often ate nothing of substance. His fifty-year-old body could not withstand the strenuous work schedule that had been his custom for decades. Although doctors warned him to sleep and eat better, he ignored their advice and suffered the physical consequences that assaulted his body.

In his usual manner, Edison focused on more than one invention at a time. Regardless of his time commitment and investment in cement, Edison also spent much of the first decade of the twentieth century developing a storage battery he intended for use in electric automobiles. Edison had a long-standing interest in battery design dating back to his time as a telegraph inventor. However, the advent of cars in the late 1890s spurred him to develop a storage battery to power them. Aware of the weight problems with batteries, Edison decided to experiment with alkaline batteries rather than the standard heavy lead-acid batteries in order to create a lightweight and long-lasting battery for automobiles. However, it took him a decade to develop a commercially viable battery, and by that time, automobiles powered by engines had become dominant.[31]

As Madeleine and Charles became older, Edison realized they could be helpful to him on those rare occasions when he had dinner with the family. Edison realized the benefit of a fifteen-minute power nap, and he often took one before dinner. Afterward, he would make up a list of ideas he wanted to work on the next day at his Lab. Edison had numerous scientific books at home to work out his thoughts. He would announce to the family, "I am on a campaign, and I have got to get all the references that I can about a certain chemical or process." Edison would insist that the children and Mina take the books, go through them, and place a paper marker wherever they found something that might be related to his research for Edison to review later. These research sessions were frequent and lengthy, sometimes spanning hours extending to bedtime. The children and Mina dreaded them and believed there was no educational merit to the exercise. Yet, typical of Edison's personality, his children's contentment was not his concern. He saw three and, later, when Theodore was older, four research assistants. Whether related, the children were rungs on his ladder to create his invention. No one's individual needs ever took precedence over his own.[32]

As he grew older, Edison appreciated the benefits of traveling to the warmer climate of Fort Myers during the colder months. The following winter, Edison had one of his colleagues wire his home for generator electricity. The local papers admired how lovely the evening lights of the Edison home showed off the sumptuous property.

By the time Charles was fourteen, he had learned the love of fishing, much like his father. At that time, the pristine Caloosahatchee River alongside Fort Myers was filled with sea life of all kinds. When they were fishing, Edison's competitive streak came. Once, when Charles caught an enormous one-hundred-pound tarpon that was more impressive than his father's forty-pound catch, Edison was so dejected he wanted to throw it back in the water. He could not stand to have his son beat him.

On the last night of their stay that winter in 1901, the Edison family ate at the Hotel. The town once again embraced the famous inventor and his family. The local paper reiterated that the city had adopted him and wrote, "Prof. Edison and his interesting family have won the hearts of all the people who have come in contact with them." Mina left satisfied that at least in Florida, Edison's reputation was "as good as ever."[33]

13

Between Two Fires

MINA ACCLIMATED TO THE TWENTIETH CENTURY AT A SLOWER PACE than the rest of her family. Nevertheless, the first flight by the Wright brothers, Henry Ford's Model-T, Albert Einstein's Theory of Relativity, and a vaccine for tuberculosis thrust the nation into the future. Although Mina appreciated these modern discoveries, she held on to the Victorian mores she had grown up with and considered her moral compass.

Madeleine and Charles had vivacious personalities, and as her children grew older, they made strong friendships. Like many young mothers, her children's social circles caused Mina to meet and interact with other families in her gated community. She was invited to teas and luncheons and began making essential friendships with women in the surrounding area. At Mina's urging, Edison joined the country club and other cultural groups, although he rarely, if ever, attended any functions associated with these organizations. Nevertheless, people adored the famed inventor they believed was responsible for changing the world. The newspapers recently reported Kaiser Wilhelm II of Germany was the first to make a political recording of a document using Edison's cylinder. Edison's busy schedule provided Mina with excuses for his frequent social absences.[1]

The children's daily obligations, along with her new social circle, allowed Mina to discover herself outside her husband's needs. Of course, it did not stop Mina from dropping everything to come to Edison's aid if he beckoned, but it lessened her loneliness in a significant way. She occupied her time at various civic or charity organization meetings to raise money to cure the sick, aid some orphans, or beautify a locale. As Edison's long workdays spilled over into weeks, months, and years, Mina realized that in Edison's world, she was accepted as a wife but rejected as a person. She lived with that dichotomy her entire life.

Glenmont had at least seven men working around the grounds in various capacities when the children were in elementary school. In addition, several women worked inside the home, including a waitress, a cook, a maid, a nurse, and a laundress. Her many servants and nannies allowed Mina the freedom to go into New York for lunch at the Waldorf Astoria, followed by a light opera or a stint of shopping.

Once the other society women realized Mina's social value, she was more than happy to participate as the years progressed. She had an acute understanding that her connections would move her and her children up the social ladder. As a result, she had memberships in many organizations, including the Women's Club of Orange, the Calvary Methodist Church, the Orange Orphan Society, the Orange Memorial Hospital, the Orange Auxiliary Red Cross, the Daughters of the American Revolution, and the New Jersey Audubon Society. These groups and others occupied her days to the point of frequent exhaustion. In addition, several of the organizations promoted her to chair or president.

Mina's dream was for Madeleine to become a socialite in her own right. With her wealthy background and prominent surname, she could marry the son of one of the women in Mina's circle. Madeleine's life could eventually mimic her own, allowing a significant amount of time to attend various fashionable social gatherings instead of having to work for a living.

For her children to carry out Mina's dream, she believed they, too, must be exposed to what high society could offer. Therefore, Mina hired tutors from all disciplines to supplement their education. Commencing in their childhood and until they all entered college, they had lessons in piano and mandolin, German and French, dancing, tennis, skating, and drawing, as well as vocal lessons.[2]

Madeleine also enjoyed horseback riding, but Edison was adamantly opposed to her riding side-saddle. As Madeleine grew older and emboldened, she pushed back. Although usually one to control the family through a few words or utter silence, Edison's anger sometimes surfaced with a vengeance. On one occasion, Edison noticed one of the countless servants helping Madeleine tie up her boots in her room. He stormed out, screaming at Mina that he refused to allow his daughter to have someone else button her boots for her. Madeleine recalled in her memoirs that she had never before seen her father so enraged. At those moments, Mina swooped in to calm the raging lion. Mina was desperate to keep the peace, and she accomplished this by allowing Edison a wide berth when he was home, often at the expense of the children's well-being.[3]

A true patriot, Edison celebrated July 4th with much gusto. He would wake up early, set off fireworks, then toss them at the children's bare feet. He enjoyed seeing his kids jump and scream. He would also set off roman candles and more potent fireworks in the evening. Mina would have guests over, and Edison would be happy and pleasant with the surrounding company.

Other holidays and birthdays were more critical to Mina than Edison. Madeleine had ornate birthday parties throughout her childhood. Mina would decorate Glenmont in feminine hues and the outside lawns with age-appropriate amusements. She ordered the best candies and confections for the occasion. Days before the event, the staff opened packages of Jordan almonds, ladyfingers, gumdrops, peppermints, and chocolate bonbons. Accompanied by a crystal bowl full of punch, each birthday would have an enormous birthday cake in the shape of the party's theme. Each year Mina felt she had to outdo the previous occasion. Mina was known to brandish one of her several settings of china and crystal stemware for her affairs.[4]

Mina used a significant amount of her $1,000 monthly allowance ($30,000 in today's money) to entertain. Holiday menus were always a multicourse, sumptuous feast of rich foods such as oysters, hard-shell crabs, and plum puddings. During Christmas, each place seating had a miniature Santa Claus figurine filled with candy. Mina loved buying lavish flower arrangements for her family, and her children received elaborate gifts from FAO Schwartz. Mina would also send Marion and Oscar a small, thoughtful keepsake for the holiday. Unfortunately, Mina and Edison chose not to include Tom Jr. and William in the Edison family festivities.[5]

Edison did not enjoy the formality of the meals and preferred to sit and read his newspapers or journals at the table. He had little interest in making small talk. Edison wanted only to speak of his interests or how he began his career and climbed to fame. When Mina hosted an adult cocktail or dinner party, Edison would walk in wearing his filthy laboratory clothes, feign a stomachache, then excuse himself to go upstairs to read. Mina, of course, was embarrassed by her husband's behavior. No matter how vital her events were, he refused to take part. Clergymen from the local Methodist Church visited on one such occasion. Not only did Edison not greet them with respect, but he also made a snide remark about religion. There was no controlling him. At times, Edison would join them at the dining room table; he would comment unfavorably about the food or the meaningless conversations the guests had among themselves. Ironically, Edison often had stomach problems brought on by his own strange eating habits. He usually became so embroiled in an idea or invention that he rarely ate. Over the years, this became a pattern that led him to consume odd choices such as milk and sardines or a plain chop. He had little interest in the delicacies Mina would have shipped in for the day.

There were few things Edison enjoyed outside of work; however, with the turn of the century, new inventions flooded the consumer market. The one that intrigued him the most was the automobile. At that time, cars were propelled by a steam engine where the fuel burned outside the machine. The autos were popular with early buyers such as Edison and like-minded individuals who understood the inner workings of trains and boats. Early steam cars required constant care and attention and took up to thirty minutes to start. Edison enjoyed having another adult toy he could tinker with when he had time.

In the early twentieth century, it was a widespread practice to use the automobile for pleasure rather than commuting or errands. There would be no rush to reach any particular destination. Edison enjoyed the Sunday car rides so much that he bought cars for the family. With no safety regulations in place on who could drive, Charles, now a young teenager, was tall enough to reach the pedals and became his father's defacto chauffeur. When automobiles were more widespread, Mina hired a full-time chauffeur, and Charles became an entitled passenger along with the rest of the family.[6]

Edison informed Charles, "I'll get a steam car. If you go down to the agency and spend three weeks there and learn how to take them apart and fix them." Charles, typical of his age, liked cars and thought they "were wonderful things, and you could go long distances, and you could go fast." Once Charles carried out what his father asked, he became the family mechanic, and warm-weather Sundays were transformed into times of great relaxation for Edison.[7]

On one such outing, the two of them drove down to the nearby town of Westfield. An insect bit Charles in the eye, and he could no longer drive for the rest of the trip. Edison, who was not a good driver, drove into the gutter, and the car got stuck in an embankment. The damaged vehicle was undrivable, so Edison instructed Charles to walk toward the town and call home. Mina had to send out a horse and carriage to retrieve them. During the three hours they waited, Charles attended to all the details despite still suffering from the insect bite while Edison "took a nap along the road near the car and went to sleep."[8]

After this incident, Edison never drove a car again. Because the vehicles were still developing and had no windshields, the family would drive through all the surrounding counties wearing dusters, veils, and goggles. The vehicle's mechanism could not handle the long drives. By lunchtime, it would break down; it would take the rest of the day to get back home. They would have five or six flat tires and had to carry five or six spare tubes. Charles remembered, "It was a backbreaking job. Every part of me was burned—my chest because you had to get under these things, and everything was hot, and oil dripped all over you. My arms were all burned, and everything else." Charles's ability to endure grueling work, along with his solid physique, earned him the nickname from his father of "Toughie."[9]

Once the family was more accustomed to automobiles, they took several road trips. Charles would drive one car, and Mina's younger brother John, who had moved to New Jersey and become a permanent fixture, drove the others. Edison often used these leisure trips for work-related activities. Once, he needed to look for cobalt, and he used it as an excuse for a vacation trip; in the back of the car, a box was placed where the seats were, with a camping outfit and a small field laboratory for testing minerals.

Many roads still were not paved, and the driving was treacherous. When things became difficult, Edison sensed hesitation and said to the family, "We came to go camping, get up into the mountains, and we're not sissies." Edison insisted that the family always travel the hard way. There were no bridges over the streams in some areas, and they often drove through the water.[10]

Edison's car was the first to be seen in some rural areas, especially in the Blue Ridge Mountains and then into the Alleghenies. The family would wire ahead that a car was coming. When they arrived in the town and stopped at the station, there would be quite a crowd waiting. The townspeople were interested in seeing Edison as much as seeing the automobile.

Because they were rarely at the laboratory, those trips were a front-row seat for the children to witness their father's approach to life. Charles recalled on these trips that if his father wanted to go somewhere, he would say, "I want to go here," and the family would go there. "He would not divert . . . he always kept the main objective in mind, and he was never side-tracked." Charles theorized that was "how he would accomplish so much." Unfortunately, the cars started to break down by the middle of the trip. So, Charles and John spent much of the time repairing them. Madeleine christened the two vehicles *Discord* and *Disaster*.[11]

Mina and the family knew the world had an acute sense of Edison's importance and contribution to society. Therefore, the Edison children needed thorough training to fulfill the mission of continuing his legacy. Mina wanted the next generation of Edisons to continue the great work of the original genius. Nothing could fall to chance; the last thing Mina wanted was for her beautiful children to turn into "ne'er-do-wells," which was how they referred to the first three children.[12]

The newspapers confirmed Mina's worldview of society. At that time, the editors had introduced a women's page that covered local culture and fashion. The newspaper's goal was to attract women as readers and subscribers by promising a new audience for consumer advertising. Mina relished the section that included society news, fashion, food, relationships, etiquette, health, homemaking, decorating, and family issues.

While home from his laboratory, Edison engaged with the children on his terms. According to Madeleine and Charles's written memoirs, he teased the children mercilessly. As a child, Madeleine had a nose that tilted to the sky, and Edison constantly teased her about it; Madeleine would run to her French governess for comfort, but the children were told they all had to please their father regardless of his taunting. Madeleine recalled times when he would dip a spoon in boiling-hot coffee and touch the back of her hand, or he would place a hot potato in Charles's hand simply because Edison was interested in teaching his children the properties of heat.[13]

Madeleine was about to finish her studies at the Oak Place School and take the college entrance exam to enter Bryn Marr. But Edison did not value formal education, especially for his daughter. He saw it as useless and a waste of money. Mina believed differently and would not acquiesce to her husband's thinking. Mina chose the school not just for its robust education but because she was sure Madeleine would be exposed to the "right people" and find a suitable husband.

Bryn Marr paired well with Mina's rearing of her daughter. It was founded as a Quaker institution in 1885 and was one of the Seven Sister colleges educating the elite. However, the administration at that time preferred to have faculty made up of only Anglo Saxons and believed in the intellectual supremacy of the white race.[14]

Charles had aged out of elementary school and spent two years at the Carteret School in Short Hills, New Jersey, run by Alfred C. Arnold from Cambridge, Massachusetts. The school's primary goal in education was "fitting boys for college." Although still not a believer in the benefits of classical education, Edison was too busy to rear children, even though this was his "second" chance. However, Mina might have convinced him because it advertised that it "prepared its boys for scientific school."[15]

After those uneventful years, Charles headed to the prestigious Hotchkiss school. Mina was pleased with how "nice all the boys looked … and was sure he would make many friends." But unfortunately, he could not attend St. Paul's regardless of its stature because Tom Jr. and William had permanently tarnished the Edison name.[16]

Another chief concern for Mina was her family in Akron. She saw herself as the de facto assistant matriarch. Now that she was a mother of three and managed a home herself, she felt confident giving advice to her aging mother and two unmarried sisters. In addition, her unending struggles with her husband had caused her to ripen. At this point, they had been married twenty years, and she had many battle scars. Mina believed that alone allowed her to dispense advice as freely as her sister Jennie had in the past.

Despite the Oak Place school's success, the once bright and shiny Miller family had lost quite a bit of its luster. After Mina's father and Theodore died, John, still in his early twenties, had returned to Akron without employment or a mentor. Mina's brother Robert was settling into life as the postmaster general in Puerto Rico. At first, he was honored by and appreciative of President McKinley. He needed the employment, yet the culture and environment were unfamiliar to him; he complained of a difficult adjustment. Louise, an eternal optimist, was just the sort of perpetually supportive wife and mother needed in this new setting. The other Miller brothers were faring worse. Edward Miller, the handsome and carefree bachelor, had been embroiled in a lawsuit with his brothers Ira and Lewis about common shares of the Canton & Massillon Street Railway Company. In time, the case was resolved. Mary Valinda kept Mina abreast of the embarrassment caused by her sons' names being dragged through the mud on the covers of the Ohio papers.[17]

Ira was mindful of the importance of keeping the dignity of his last name. Besides marrying a local girl and living nearby, he supported his mother and enrolled his daughters at Oak Place. When Lewis Miller was alive, Ira worked alongside him in his businesses. Dutifully, Ira continued to honor his memory and life's work with the Chautauqua Institution. When President Roosevelt visited the grounds in 1905, Ira made sure he was standing next to Rev. Vincent to greet him as part of the founding families.

Edison had always been fond of John, and when John had completed the engineering program at Cornell, he boldly asked Edison for employment. Edison hired John to work at the West Orange Laboratory and subsequently sent him to the Ortiz mine near Santa Fe, New

Mexico, to prospect and supervise the construction of an experimental ore-processing mill.

After Edison closed that operation, he sent John and others to manage magnetic surveys, diamond drilling operations, and nickel searches in the Sudbury District of Ontario, Canada. John also served as an agent of Edison's Mining Exploration Co. of New Jersey. In 1903, he was elected president of the newly organized New Jersey Patent Company, which controlled phonograph-related patents for Edison's interests. In 1907, he was put in charge of Edison's Canadian properties and administered the Darby Mine, a cobalt-bearing property in Ontario. He then returned home and served as division manager of the Chemical Works Division at the laboratory.

Edison remained busy with a variety of experimental projects. His fame was so widespread that he would receive hundreds of unsolicited letters from aspiring inventors, individuals seeking autographs, or those requesting charitable contributions. Edison often wrote perfunctory marginalia on letters to them and informed his secretary that he was too busy or was not feeling well enough to attend social functions.

Edison's fame had become so widespread that his name in the headlines alone sold newspapers. His image helped cement the myth that his inventions stemmed from the power of individual genius. Edison thought of himself as a paradigm that others should imitate. He believed in the ideals of American individualism, ingenuity, and self-reliance. Hundreds of people wanted his opinion, and Edison began to express his views to the public on a variety of subjects, including religion.[18]

While Edison focused on his inventive projects, Madeleine headed off to college. During her time there, she did not write home as often as Mina wished. Mina was not primed for a strong-willed daughter such as Madeleine. Mina would begin her letters to Madeleine with an admonishment: "Not a letter from you this whole week, and I feel out of sight out of mind. It is all right, for someday you will probably wish you could have some letters, and then you will know how it seems." Madeleine wrote, "I feel I must say something shocking today—so I guess you are the best person to say it to."[19]

Mina began missing her children, especially Charles. In his letters home, he commented on how fragile his mother was. Despite her packed schedule, with all her lady friends and Theodore still at home, he told her, "You must get over having blues as they aren't healthy." Hoping he could influence Mina's behavior, Charles informed his mother, "you worry me more than anyone I know." Charles was ambitious and had a firm social sense. He tried out for various extracurricular activities at Hotchkiss, including the newspaper, *The Record*, and the Literary Society, the football team, and other clubs.[20]

Mina always worried about their direction and outcome when planning her children's future. However, she knew she could not share her thoughts with her husband; he would dismiss her fears as foolish. In vogue at that time, especially with the upper classes, astrology served as a means of solace for Mina. Therefore, Mina paid to have her and her children's planetary indications evaluated. She supplied the dates and times of their births and received a report about their future for a given period.

Mina appreciated the multi-page reports she received about her and her children's lives and believed what she read. The topics covered were "General Outlook," "Reaping of Good Seed Sown," "The Things of Saturn," and topics of a similar tone: "The positions of your planets at this time are conducive for inner growth stability of character material prosperity and especially a keen desire for understanding." Furthermore, the concepts dovetailed perfectly with her Methodist teaching: "The soul is now reaping results of good work . . . must make all the opportunities to build wells for the future in material as well as spiritual ways."[21]

Mina struggled daily and yearned for guidance to understand her children and herself. She believed the influence of planets and other celestial objects would help her determine their future and actions. Mina clung to the idea that the alignment of stars and planets affected every individual's mood, personality, and environment depending on when the individual was born. The blanket statements she received in her reports were helpful because she needed to understand the world and look for connections. Her mind needed to see a link—even when there was none.

Likewise, Mina was an avid reader and bought books monthly. Edison often mocked her for reading the current fiction or romance, such as *Vanity Fair* and other books by Thackery. But she bought many books for Glenmont or brought them down to Fort Myers. Mina yearned to keep up her social standing, and she purchased an annual subscription to *The Social Directory of the Oranges* and *Table Talk*, which had essays on men and manners. She bought *The Blues* and *Everybody's Lonesome* for her unrelenting and incessant miserable periods.

However, Mina's essential goal was perfecting her children. For guidance for the family, she bought *Brain and Personality* and *Principles of Hereditary*, *Thinking Feeling Doing*, and *What Every Child Should Know*. Besides worrying about her own matters, Mina had to contend with Edison's ongoing intestinal problems. So, she referred to *Diseases of Stomach and Intestine* and *Age Growth and Death*. Mina's life had been a series of hurdles she'd had to overcome most of the time, and *Walks with Jesus* kept her prepared for those moments.[22]

Edison's robust health was a matter of the past. He did not trust doctors, and his weakened body could not keep up with his long hours. So, Mina purchased large quantities of opium, codeine, and hypodermic needles from the drugstore to help him.

The singular constant consolation for Mina was not a family member, but a recent addition to the Glenmont milieu. When the children started taking piano lessons, Mina hired Lucy Bogue. The family fell in love with her engaging and loving personality. Within months of her arrival, she earned the moniker "Bogey" or "Boguelette." She became a personal fixture in the household and often traveled with the Edisons to Florida. When the children stopped piano lessons, her role evolved into that of Mina's companion, and she remained part of the family her entire life. Mina shared her fondness for Lucy with her brother John, stating that she did not know anyone "who has done so much for inner self as she has." Other friends such as "Mrs. Franks made me dissatisfied with myself. . . . She always stirs up the rebellious or worse side in me some way." But, on the other hand, she felt that good friends like Lucy "awaken things in me, and it makes my circumstances all the more apparent."[23]

Mina needed Lucy that year more than ever. Edison awoke to a "terrible shock one early cold February morning." John Randolph, Edison's secretary of over thirty years, took a shotgun, walked down to his cellar, and shot himself in the heart. Before the suicide, he had walked outside and told his driver that he would only be a minute. His wife and younger daughter admitted to hearing him walk down to the basement and thought it rather unusual. A moment later, his wife heard the shot, ran down to the cellar, and saw his "body stretched out on the coal." Edison was "saddened," and Mina knew she had already enough to deal with before, "but now it is worse the books all in the hands of strangers and everything unsettled." When Edison arrived at the house, Mrs. Randolph was so beside herself that she climbed upstairs and tried to throw herself out the second-floor window. Edison grabbed her away from the window and tried to calm her down. The ordeal, coupled with Edison's poor health, sent the Edison family to recover in Fort Myers.[24]

Another duty Mina sought to impose on her children was to engage with their father regardless of whether or not he reciprocated. Thus, she urged Charles to "Write to papa occasionally; it will please him." Unfortunately, that request was not as easy to fulfill. Charles had an active social life, and his grades were not newsworthy. Although Charles was a middling student at MIT, in contrast to the letters Mina had written to Tom Jr. and William, she always provided Charles with substantial positive reinforcement, encouraging him to keep improving so as to reach the top of the class. "Try to do your best, Charles, because it puts a feather in your mother's cap. I wouldn't like to disappoint your father." As the years progressed, Charles proved to be only an average student. He often received grades in the C range, but Edison believed that Charles was not taking enough classes. Charles told Mina that he would rather take "fewer classes and do well."[25]

Charles and Madeleine were close as teens, and he often referred to her as "Lynn." There were times when they were in cahoots to leave school for a day and enjoy the comforts of home. Charles did the planning and claimed he needed "a dentist appointment and a new overcoat," hoping to get permission to return by "working his end" and telling the "the king" he had no wearable clothes for the upcoming week.[26]

Aware of their self-importance, Madeleine and Charles often used their ample allowance of $150 a month ($4,000 in today's money) to roam around in New York City. Often the siblings would visit the Plaza Hotel for lunch, ordering everything on the menu that began with the same letter. When traveling with suitcases in Pennsylvania Station, Charles and his friends would buy ten or more magazines. Then they would purposely drop them every few feet. The porter would stop, put down the suitcase, and pick up the magazines. Charles and his friends would continue to drop them until they reached their train. Eventually, the porter would carry the bags and all the magazines. After the gag was over, Charles would give the porter a very generous tip.

Taking advantage of funds from Edison's phonograph and other successful inventions, Mina decided to make significant additions to Glenmont in addition to purchasing a new car. One of her essential projects was building a new greenhouse and enlarging the garage. But much like all construction work, the project took longer to finish than anticipated. She got caught up in the outward appearance of the entire undertaking and turned despondent that things were not done on time. Charles would be privy to her disposition. As he matured, he was keenly aware of her mood fluctuations and repeatedly told her to "cheer up."[27]

Tom Jr., absent still of any successful endeavors and familial love, turned to alcohol to self-soothe. He lived in Orange County, New York, and suffered from weakness, nerve problems, and painful headaches. Tom Jr. hired nurse Beatrice Willard to attend to his ailments. After the pain would not subside, he entered the Cornwall Sanitarium in Cornwall-on-Hudson for the Treatment and Permanent Cure of the Liquor, Narcotic Drug Addiction, and Nervous Diseases. Beatrice, a widow, eventually became his love interest and accompanied Tom Jr. to the sanitarium. Edison's secretary knew Edison would eventually hear of his son's most recent incident. Ripe for a story, newspaper journalists were swarming his residence, hoping to sell a story by recapping his prior financial malfeasance. Despite his addictions, he was cognizant enough that his father would have to foot the bill, and he could not embarrass him again. Hoping to avoid involving Edison and his ire, the couple registered under the assumed names of Burton and Beatrice Willard. Edison wanted nothing of this episode to be in the press; he paid for the entire treatment and Beatrice's room and board.

After leaving the sanitarium, Tom Jr. wrote his father with effusive praise: "Words are certainly inadequate to express my appreciation for all of your kindness." Tom Jr. wanted to show his father that, at last, he was making better decisions: "My entire system has forever and eternally rid itself of the poison . . . that was eating life away." He further assured his father that with "his new name, my new life and new acquaintances—I am ready . . . to meet the demands of my business ability." His recent confession meant that Tom Jr. wanted his father to back him in his next venture.[28]

Although he was in love, Tom Jr. could not marry his nurse because his previous wife, a Catholic, had never secured a suitable divorce. However, he received some astonishing good luck when Marie Toohey unexpectedly died at the age of twenty-six. Some prominent newspapers picked up the story and rehashed the chaotic marriage details. Edison, fearful of a media frenzy and hoping to put that dreadful saga to rest, paid for her funeral. Mina and Edison felt concerned about Tom Jr.'s plight and appreciated that he was attempting to straighten out his life. However, although Edison paid for the hospital stay, Tom Jr. owed his nurse money for her care. Willing to do anything to rekindle his relationship with his father, Tom Jr. agreed to assign the $40 weekly allowance ($1,200 in today's money) he was receiving from his father to Mrs. Willard until his debt was paid off.

Subsequently, Tom Jr. married his nurse and permanently changed his name to Burton Willard. Edison bought him a mushroom farm in Burlington, New Jersey, that year. Tom Jr. felt grateful that he was starting life anew and began to rekindle his fragile relationship with Mina, writing vivid expressions of affection for his stepmother. Tom Jr. expressed how proud he was to have married a college graduate and that he hoped to entertain his mother at the farm. Mina and Edison hoped this educated and domesticated new wife would keep Tom Jr. "straight." Unfortunately, he punctuated his letters with his health problems, still hoping to gain sympathy.[29]

When William heard of the reconciliation between his brother and parents, he thought he might have a chance as well. Although married and more psychologically balanced, he had no success working in various automobile businesses. It seemed that he and his family, too, were destined to be farmers. The couple moved to Virginia and became administrators of the Punch Bowl Island Game & Poultry Farm, where they raised turkeys, pheasants, pigeons, ducks, and quail. No one could be sure that William was satisfied with his occupation as he was constantly dropping comments about other opportunities. In his few letters, he begged Mina for pictures of his siblings. He claimed he would not recognize them if he passed them on the street.

Tom Jr.'s wife, Beatrice, positively affected his persona, but she could not teach him business acumen. The farm was complex, and he would not work hard enough to achieve a profit and support the family. Moreover, Edison lost patience with his son, whom he believed was too lazy to succeed in any business. Edison's final trace of patience for his son was gone. He refused to talk to him directly and had one of his lawyers intervene. The lawyer reiterated Edison's wishes that he did not want his son near any of his businesses or factories and described his son as a "degenerate." Edison's lawyer tried to get the inventor to be more kindhearted to his flesh and blood but was unsuccessful. He later wrote, "It seems remarkable . . . that Edison should be so cold and vindictive."[30]

William and Blanche continued to disappoint Edison as well. The couple always lived larger than their means and used Edison's allowance on wasteful trips. Edison had the same lawyer mediate between himself and William's constant extravagant requests for cars and clothes. He gave up teaching him the value of money and admonished him, "if we turned $100,000 over to you, it would be spent in idle foolishness." The lawyer was sympathetic to Tom Jr., who asked for funds for a broken furnace and to help pay doctors for his appendicitis, but William was a different story. Edison believed William could not mature and continued to act "like a child."[31]

Tom Jr. and William were of little concern to Mina at that time. She was far too involved with her own children. Charles had grown into a handsome young man and joined a fraternity. Having visited his sister at Bryn Marr, he was known among the many young ladies in their social circle. Theodore was much more thoughtful, with a propensity to show his sensitive side. He was compassionate about the environment, nature, and animal life. He was often sickly and anxious as a child, and Mina worried about Theodore being so far from home. Rather than have him follow Charles's path, she sent Theodore to Montclair Military Academy nearby.

Mina stayed true to her Victorian convictions about nature's moral and physical benefits; she sent Theodore to sleepaway camp in the summer. She chose Camp Pasquaney, set up in 1895 near Squam Lake in New Hampshire. It was a small, private camp for older boys that catered to the sons of elite families. Although the physical character of these camps was highly rustic, at Pasquaney a professional cook served meals on china. It became an international phenomenon, supported by organizations with varied social, political, religious, and pedagogical agendas.

At the outset, Mina and Theodore wrote to each other often. At first, he was homesick, but he eventually acclimated to the "icy lake" and competitive sports. Ten-year-old Theodore's letters concerned his dog, Snowy, and his ducks, chicken, and rabbits. Mina was conscientious of writing him back, but she could not visit him at camp because Edison needed her at his side for some phonograph business obligations. Finally, after two full months away, Theodore returned on the first Wednesday in September, but Edison still needed Mina, so she could not be there to greet him. Instead, she sent Charles and Madeleine to pick him up at the station. Mina knew it was a mistake not to be there to welcome her son at the train or at the house. Embarrassed, she admitted to her delicate son that she could not "bear the idea" that she would not be at home when he arrived. To soothe her conscience, she wrote, "You understand, don't you." There is no record of whether or not Theodore fully understood that his famous father's constant and unending needs would always supersede his own. What is evident is that Theodore would make his own needs clear during his teenage years and beyond. Moreover, he would prove to be as stubborn as his father and refuse to budge.[32]

Dutiful as ever, Mina attended to her beloved Edison. It was clear that Edison was not as physically robust as he once was. At the age of fifty-seven, he reentered the hospital to remove a mastoid abscess behind the ear that was "very close to the brain." He had been suffering for a long time, and it had become pretty painful for him. Edison's hearing had been damaged much of his life, and this new operation took his hearing level to next to nothing. The procedure also left him with blurred vision. Mina was a thirty-seven-year-old woman who now had to navigate life with a physically hindered husband. The doctors told him to relax and recuperate after the operation, but he refused. Furthermore, Edison shut down any suggestions to go to Fort Myers for the winter. Three years later, he developed another mastoid abscess requiring surgical drainage.[33]

While Mina was only allowed to monitor her husband's ailments from afar, she could observe and supervise Madeleine's progress. Unfortunately, Madeleine could not pass all the required entrance exams and had to retake the geometry and Latin sections. Once entering Bryn Mawr, she never achieved high grades, preferring dramatics and English rather than the more robust classes like physics or torts.

In her first year, Madeleine told Mina that she'd learned to write notes of invitation, acceptance, and regret. The following week, Madeleine was able to recommend a servant who was applying for a position elsewhere. Mina was pleased that her daughter was learning practical skills.

Madeleine's love became the theatre. She acted in all the school plays and saved the playbills as souvenirs. However, when it came to her athletics classes, she preferred to miss them rather than attend. Charles wrote his sister often and realized her strength was not academics; he "wished her the best" for a "brilliant society career."[34]

Madeleine was attractive, outspoken, and popular. Her college scrapbook had countless invitations to social events and thank-you notes. Besides acting, she played tennis and was a glee club member. Her best friends were Julia Thompson and Peggy James, niece of Henry James. She and her gaggle of girls attended the Yale-Princeton football game at Columbia.

Along with these trips came countless invitations from what Mina would call a "suitable mate." Two boys in particular wanted Madeleine's hand in marriage: Paul Jones of Louisville and Joseph Batten of nearby Montclair.[35]

Madeleine's plucky, self-governing personality clashed with Mina's reserved, conservative nature. After returning to college after a break, Madeleine apologized to her mother: "Sorry I was nasty to you. . . . Made you nervous, my natural gift." Madeleine contemplated leaving college and shared, "I don't have time at college to spend on my character, and that's why I insist on coming home to stay next year." Mina wanted her daughter to finish her education. However, Madeleine needed to challenge her mother. She declared, "I also realize your position in wanting me to stay here as the preliminary stages of developing a sweet disposition will probably be painful in the extreme, but perhaps with resolute application and profound research into ways and means, I may cure my chronic distemper."[36]

Mina resisted Madeleine's attempt to drop out of college. It would be challenging to have Madeleine at home with constant bickering. Madeleine filled her time with parties and balls at the mansions of Newport, Charleston, and Richmond. Appreciating the fine art of entertaining without a budget, she invited all her friends for an over-the-top Halloween party. She and Charles converted the barn and parts of the home into a haunted house and had Theodore dress up like a girl to even out the couples for dancing. She decorated the house with ghosts, lights, pumpkins, and mazes. Madeleine and Charles even created a small electric-shocking mechanism when guests touched the banister. The party was spectacular; friends recalled it years later.

Madeleine's sparkling personality and classic good looks generated countless invitations to travel as well. Her last name heightened the trips for her friends. On one occasion, they dragged Madeleine to meet Mark Twain on a dance floor on a ship to Bermuda. He invited Madeleine to sit on his lap, which she declined. Instead, he told her he thought Edison was a great man, and in turn, Edison believed he was one, too. Madeleine, however, described Twain as a "dirty old man."[37]

Madeleine had countless suitors from all the finest schools. Although they wrote long, romantic letters, Madeleine claimed they all missed the mark for one reason or another. While she continued to be active in the theatrical world of the Oranges, she received an invitation to a dance by a local man named John Sloane. At twenty-two, Madeleine was never in need of a date. She turned him down because she had already accepted a prior invitation. He asked her to go for a "ride with him on another evening" and courted her with gusto. He often used any opportunity to send flowers.[38]

However, Mina disapproved of John Sloane; she thought he was far from a suitable husband. As the relationship became more serious, Mina told Madeleine, "He never seems to be particularly tender of you."

Madeleine told her mother not to worry: "You will like John Sloane once you get to know him better." Charles thought he was too young for her. Mina used every opportunity to tell Madeleine that John was unaffectionate and unappreciative. In truth, John routinely became consumed in his work. He was a budding engineer and often forgot the young couple's appointments to see each other. Even in her mid-thirties, Mina could not recognize the irony of the situation.[39]

Mina wrote Charles in confidence regarding a possible engagement: "If the inevitable must happen, I think the clouds will be very black. . . . Madeleine is absorbed in John, and it is a sad case, and Papa is wholly disappointed in Madeleine's judgment—What are we going to do? I, too, am far from satisfied, but he seems to be Madeleine's choice. . . . I do not see why?"[40]

Recent family obligations punctuated the dating and parties. Edison needed someone to accompany him to his corporate events, and lately, Mina was unavailable. Madeleine was required to fill her role. The Miller family was having another crisis, and obedient Mina had to restore the stability at Oak Place.

Mina's sister Mame was having trouble sleeping, and her nervous nature presented itself to the family in a heightened state. Her anxiety reached a level that disrupted her daily life. The tremendous financial concerns of running Oak Place and prolonged stress brought on by the deaths of Jennie, Theodore, and their father, Lewis, finally gave Mame a nervous breakdown. Ira's wife and Cora accompanied Mame to Battle Creek Michigan Sanitarium. There, she was placed under the care of three physicians.[41]

Robert, known as the most straightforward and perceptive of the five remaining Miller brothers, wrote frequent letters to his mother from his home in Puerto Rico: "I am thinking about you and Mame and hoping she will get better at once and soon will be all right. It is surely too bad she worries over things so much." Cora sent regular reports home and shared that on Mame's fourth night, she was able to sleep "with no sign of tears." The doctors had her wear a kimono and be on an all-fruit diet. The nurses wheeled her around in a wheelchair, making her self-conscious.[42]

In Mame's report home, she disclosed she was doing everything prescribed, including "the bitter." The various treatments included electricity baths believed to "draw the blood from the brain" and other therapies for the stomach and spine. The doctors indicated that Mame's "nerves are in run-down condition." By the second week, Mame was guilt-ridden and apologized that she had "created such a commotion." Her crying did not subside, however. She often cried during her talking sessions with the doctors, and the nurses needed to soothe her mind during the day constantly. Mame required to remain at the sanitarium for the near future.[43]

Two months later, a week before Christmas, she was discharged. Mary declared to her family, "cage door is open, and the dove has escaped." Having heard the news, Robert sent words of wisdom that evoked their father's sage advice: "One should avoid worry in ourselves . . . if we don't help to heal Mary from worry, she goes back to worse than ever . . . it is up to you, me, and the rest to accept what she does as the best that can be done . . . encouragement and praise accomplish more than a complaint."[44]

The family heeded Robert's warning and gave Mame a wide berth. After the holidays, she went to Glenmont to be with Mina. After disintegrating within hours of her arrival, she broke down in uncontrollable tears. Mary was still unable to understand why she felt so severely depressed. Dutiful, she kept her mother abreast of her moods: When "one is blue . . . I couldn't get my strength to do anything. So, I've just stayed in bed and had a second rest cure."[45]

The disruptive Miller family commotion caused Edison to give his assessment. He informed his unsound sister-in-law that he has so "darn much to attend to that he hasn't time to worry over any." Yet, even in her nervous state, she exalted Edison for his wise observation of life's troubles.[46]

Mina paid the bill at Battle Creek, Michigan, and for a series of trips for Mary throughout the year. Mame first went to Bermuda, then she joined the Edisons at Fort Myers and at Mohegan Lake, a more recent destination for Mina and the children. These trips had mixed results. Mary could not sustain psychological strength and often became panic-stricken when encountering something unfamiliar. She returned to the sanitarium the following spring.

The nature of Edison's interviews changed from dissecting his inventive work to more global ideas. Reporters were always gunning for Edison's provocative statements to sell more papers. Edison gave an interview to the *New York Times* in which he denied the immortality of the human soul. The confrontational nature of his comments and the revelation of his unorthodox religious beliefs caused public outcry and controversy. Reporters across the nation were eager to follow up with Edison. In a subsequent interview, Edison stated: "I believe in a supreme intelligence, but I have grave doubts as to whether you and I and other good folks of this year are going to be roused from our grave to go to some shining heaven up above. . . . Don't see it, can't understand it, and neither do these minsters of fashionable churches. They don't say what they think. Often they don't even think; it is all business with 'em." Then Edison raised a hand of scorn. "They tell me I am heading straight for hell; maybe I am. But I'll take my chances with the fashionable minister, and if there is a spot such as heaven, I bet I'll get there first."[47]

The negative publicity distressed Mina, and she shared her unhappiness with Charles. "He has gotten himself in trouble by publishing his ideas on immortality. . . . Have you seen the articles?" In Boston, the papers stated that Edison thought there was "no future life [or] god." The harmful exposure affected the entire family. Madeleine became moody and frenetic and shared her disdain for her father's comments with her new confidant, John Sloane: "Will I ever get away from that controversy?"[48]

Adding to the flames, John asked Madeleine to marry him behind Mina and Edison's back. Deeply in love with a man her parents described as an "undesirable Catholic," Madeleine replied, "yes." Despondent and cheerless, Mina wrote her mother that she is "between two fires, and it's hard not to be burnt."[49]

14

Concealing the Truth

ONCE AGAIN, THE EDISON NAME OPENED DOORS TO A PRESTIGIOUS EDU-cation—the Massachusetts Institute of Technology. Had the candidate been born with a different last name, his application would have been relegated to the "do not admit" pile. His grades were poor, and he never proved to excel in anything other than socializing and mingling. But Charles Edison did not need to be driven when it came to academics. He was more than familiar with where he would be working for the rest of his life. Knowing he would be forced to work alongside the world's most ambitious workaholic, he would make the most of his freedom before his life in golden handcuffs began. Luckily, MIT had an academic track for Charles Edison and his ilk—general science. Although Charles's university load was far from rigorous, he still complained about his work to his mother. Mina, sympathetic to Charles's needs, hated to see her lovely son suffer.[1]

It was easy for Charles to manipulate his mother, yet he still apologized that his grades were not what his parents had hoped he would achieve. Charles unabashedly confessed to his mother, "I can't get my mind on to anything I don't want to do." This was one of the few points that he and he and his father had in common. What was important to Charles was his fraternity, Delta Psi, close to the tony Beacon Hill, not far from where Mina had received her own Boston education. After his sophomore year, he described the other men as the "saddest bunch that ever came together." Was Mina surprised about his snobbish remarks?

She wanted him to be exposed to the finer things in life. But was he insulting his fellow man without hesitancy? That was not very Christian of him. Mina could not admit that Charles was not like her Methodist younger brother John. He admitted he could not wait till his twenty-first birthday, if for no other reason than to smoke cigarettes in front of his parents, something he did in excess.[2]

Along with life at the fraternity came alcohol and banter, subjects in which Charles knew how to excel. But with this lifestyle, one had to dress the part. Charles attempted to impress his mother with his budgetary savvy and explained how expensive his books cost. As a result, he claimed he needed a larger allowance. Mina hoped that the heir apparent to the Edison empire was inching his way closer to meeting a lady from the suitable class and continuing the legacy. She acquiesced to a monthly allowance of $125 ($3,700 in today's money). Even with Charles failing three of his classes, he seemed not concerned; he would only have to return to school a little earlier than usual the following term for some extra tutoring.

If Charles learned anything at university besides how to hold his liquor, it was how to hone his self-confidence. Mina's letters primarily consisted of positive encouragement and nothing harsh enough to cause Charles to work harder: "Don't get discouraged, Charlsie dear; you are coming out all right." The family knew Edison had laid the path for Charles's life. Regardless of the secured position at his father's laboratory, someone would cover for him if he did not understand the chemistry or engineering needed. That was the idea.[3]

Charles felt even more secure about his prospects after college after becoming aware that his father's company was getting a new name—Thomas Edison Inc. Whenever a company changes its name, it comes with both positive and negative consequences. According to Edison, there was a total share of both. The Phonograph Company made more money than the other inventions he'd patented in his career. Yet, at the same time, it was losing money from the smaller companies, such as the cement and storage battery enterprises. Eventually, they earned profits that washed their startup cost, but it took a considerable amount of time.

As with Edison's other inventions, there was competition in the market for the phonograph. And although Edison's phonograph cylinders were superior in sound quality, the Victor company had recently introduced the flat records, and consumers preferred those over the antiquated heavier cylinders. Edison was a purist and felt the public was foolish not to choose the better-sounding device. The people wanted to listen to music, and although they did have the discerning ear to tell the difference, they wanted to dance in their living rooms, patios, or nearby social halls more. The public preferred the flat record so much so that the Victor company earned $8.25 million to Edison's $2.67 million ($250 million to $80 million in today's money). When a colleague pointed out his profit difference, Edison agreed he needed to adapt to the newer technology or go bankrupt. He had invested a great deal of his capital already, and he would need outside investors to keep going in this competitive market. The advantage he had over Victor was his name, which in the public mind was synonymous with quality. It was for this reason that the company's name was changed from National Phonograph to Thomas Edison, Inc. It would now essentially be a wholly owned personal corporation. Instead of focusing on innovation, Edison focused on quality control. He was intent on perfecting the disc phonograph. His main interests were largely about improving the sound product and determining who was going to record the music.

The new company was capitalized with $12 million and 3,600 employees. Mina had hoped Edison would consider slowing down and working less after the significant change, but he refused. He still worked late and came home the following day, even with the corporation status. More confident with three children under her belt, Mina was now forceful enough to push Edison to shower and shave before returning to the laboratory the next day. One evening that year, Mina also managed to get Edison to spend more time at home. A week before the company changed names, Edison and Mina celebrated their twenty-fifth wedding anniversary. Madeleine happily decorated the house, and the family had a celebratory dinner. Instead of returning to the laboratory after dinner, Edison stayed home to play his favorite game, Parcheesi, with the family. But like everything else in his life, he only played if the family followed his rules.[4]

Mina was desperate for respite from her daughter's intense romance with a man whom she deemed an unworthy Catholic, and Edison, now sixty-four years old, had no intention of reducing his work schedule. Still, Mina needed a vacation, away from home concerns, and Fort Myers never proved to be a place of leisure for her husband but rather just a winter laboratory. Mina thought Europe would be the best place for the family's escape. Realizing he had not been on a real vacation for twelve years, Edison agreed to the trip. Theodore could meet Marion for the first time, and Mina prayed that Madeleine might change her mind about marrying John Sloane.

The fact that Edison had not seen his daughter Marion for seventeen years was not at the forefront of his mind. Although Mina trusted herself to plan the trip and the itinerary, Edison had stipulations. He did not want to go to any popular cities to avoid attracting publicity. The journey was set for England, Belgium, Holland, and Boulogne. There was no intention of going to Germany to see Marion and her home. If she wanted to see Edison and the family, she would need to travel to them.

Marion, so desperate to connect to the family personally, was thrilled when she heard the news of the family trip. Marion assumed that Edison would want to visit her at her home, and she even enrolled her husband, Oscar, in English lessons so he could communicate better with the family. But Marion soon realized that, once again, her father's love was doled out to her only in the tiniest increments, and she had to force herself to cope with his ways. Once she found out about the trip's itinerary, she made it her business to meet her father where he preferred.[5]

An additional requirement of the trip was that the family would travel separately. According to Madeleine's oral history interview, her father was worried that if the family had traveled together and had some terrible accident, they would all die together. Divided travel would allow for some survivors if the worst did occur. The news of the *Titanic* sinking was not until later years; however, smaller ships had sunk, which may have given Edison pause. Charles explained that independent travel was more of a function of his school schedule. Madeleine and Theodore, however, did not travel until June 24th. Charles had finished school by then. Still, the decision was never up for discussion. Both explanations might have been valid reasons; however, the underlying reason might have been that Edison never wanted to leave his beloved lab and was not looking forward to being away from work for such a lengthy time. Like everything else, the trip had to be made on Edison's terms. Madeleine stated, "We tried to please father in all ways. He was next to G-d."[6]

Edison and Charles left in August on the *Mauretania*, a ship designed to suit Edwardian tastes. Women still wore corsets and long skirts. Men still wore suits. A complete wardrobe included hats and gloves and, for women, often an umbrella. Edwardian fashion was opulent and formal with expensive fabrics and trimmings. Mina favored a distinguished, mature look and wanted the same for her family. Edwardian style was known for its dramatically large hats, such as wide-brimmed, and for driving, some women tied long, sheer veils over silk motoring hats.

These enormous hats required hairstyles to support them, and Mina ensured that her hair was kept long to accommodate the most popular hairstyle. It was a full pompadour, with hair swept loosely up into coils or buns. It also was stylish to tuck fresh flowers or decorative combs or hatpins into styled hair. In some of the photographs of Mina, one can see she has affixed these accoutrements to her hair.

The ship's interior was designed with twenty-eight different types of wood, along with marble, tapestries, and other furnishings, such as the stunning octagon table in the smoking room. Wood paneling graced the walls for the first-class public spaces. Topped by a large dome skylight, the multilevel, first-class dining saloon made of straw oak was decorated in Francis I style, including columns, a wide variety of decorative plaques, and sculptural decorations. In addition, there was a series of elevators, then a rare new feature for liners; and grilles composed of the relatively new lightweight aluminum were installed next to the *Mauretania*'s grand walnut staircase. Finally, the Verandah Café on the boat deck was a new feature, where waiters served passengers in a weather-protected environment.

This opulent ship was the precise method of travel that Mina wanted for her children. The passengers were people with means. They worked hard, and their discretionary income allowed them to enjoy such luxuries. Mina hoped the lavish and opulent décor would make a lasting impression.

Edison's European business associates arranged to have a Daimler automobile with a chauffeur to take Mina, Madeleine, and Theodore touring in Europe before the others arrived. In those few weeks before Edison's arrival, the trip was not as effortless as Mina had hoped. Madeleine was twenty-three, and Theodore was just thirteen years old. Their interests varied, making specific sites tedious for some and exciting for others.[7]

Mina's primary goal of distracting Madeleine from John Sloane, her love interest, backfired. Madeleine and John wrote to each other often. Their letters covered religion, John's stress from work, their intimate feelings for each other, and general news of the trip. If anything, the distance bonded them closer together. Madeleine visited John's aunt, a nun, in Italy. The meeting brought up all sorts of discussions about theology and sin, which any lovestruck sensitive young woman would take personally. John's mother and Mina, who were both against the mixed marriage, thought the meeting with a nun would discourage them. Instead, it opened Pandora's box and made the religious question a preoccupation for the entire trip. Madeleine and John compared the virtues and difficulties of the Catholic and Protestant churches and their members.

Madeleine described herself as a "grief bringer to her mother, a distracting parasite to her lover, an underachiever to herself." Her anxiety and tension thrust their way toward Mina, who rarely knew any other way to live. Madeleine ended up with endless headaches, and Mina suffered a general malaise. Mina suggested that Madeleine remain in Europe after Christmas instead of returning home with the family in the late fall. The reason for the further separation, as told by Madeleine, was that it would "gratify Mother ... and that I would not be frittering away the time dancing, etc., as she thinks I have been doing for the last two years. Also, it would give her rest from me and form the immediate pressure of the worry that I cause her."[8]

By the time Mina, Madeleine, and Theodore met up with Edison and Charles, it was August. The plan was to meet in Boulogne; however, Mina and the children were still traveling and had to get to Paris first before Edison arrived. Edison refused to go back the City of Lights. He was fearful that they would give him "dinners and things." Madeleine expressed to John, "Lots of good it does to travel with a celebrated Pa if one can't hobnob with the elite. I think a little excitement of that nature would rather be fine—but Pa thinks differently."[9]

Madeleine was correct; all the pomp and circumstance around Edison would have distracted Mina and lifted her spirits. Instead, she brooded all day about the doomed future her daughter was to have with a Catholic man who had few, if any, successful business prospects. All the effort she'd put into raising a debutante from superior stock seemed to be for naught.

Getting to Paris became a nightmare for Mina. They had car trouble in Brussels and ran a day late. While driving, three government officials turned them back to an alternate route, and they missed the crossing into France. They finally decided to leave the car and cross into the country on foot. Few hotels were up to Mina's standards, but they agreed to stay at a place reminiscent of the dingy days of Florida. They slept on top of the beds because the sheets were too filthy to use. They barely had a proper dinner and were frightened to hear that "a man was shot on the German-Swiss border for picking strawberries on the wrong side."[10]

They arrived in Paris during a thunderstorm. Madeleine had a horrible cold, and Mina was beside herself. She and Madeleine knew they still had to sightsee quite a bit, because when Edison would arrive, he would refuse to visit the places they wanted to see, and they would have to capitulate to his requests. Madeleine wrote John about her mother's state regarding Edison's arrival: "She's been looking forward to it so violently, and her one ambition in life is to give him a good time."[11]

Mina was frantic after she misplaced the claim checks for the Edison steamer trunks containing all the coats. She was beside herself with worry. But that minor disaster became an afterthought when Mina received word from home that her brother Robert, recently returned home from Puerto Rico, had unexpectedly become sick and died. The news put Mina in a state of shock. Her sister Grace hoped that Edison's arrival would help her "bear the news."[12]

Mina couldn't return for the funeral. Instead, she grieved alone on the other side of the world. Her dear friend and confidant Louise was now a widow. Her mother had to bury her fourth child. It was unfathomable.

In a "daze," Mina wrote home to her mother, admitting how guilty she felt being in Europe while the family was grieving at Oak Place without her. Hoping to comfort her mother, Mina told her that Robert was the brother who always gave her "so many words of encouragement and the right way to live . . . one more bright star was taken from the circle." She confessed to her mother that she genuinely wanted to return to Akron to be with her family, but she was conflicted. Edison was arriving that day, and he desperately needed the rest and change. She asked her mother to keep her abreast of the family news because it made "her anxious" when she was "left in the dark."[13]

Louise could not come to terms with his death and said, "It seems crueler every day." Not only was Robert a loving father and husband, but the family had relied on him to manage financial matters for Mary Valinda and Grace at Oak Place.[14]

By mid-August, the Edison family was reunited sans Marion. William and Tom Jr. were not invited on the trip. Edison and Charles had docked in Liverpool upon arrival. Many of the passengers on the ship were quite seasick, but that never affected Edison, who rarely ate regular meals. His eating habits always upset the stewards and chefs, who would go to great lengths to make their best dishes for him.

Aboard the ship, Edison conversed with Peter Cooper Hewitt and Henry James, who were also traveling abroad. Upon arrival, a member of Parliament greeted Charles and Edison. They wanted to abolish the veto power of the House of Lords that very evening, and Edison and Charles were invited to watch the historic event. Charles found the evening fascinating. The debates between the House of Commons and Lords stayed with him his entire life, unconsciously affecting his political trajectory later in life.

The next day, Edison and Charles met Mina and the others in Boulogne. The first thing Edison said to Madeleine was that she appeared pale and malnourished. Edison also admitted exhaustion from the travel. He acknowledged he had caught a bronchial cold on the ship. The family went south, keeping with Edison's needs and visiting small towns along the coast of Normandy. Edison appreciated the absence of the crowd and was somewhat content, even away from his beloved laboratory.

As the trip continued, the family encountered numerous mishaps. The heat was reaching record highs and wreaking havoc on their cars. The family was constantly fixing tires. The weather led to countless missed meals and getting stuck in unpopulated towns without necessary provisions. Edison, who never believed in maps, finally decided to go to Paris and endure the crowds and adoring fans.

Upon meeting up with Marion and Oscar, the family was relatively cordial and on their best behavior. Marion, however, unloaded years of exacerbation toward her father's apathy toward her. She complained that she was "miserable from nights of sleeplessness" staying in hotel after hotel to be able to come and meet them. In addition, the expense was burdensome on Oscar's meager salary. Oscar responded differently. It was his first time meeting the famous Papa, and he was enthralled. Oscar appeared jolly and quite personable, and the entire family noticed how much he adored Marion. She had blossomed. Marion was beautiful and vivacious, and Oscar commented that all the lieutenants in his unit loved her. Marion requested again that her father come to her home and see how she lived, but Edison refused to deviate from the set plan. Feeling somewhat guilty, the Edisons eventually paid for most of the travel arrangements for Marion and Oscar once they were together. After Marion had the opportunity to traipse through Europe and travel like an Edison once again, she was more upbeat and appreciative.[15]

Unfortunately, the Paris family reunion lacked any privacy. One eager reporter followed the Edisons throughout Europe. Overly anxious to please his publisher, the reporter attempted to cover the Edisons' trip despite becoming deathly ill. Mina, who never traveled far without her first aid kit, nursed him back to health. Charles sympathized with his blight and helped him write the story to submit by his deadline. Then, owing his life and job to the Edisons, the reporter helped drive them throughout Europe for the rest of their trip.

Spectators mobbed them as the family continued to Vienna, Budapest, and Prague. Mounted policemen were often needed to keep the throngs of people at bay. Mayors and government officials of various cities showed them the highlights. The family was invited to lavish dinners, which Edison hated, but Mina insisted they could not refuse.

Madeleine and Charles hoped to warm up and joke around with Oscar, but they could not because of the language barrier. Madeleine thought that Marion was a "weird and strange lady." The two sisters lived in two different worlds, yet they had the same father. Marion had been robbed of the life that Madeleine inhabited. It would not be until years later that the two half-sisters would be able to relate to one another. In a rare moment of closeness, Mina shared with Marion that one of the purposes of the trip was for Madeleine to realize there were superior men in the world to choose for her husband besides John Sloane. Marion thought a young and handsome German lieutenant would be attracted to Madeleine. The attention could have opened her eyes to other possibilities. Unfortunately, Edison refused a meeting because, again, it deviated from his set travel plans.

Mina wanted to attend Sunday church services, but Edison insisted on going to the horse races despite her opposition. A cameraman spotted them in the stands and took several photos. Edison was overjoyed that Mina's attendance was public and stated, "When the Methodists find out she was at the races on Sunday, she will be excommunicated." Mina responded that she "would resign from her Sunday school class before they have a chance to fire me."[16]

But the worst part of the vacation was yet to come—and the press was right there to publicize to the world the dreadful blunders of the Edison family. In Nuremberg, Edison's car ran over a little boy running across the street. Madeleine claimed the driver probably ran over "his neck." The boy had a club foot and could not dash out of the way fast enough. After seeing the dreadful incident, Mina and Edison exited the car to save him, but it was too late. The boy was already dead. Angry crowds immediately surrounded the car, yelling at the family. Oscar and Marion, who were in a car behind them, took some time to arrive at the scene. They were able to pacify the situation somewhat because of their fluency in German. The following day's inquest cleared the Edisons of negligence. Edison gave 400 marks to the boy's impoverished mother. Ashamed by what had transpired, the Edisons cabled home to warn their family of the news.[17]

A depressing tone cast a shadow on the last ten days of the trip. Mina wanted Madeleine to remain in Europe and tour Italy, but Madeleine wished to return home to see John. Mina's uneasy emotional state was too much to match the will of her lovestruck daughter. Madeleine returned with the family. Marion also took advantage of the current situation. Her proficiency in German had saved the family from a legal entanglement that would have been disastrous to the Edison name. Emboldened as she could be around her father, she hinted at her need for a car, which she and Oscar could never afford on his salary. Edison, familiar with throwing money at problems and children so they would go away, told Marion to pick out a Mercedes, and he would pay for it.

Upon returning home, Edison relished the hovering newspapermen begging for a quote from the icon about his views regarding Europe. Always a Yankee, he told the world that America's work ethic far exceeded those he had seen in Europe. Yet again, Mina had to do some corrective surgery regarding her husband's remarks. After insulting many of his colleagues and bankers overseas. Edison then sent updated comments to *Scientific American* magazine. In addition, Marion penned an article entitled "Edison's Daughter on Her Father"; it was written in German for the local papers and translated for the *New York World*. In the article, she effusively stated that her father "had much too much tact and kindness in his heart . . . could never show such unkindness toward a land that has honored him so greatly."[18]

Fortunately, Mina would find a reprieve with the Millers. After recuperating from her breakdown, Mame had met William Nichols, a supportive divorcee from New York City. William, who was embroiled in a custody battle over his daughter, understood life's vicissitudes and was sympathetic and encouraging to Mame during her depressive periods. Although she was now too old to have children at the age of forty-four, the Millers were overjoyed that Mame had found true love.

Even without the kind of riches the Miller family had long enjoyed, the wedding was lavish by anyone's standards. Mary Valinda paid to have Oak Place decorated with roses, peonies, and orchids. Upon entering the home, "Ave Maria," played by violinists and harpists, along with other fine music, greeted the guests. Mina's brother Lewis knew of the financial constraints that beset their mother and helped pay for a considerable amount of the affair.[19]

In the meantime, Mina was convinced that her mother's days were numbered. She informed her family she would spend as much time as needed in Akron at her mother's bedside. After missing her brother Robert's funeral, Mina could exemplify the supportive daughter she envisioned herself as being. This time in Akron was the longest of any time she spent there, exceeding any time she'd been away from her husband in their entire marriage of twenty-six years.

Mame's wedding was the last cheerful moment for Mary Valinda. It was as though she mustered her previous strength to be lively for her namesake's big day. After burying a husband and four children, her heart no longer had the will or the strength to go any further, and she would not live to see her last four unmarried children find spouses. In one of her last letters to her newly married daughter, she wrote words filled with a lifetime of experience and wisdom: "I find if we want things bright and pleasant, we have to be that ourselves." Mary Valinda died at the age of eighty-two, after bearing eleven children.[20]

The family returned to Glenmont downcast. Madeleine was pushing Mina to announce her engagement to John. Madeleine was determined to win this test of will between her and her mother. She told John that her mother had "got so into the habit of disapproving of anything that you and I are connected with, and I simply dread telling her the simplest thing." John was Madeleine's ticket out of Glenmont to start a new happy, upbeat life—not a life surrounded by a nervous and depressed mother who walked around with a literal and metaphorical first aid box, hoping to repair everything and everybody broken or not. Madeleine did not want her personality to be mended. She dreaded her mother's "disapproval spilled all over me all the time."[21]

While at home, she wanted to do part-time work to fill her days. Edison and Mina both thought a woman should not have to work, especially if she were an "Edison." Yet, Madeleine was twenty-three years old, and she did not want to lie around the house eating chocolates. Madeleine wanted to continue her promising acting career. Local directors saw her acute ability to transform herself into various characters. But when the parts became a little too racy, such as involving a possible kissing scene, Edison and Mina ended her acting days. Instead, Mina suggested she volunteer for local organizations such as the library. Madeleine was internally conflicted. Mina had brainwashed her regarding the importance of whom she represented. Her last name was not just a name; it was an emblem of the nation. She had to be an ambassador to the public. Working and acting did not fit into the life Mina had planned for her.[22]

Her struggle was real. It pained Madeleine, and she felt trapped. She knew her life was different from others, but when she had an opportunity to see how others viewed her family, she learned a different truth, which was difficult to swallow. John's mother commented that Mina was "not normal." Madeleine was carrying so much guilt about wanting a different life, but deliberately going against her parents' wishes to follow her heart was often too much to bear.[23]

Taking a defensive attitude, Madeleine told John, "Dearest, it's alright for me to make remarks about mother's strange variation of thought, but I don't want you to, or I won't love you anymore." John had to stand firm regarding Madeleine's mood swings and comments. He knew if he wanted to marry Madeleine, he would have to manage the currents. Unfortunately, he neglected to call Madeleine after Mary Valinda died. Madeleine was close to her grandmother; she had lived at Oak Place during her high school years. For John to be so insensitive or forget that fact was unacceptable. The family witnessed that faux pas and used it to help build their case against him.[24]

John was under pressure to start his own business and make it successful. Edison had no intention of letting John land a spot at his company. That was solely for Charles and eventually Theodore. John was not respected enough to get a piece of the Edison pie. While traveling in Europe, Madeleine was sure to write home that her father took to Marion's husband because he had no intention of sponging her father. That information permeated John's psyche. He would have to work extra hard to make a name for himself, but in that way he would gain respect from his future father-in-law. Attaining his success was an impossible task, however, and while he attempted to achieve it, he often forgot to check in with Madeleine. When he was too busy with work, she became incensed. Madeleine did not realize that she was on the same life path as her mother had been.

Charles finished his second year at MIT with poor grades. The following year, the school required him to choose a specialized field in engineering: mechanical or civil. Charles did not have the predisposition to succeed in either of those fields. Rather than talk to his father about the decision, he consulted an executive he knew at the local Boston Edison Company. Familiar with Edison's opinion of formal education, he suggested that Charles not waste a year in the classroom and instead work directly at their offices. Charles was relieved, and Edison "was delighted." Mina, however, was not happy. Her dream of her son becoming a college graduate had just slipped out of her hands. Mina faced this "heartache" as she had so many others and yielded to her husband. She had no say in the matter.[25]

Charles enjoyed working at Boston Edison the following year. He learned to keep track of sales, accounting, and other service jobs that were more of an organizational and clerical nature. The executives realized that Charles was more suited to an administrative position than a technical one. In addition, Charles had natural social skills; he would have a future keeping customers and other employees content.

After the year, Charles felt entitled to take road trips across the country with his buddies. He knew this would be the last time he would have the lifestyle and freedom to travel. Working at the West Orange laboratory would occupy the rest of his life. Charles knew that the way to get permission from his father to act was not to ask for money. Edison always approved of his children roughing it—realizing that they valued the same ideas as him.

Edison agreed to the trip, but he thought "Charles would be writing home begging for money within a couple of weeks." Charles had saved up $400 and believed that would be enough to sustain him for months. He and his friends traveled west toward "San Fransisco by way of the Grand Canyon and Los Angeles." The boys loved "the fifty-cent a day budget" and treating themselves to "nickel beers." Wherever Charles traveled, the public quickly recognized him as Edison's son. Newspaper journalists approached him and thought he was there to work on his father's behalf. Word got around that they were there, and Edison's business associates picked up various lunches and dinners along the trip. Charles returned home with newfound respect from his father because he had never wired home for money.[26]

Mina insisted that Madeleine join her and Theodore on a short vacation at Mohegan Lake in Maine. The area had recently become a favorite relatively nearby vacation respite for the Edison family. As of late, Mina was becoming increasingly aware of Charles's lively social life, and she worried about which of his many girlfriends would steal her son's heart. Whenever Mina felt a pang of anxiety, she planned a family getaway. She was under the false impression that changing locations would make her worries disappear. Edison would eventually join them on his own timetable; however, he arrived sick after a sleepless night and a three-day car journey. He again complained to Mina to help with his chronic and intense abdominal pain. He was eventually diagnosed with "gall stones or abscess on his gall bladder." Mina began to prepare for an operation, but Edison treated his pain with ice and returned to his regular work schedule.[27]

Edison did admit that he was distressed that the family was paying attention to John Sloane. Edison displayed jealousy when attention was taken from him by family members. John Sloane did consume much of the family discussions. Mina was anxious about the inevitable wedding and disclosed to Grace that the engagement made her sick. She knew that the time at Mohegan Lake would be their last family vacation. Now Mina felt all her hard work spent rearing Madeleine was for nothing; the marriage to John Sloane would be doomed.

Madeleine and John convinced their family to make the engagement public before the year's end. Then, in November, the couple decided to announce it then, to make the holiday season less tumultuous. Madeleine now gave John an almost-impossible task: "Mother is dear and sweet, and you two must love each other sooner or later, or I will never be happy. . . . I know it's hard for both of you, though." Madeleine could not evade her guilty conscience and blamed herself for their acrimonious relationship.[28]

Theodore was still in Montclair Academy. Although he received better grades than his siblings, the teachers still complained of the slow pace of his work.

Mina's last moment of pride and happiness about her daughter appeared in the papers a month before Madeleine's engagement went public. Madeleine was always mixing in the right social circles, and she had befriended Genieve Clark, the daughter of Camp Clark, the speaker of the house in the House of Representatives. The two girls were close and hosted a party together in New Jersey. The speaker and his wife were guests of the Edisons at Glenmont. After their lavish party, the papers picked up that the socialites were searching for a wedding present for another prominent young lady of society—Miss Jessie Woodrow Wilson, the daughter of the president. She would marry Francis Sayre, whose father had built the Leigh Railroad that summer.[29]

Mina was overjoyed that her daughter was cited in the same breath as these renowned young ladies. Yet, realizing that Madeleine's life would diverge, she confessed to her sister, "I had imagined Madeleine gracing some fine intellectual house, but to think of her as an ordinary man's wife, a mere clerk mind makes me sick."[30]

"Thomas Edison's Daughter to Marry" was the headline Mina supplied the press. The announcement included John's work in aviation and that he was a doctor's son. Born in South Orange, he had attended the Dearborn-Morgan School at Orange just as the Edison children had. Later, he entered the Carteret Academy of Orange, graduating in 1904. After graduating from Columbia University, his interest in aviation led him to establish one of the first airplane plants in the country in Long Island City in 1912. He also did considerable work in the design and construction of gas engines. In the same year as their engagement, John established Sloane Aeroplane Co., which manufactured airplanes in Plainfield, New Jersey.

John's father was a scientist, inventor, author, editor, educator, and linguist, perhaps best known as the author of *The Standard Electrical Dictionary* and the editor of *Scientific American*. He was also an editor of the first science-fiction magazine, *Amazing Stories*. He had a PhD in electrical engineering from Columbia University and an LLD from the College of St. Francis Xavier. In addition, he was a natural science and higher mathematics professor. The Edisons, however, could not see beyond their insular realm to realize that John came from an impressive family.[31]

Once Edison went public with the news, Mina had to accept her daughter's future. However, it was also time to shift the conversation about Edison from Madeleine's impending wedding back to Edison, the famous inventor.

Mina enjoyed the celebrated and eminent visitors' constant desire to meet her brilliant husband. Some wanted to become lifelong friends, but Edison did not cultivate friendships. His laboratory was his best friend, yet he was willing to engage with those who took a keen interest in his mind and treated him with reverence. One dogged engineer with the Edison Illuminating Company of Detroit had an opportunity to meet Edison and share his ideas and experiments, specifically with regard to gasoline engines, which proved successful, eventually becoming a self-propelled vehicle. Edison saw his drive and encouraged the engineer to build a second vehicle. The vehicle was a success and ultimately revolutionized transportation. The engineer, Henry Ford, became quite wealthy and famous, practically rivaling Edison. That same winter, the engineer-turned-industry-leader and his wife joined the Edisons in Fort Myers. The men became friends, forcing the wives to get along. The families' friendship would last years, often pushing Mina out of the picture. She always put on a smiling face for the public, though, secretly harboring her resentment.

Along with the Fords came a genuine friend, John Burroughs, the naturalist. He had met Mina before Edison. She knew what a unique and thoughtful individual he was, and she thought her husband would enjoy his opinions and his company. Ford had also admired the works of Burroughs and, like Edison, sought out his company. Ford loved birds and nature, and the men bonded over their shared interests.

Edison invited the Burroughs to visit Fort Myers during the winter before Madeleine's wedding. While they were there, they toured the Everglades. Edison enjoyed the camaraderie and extended the invitation to visit California for the Panama-Pacific Exposition the following year. He also included the family of the industrialist Harvey Firestone. The fairs celebrated new and cutting-edge technology of the time. Edison, the inventor of the light bulb, phonograph, and motion picture camera, was praised by all.

After the exposition, Ford and Edison traveled with their families to Ford's private rail car after fans celebrated Edison's achievements, then headed north to Santa Rosa in a vehicle to visit another celebrated innovator, the horticulturist Luther Burbank, who also had been celebrated at the exposition. After touring Burbank's experimental garden, Edison, Ford, and Firestone headed south on a tour of California on their way to the state's sister fair, San Diego's Panama-California Exposition.

The men enjoyed each other's companionship and decided to travel each subsequent year. The group mainly consisted of Ford, Firestone, and Burroughs. The men staged the ruggedness of the camping trips. Along with the men was an entourage that included fifty of Ford's vehicles, supplies, staff, and enough illumination to light the summer nights. The press was also there to share it with the world. Burroughs claimed, "It often seemed to me that we were a luxuriously equipped expedition going forth to seek discomfort." The women were excluded from most of the trips they took over the next ten years. Mina complained to her sister about Edison, "I never can see why they think we never want to do some of the interesting things too." When Edison chose to spend time with his guests rather than his wife, Mina was hurt. Instead of speaking up, she vented to Grace, "I am getting calmer, and I hope more sensible, but it comes hard. . . . I am longing to be first in my husband's thoughts. It's a hard lesson to learn."[32]

Mina was frazzled with the guests that winter in Fort Myers. Ford was the wealthiest man, and the town welcomed the "distinguished guest" with a brass band and forty-five Ford cars, then paraded through the streets. Madeleine unhappily recalled the event. The quiet time she associated with Fort Myers had been stolen from her by her father's new friends, whom she deemed interlopers. Once the news spread about the Edisons' guests, others felt inclined to visit, including Dr. John Harvey Kellogg from the Battle Creek Sanitarium, where Mina's sister punctuated her depressive cycles. The doctor was also famous and espoused his various habits to live a healthy lifestyle. He brought Mina pounds of medicated chocolates that Madeleine thought "we shall never get rid of."[33]

While spending much of her trip with outsiders, Mina kept up a happy façade for the guests. In the evenings, she unloaded her true feelings to her sister, stating she was "down in the depths." She was still dreading the fights she would have with John. She wanted to be a "delightful creature" but did not think she could correct her behavior.[34]

After Mina returned to Glenmont, the planning was in full force. Mina could not free herself from the religious conflict. It ate at her core. The Sloanes insisted on a Catholic ceremony, but Mina pushed for a Protestant service. She told Madeleine to have a "quiet Catholic service just to make things legal" with John's family and that the fundamental part of the wedding should be Protestant. Again, Mina vented to her sister that she would be "absolutely sick if she had to countenance the Catholic idea in our house."[35]

The planning of a large wedding staggered Mina. She still dreaded all the details and "hoped it would be perfect." Madeleine chose the bridesmaids and their dresses. Mina hired the finest decorators and caterers of New York for the affair.[36]

John's mother entertained Madeleine and her wedding party at a formal luncheon the day before the wedding. Mina's friend Mrs. Richard Colgate hosted the rehearsal dinner, followed by a sumptuous dinner dance at the Eagle Rock Pavilion, also called "The Casino." It was built on the crest of Eagle Rock Reservation, with half the structure residing in Montclair and the other half in West Orange. "Casino" referred to an Italian-style county dwelling or gathering place. Mina had the entire building adorned with decorative Japanese lanterns and spring flowers. Guests were able to see the lights of New York City from the hall.[37]

Private cars were sent from Llewellyn Park to the railroad to pick up the out-of-town guests. Mina also hired seven police officers to guard Glenmont during the ceremony and reception. When it came to the religious aspect, Mina got her way. Monsignor Henry Brann of St. Agnes Catholic Church of New York performed the ceremony, attended only by relatives and a few friends. Madeleine and John were married in front of a large mirror in the alcove. The mirror was covered with a tapestry with oversized candlesticks on each side to provide a subdued light. Mina wanted to mimic a chapel without actually being in one.

The wedding was lavish, with eight bridesmaids in lavender taffeta dresses with overskirts of light blue tulle and large fashionable straw hats. The corsages were made of orchids and freesia. The procession started upstairs with each bridesmaid carrying a fountain of flowers in similar colors. Edison and Madeleine then followed. Madeleine had a "terrible time keeping Edison in step with the music during the rehearsals." However, he surprised Madeleine at the wedding and escorted his daughter perfectly.[38]

Madeleine wore a beautiful lace and white velvet dress adorned with laces from Mina's own wedding gown. She carried a bouquet of orchids, lilies of the valley, and freesia. The florist filled the home's front hall with American Beauty roses and garlands and enclosed the porches with floral canopies of ferns and orchids. American Beauty roses and garlands filled the front entrance. Six hundred fifty guests danced on a custom-made green platform and celebrated the famous inventor's daughter. By newspaper reports, the affair went off smoothly. However, in the wedding photos of the day, it is easy to discern the downhearted expressions of both Mina and Edison.

With the wedding over, Mina "dreaded" showing Edison the bills from the wedding expenses. The newlyweds moved to a small apartment in downtown Manhattan on West 8th Street in the Village. Madeleine did not have a maid and was happy doing the housework herself in her apron. Mina was interested in how she could manage. Madeleine's one-bedroom apartment was a far cry from the mansion Mina had moved into as a young bride. Unsatisfied with the standard of cleanliness, or rather Madeleine's housekeeping abilities, Mina sent her maid to the apartment to do the necessary "scrubbing."[39]

Eleven days after Madeleine's opulent wedding, the world would change forever. While Madeleine was still swirling around in newlywed bliss, an archduke named Franz Ferdinand was visiting Sarajevo on the other side of the world. Six men followed him along his motorcade. Their goal was to assassinate him, hoping his death would free Bosnia from what, at that time, was Austrian rule. One of them threw a grenade at the archduke's car and injured two of his aides, who went to the hospital while the convoy carried on. Ferdinand survived, but an hour later, as he was returning from visiting the injured officers, his car turned into a street, where he stepped forward and received two bullets, which fatally wounded both Ferdinand and his wife, Sophie.

The news was only a headline about the volatility of Europe—a continent away for Mina. She was far from prescient. She might have read the headline, but it made no lasting impression. Her chronic inability to understand the needs and aspirations of her three children confounded her. Moreover, one would never expect Mina to predict the trajectory of world power. Glenmont was her oyster, and it had only just expanded to a small apartment in Manhattan.

15

Domestic Life in the Trenches

MADELEINE'S NEW NEIGHBORHOOD WAS NOT TO MINA'S LIKING. At that time, Greenwich Village became widely identified as America's Bohemia. The radicals who lived there rejected traditionally structured society and preferred informality. Each corner store and café became dens to discuss ideas about art and revolution. Not only were Madeleine and John enjoying their new neighborhood, but after Charles returned from traveling out West, he also gravitated to this unconventional and quirky destination. Charles had a taste for the arts. He was talented in playing both mandolin and piano, and he had a knack for poetry, often humorous or containing a quick-witted tone. Those traits made him a natural fit in the Greenwich Village community.

Mina continued to be baffled by her children's pursuits. She considered it a form of mutiny against the past twenty years of rearing. Both Charles and Madeleine had formed fierce personalities. A sensible person could not expect otherwise. As children, they had no choice but to live in the limelight, constantly accosted by the flashbulbs of the press. Each of them was questioned ad nauseum: what was it like living with the most famous man in the world? As a result, their skin thickened at a young age. Besides, Madeleine had to fight her parents to marry the love of her life. Together, these experiences provided her with independent thought, strength, and confidence. As for Charles, he wanted to explore and expand his horizons beyond the prescribed walls of Glenmont's Methodist fortress.

Madeleine and Charles were more insightful and shrewder than their straitlaced mother. They realized they could easily manipulate her gullible and prudish style. When they were forceful with her about expressing their needs, she never had the fortitude to push back. The arguments always ended in her children getting their way, then she would recoil and write her family of her defeat. The years of contending with Edison had made her a mere shell of herself. Her children understood this and used it to their advantage. Mina did not bring in Edison for fortification. Throughout his life, and now more than ever, he cared more about his work than the day-to-day details of his children's domestic interests.[1]

Charles witnessed how Mina attempted to micromanage every day of Madeleine's life after leaving Bryn Marr until her wedding day. Charles was not going to live in that cage. It was 1915, and it was a white male-dominated world; he had more freedom than his sister. He had every intention of taking advantage of that.

Edison soon realized that Charles did not have a mind for engineering or chemistry, but he hoped the business side of the company would interest him. However, Charles knew his strengths and admitted that "he couldn't even balance his checkbook." Edison was unsure where to situate Charles at the outset of his career. A colleague suggested he investigate a building Edison had purchased downtown in Mina's name. Edison had put Glenmont and other investments in her name. It was primarily for protection against bankruptcy and, to a lesser degree, to provide income to Mina after Edison's death. Located at 10 Fifth Avenue in New York City, the entire building was for "some offices for export business."[2]

When Charles headed downtown, he was captivated by the previously "undiscovered area." He said that, unlike West Orange, "It had atmosphere." He suggested the company could place a phonograph record shop in that building, and the profits would cover the property taxes. In the lower level of the building, Charles "conceived of an idea of having a little theatre on the second floor." In making the theatre, Charles would need someone to run it while he worked at the laboratory in West Orange during the day. He could only return to the city at night after a day's work.[3]

The enticing narrow streets of the area summoned him. Then, finally, he "encountered a farmhouse at the corner of Washinton Square and Thompson Street flanked with limousines and cars." As he entered, his eyes glazed on a "swarthy fellow" who stood "six foot three" reading excerpts from Oscar Wilde.[4]

The swarthy man—Guido Bruno, soon became Charles's close friend. Torn from a different cloth than Charles, he spoke six languages and had a strong understanding of public relations. Bruno saw potential in Charles and his last name and partnered with him in the operation of the Little Thimble Theater. Charles's theatre goal was to give an audience to young American musicians, composers, poets, and playwrights who did not have the means to hire an agent. As a result, the performers had the opportunity to act in a free forum accessible to everyone, with the chance to be heard by an unprejudiced audience.

Bruno also published *Bruno's Weekly*, a literary magazine that celebrated Greenwich Village and its people. It contained local news, gossip, poetry, short stories, and artwork by the neighborhood inhabitants. In addition, Charles regularly contributed poetry under the nom de plume of Tom Sleeper. The name suggested the two superior forces that ruled his existence: his father, "Tom" Edison, and the lack of sleep he often alluded to in his various poems. Still, it was easy to see his love for life in the Village. It was the furthest point from his mother's structured world around him.[5]

In those years, Charles's youthful energy was used every hour of his day. First, he would work at his father's plant until four or five in the afternoon. He would then take the train downtown and prepare for the evening show. After grabbing a bite to eat with friends, he would then go back to the theatre for the production. After the show, he would write poetry for Bruno's magazine, take the train back to West Orange, return home at three-thirty in the morning, then return to work for his father five hours later.

Charles knew that Mina felt excluded and mortified by the contemporary world he now inhabited. Hoping to lessen the shock, he invited her to some performances. Mina often demurred with various excuses, but she made one surprise appearance. Unfortunately, the timing could not have been worse. That evening was a one-act play entitled "The State Forbids," an avant-garde production by Sada Cowan. She was an up-and-coming playwright whose plays and later films revolved around marriage, divorce, love, and infidelity. The theme of the play espoused the need for birth control. Margaret Sanger, an American birth control activist, sex educator, writer, and nurse, had helped bring about the public understanding and need for birth control in the United States.[6]

When Mina showed up at the theatre, Charles's expression fell. He remained anxious throughout the play and could not fathom what his cloistered, Victorian, Methodist mother would perceive of the show. Charles's fears were not unfounded. Mina had recently done public interviews for the press about women's contemporary dress styles. She condemned the sudden appearance of women's knees or calves while walking in the city streets. Moreover, at a social function in the New Jersey suburbs, she had started a campaign against wearing low-cut dresses.

The actors, actresses, and Charles's friends were eager to hear the famous Mrs. Edison's review. Mina, aware of her onlookers—especially her beloved son and his friends—stated, "That play was the finest and strongest little play I've ever seen." Charles was relieved by his mother's appraisal and knew she would not dare make a scene in public.[7]

One of the most important of Charles's friends who frequently accompanied him in that scene was his new girlfriend, Carolyn Hawkins. Charles was good-looking and charismatic and had brought many young ladies home. Carolyn, however, had outlasted all of them. They met while at school in Boston. She would often travel to New York to enjoy the Village scene with Charles. Often, they would get together with Edna St. Vincent Millay, a famous poet and political activist noted for her uninhibited lifestyle, forming romantic relationships with both men and women. Carolyn was a modern woman who was not reticent in meeting and engaging with the progressive group that Charles found enticing.[8]

Mina barely survived the Madeleine and John courtship debacle. She would try not to now alienate Charles by looking down her nose at Carolyn because she had different sensibilities. But try as she might, Mina would not succeed.

When Charles started bringing Carolyn to Glenmont regularly, she earnestly tried to ingratiate herself with her boyfriend's famous parents. Unfortunately, Carolyn was unfamiliar with Mina and how she politely conducted herself among society, and she mistakenly confused Mina's initially agreeable posture with fondness. She decided to confide in Mina about her family: Carolyn's father, Horatio Hawkins, was a physician. Unfortunately, he'd become an alcoholic and morphine addict who abused his wife and was eventually committed to a sanitarium. When he checked himself out and attempted to return home, Carolyn threw him out of the house to protect her mother and sisters. Three days later, he committed suicide by drowning in the Connecticut River. Carolyn blamed herself for her father's death. As Mina listenend to the saga and outpouring of grief, she kept her composure.

Mina relayed the sordid tale to Edison, who "hoped that Charles had not fallen in love with that girl." When hearing about the family's tragedy, Madeleine wondered to her husband, John, "how far the affair has progressed," yet she was impressed with Carolyn's "strength" and "character." Mina let the information about Carolyn simmer. At that time, Charles was in no position to get married, especially with his schedule and Carolyn living in Boston and working as a secretary for a local physician.[9]

Mina was soon cheered by the news that her unmarried sister Grace had found someone with whom she wanted to spend the rest of her life. His name was Halbert Hitchcock, an engineer and fellow Ohioan. The one smudge on his résumé was that he had been previously married. The good news to Mina was that he had no children. Mina often listened to her sister Mame compete for her husband's attention with his daughter from a previous marriage. Mina, of course, had also had a negative experience with children from her previous marriage. Hal was a self-confident and ideal match for Grace, who desperately needed a companion and a perfectionist. Madeleine, a keen observer, was never fond of him and later stated, "When you were in his presence, he had a perfect belief that everything he has is the best there is and his determination to make you agree with him when most of the time you don't."[10]

Mina was overjoyed to share the news with the family. Grace's fiancé was someone whom Mina could be proud to mention to her lady friends.

Making Mina even happier, Halbert's brother Lucius was a well-known artist whose illustrations appeared in some of the works of Mark Twain. Mina would later request that he paint a portrait of Edison, which would be prominently displayed at Glenmont.

With Grace getting married and moving to Pittsburgh with Hal, Lewis Jr. would be the last Miller child still residing in Oak Place. Well into his fifties now, Lewis was regrettably still unmarried. Her two other brothers, Edward and John, were also single men. The family considered Edward a confirmed bachelor. Even after being introduced to countless women, he would lose interest and claim the young ladies were not attractive enough.[11]

Mina also introduced John to various women, and the family did not understand why he would not take the leap. For close to twenty years, he had earned a place within the immediate family working for Edison. Along with his daily duties, he ran interference between the family members, often forestalling impending blowups.

Mame had a happy marriage despite her new stepdaughter's needs. Mame settled in Scarsdale and was living a very comfortable and care-free life. She deserved a relaxed lifestyle after countless years of intense anxiety, sanitariums, and the accompanying stigma. She and her husband traveled extensively and often asked Mina to join them on their trips. Mina always had to decline. She wished her husband would retire, but she knew Edison would never leave his laboratory.

The future of Oak Place hung in the balance. While Mary Valinda was still alive, she'd made a committee of her three children—Edward, John, and Grace—to select an appraiser to value Oak Place and its contents for sale. In addition to the home, there were 350 shares of stock in the Chautauqua Hotel to be divided among the children. Grace had suggested all the items in the house be appraised, and in a method of lots, the Miller children would choose what they wanted. But, in the back of Mina's mind, she wanted her mother's furniture for Madeleine; she knew Madeleine and John. She knew they would never have the financial means to buy such things.

It was always a struggle to get Edison to agree to buy new furniture, however. She would have to use her allowance to buy her mother's old furniture from the estate and ship it to Madeleine and John to store until they settled into a new home. Sadness overcame Mina. She could not bear to think about selling her parents' house; she always considered it her "home with all its associations and joys."[12]

Mina took the social reins with most family events and suggested that Grace and Hal marry at Glenmont. She could ensure the family would come together. Mina decorated her conservatory with many American Beauty roses to create a sumptuous garden. Grace wore orange blossoms in her hair and a white crepe de chine gown trimmed with lace. Mina used her active position at her church to have the local reverend perform the ceremony. Well into his seventies, Edison was turning increasingly deaf, but Mina wanted him to be part of the ceremony rather than off to the side in his own thoughts. She asked Edison to give Grace away; surprisingly, he complied. The ceremony was intimate, intended only for immediate family. For friends who remained in Ohio, Grace and Hal planned a larger reception at Oak Place before its sale to new owners.

After the wedding, and only a few days before Thanksgiving, Mina's older brother Lewis Jr. astonished her with news he planned to marry his twenty-three-year-old secretary, Cotta Smyser. He informed Mina it would not be a large wedding, just a small ceremony at her mother's home. At only twenty-three years old, Cotta was younger than Madeleine. Lewis knew that Mina would disapprove and told his younger sister, "Please keep your thoughts to yourself . . . everything has been talked over, and I wish you will welcome her into the family and will come to see me married, if you can't come, please write a good welcome and happy letter to her." After the wedding, he and his bride planned to move to California. He further stressed to Mina that he had not told anyone about the marriage and would like to "keep it a secret" until after the wedding.[13]

Lewis entrusted Mina with personal information. Mina, grounded in the past, thought of the relationship she and her brother had as children, ultimately keeping his secret and attending the wedding. Once the couple was settled in Pasadena, where Lewis would own a lemon and orange grove, he shared another secret: He was to become a father at fifty-three. The child had been conceived before their wedding—a genuine scandal for the Methodist Millers. But if Mina and the others knew this fact, they swept it under the Miller rug.

Six months after the wedding, the stately Oak Place left the hands of the Miller family. Two businessmen, one in the rubber industry and the other in real estate, had various plans for the stately mansion. After previous sales of property and land, the home and the last remaining six acres of land were still under discussion.

After years of managing Glenmont and her children with her monthly allowance, Mina developed into the family bookkeeper. Careful records of her purchases had to be kept and reviewed by Edison or his secretary. As other women became more and more modern and entered the workforce, Mina publicly referred to herself as a "home executive."

Concerned about her siblings since her father's business had gone bankrupt, Mina would send parts of her monthly stipend to help her siblings financially. Grace and Mame now lived comfortably, but her other siblings never regained the same financial stability they had before the crash. Furthermore, Mina's discretionary income enabled her to maintain her parents' house in Chautauqua, and she made the Institution's solvency a priority of hers. She felt assured that she could preserve her father's legacy while maintaining her involvement.

While Mina remained engaged with Chautauqua for the next generation, George Vincent did the same. Both of them had internalized its importance. Mina's children appreciated its significance but had never fully embraced its religious and conservative worldview. Rev. Vincent had indoctrinated George, and he followed his father's teachings by staying true to the mission and ensuring its future. Ultimately, he became the president of the Chautauqua Institution.

After Mina had discarded him those many years before, his broken heart and keen mind had led him into academia. His career started at the University of Chicago, and he climbed up the ranks to become dean. Eventually, he moved to the University of Minnesota to become its third president, where George introduced innovative programming, including lecture concerts and debates similar to those at Chautauqua Institution. Much like his father and Lewis Miller, he cared about increasing educational and cultural opportunities for the general public. His admired reputation in academics spread, and Rockefeller University asked George to become its president, an offer he happily accepted.

Observing George's career arc suggests he was more like Mina's father and his life outlook was similar to her own. She knew he had married and had three children, but Mina and George rarely crossed paths.

Despite Mina's love for her siblings, her first concern was always her children. Madeleine and John had moved to Plainfield, New Jersey, to be close to John's airplane manufacturing business, the Sloane Aeroplane Company. Within two years of the marriage, the company dissolved. It was devastating for the newly married Madeleine to watch her husband's energy and work fade into nothing. The disaster crushed John, and he never fully recovered from the amount of time and money he put into it. Before the company went under, John was "on the edge of success," but he did not have "enough capital to cover his debts and was getting deeper all the time." John's Achilles' heel was that he "could not land orders."[14]

Throughout John's business failures, Edison sat on the sidelines. Not once did he offer to help make connections for John with his countless associates. His view that each man should make his way in the world fueled his detachment. His position remained resolute while he watched his daughter suffer financially. Ostensibly, Edison punished Madeleine and John because they had married against his wishes. Edison lumped them in the same pile as William and Tom Jr., with whom Mina had recently corresponded after years of exile. Madeleine would be allowed infrequent gifts, which often transformed ex post facto into loans that had to be paid back with interest, like Edison's loans to her stepbrothers.

Mina did not go along with this identical persecuting and pecuniary punishment. Madeleine was her flesh and blood; Tom Jr. and William were not. Moreover, Madeleine had given birth to a boy. Despite Edison's displeasure with the couple, he was the godfather of their first son, Thomas Edison Sloane.

Mina had previously confided in Charles that when Madeleine wanted to marry John, "It grieves me beyond expression, and the worst of it is that Madeleine is perfectly indifferent to either of us." She knew Madeleine had chosen John against their wishes, but she wanted to entice her back into the fold. She wanted Madeleine to remain at Glenmont for a month to recuperate after the difficult birth. At that time, Mina and Edison planned a trip to Fort Myers for the winter months, allowing Madeleine to recover without their interference.[15]

This dynamic was a common theme in Mina and Madeleine's relationship. Mina would painfully watch Madeleine bring up her children in an environment that distressed Mina. Moreover, she would watch Madeleine struggle financially without any help. Within two years, a second son arrived after another problematic pregnancy and birth. Mina once again insisted that Madeleine give birth at the house. Afterward, Mina would send a nanny and a maid to help her daughter with early motherhood.

While Madeleine and Mina were jockeying for Edison's attention, the United States had formally entered World War I. To secure a continual source of income, John enlisted in the army in a clerical position. So, Madeleine and John and the two babies moved to Washington, DC. John now had a pro forma title and served as a lieutenant in the Army Air Service, the Signal Corps in Washington, DC. He received a steady income to support Madeleine and his two sons.

At that time, Theodore was graduating from high school and developing into a keen observer of human nature, especially the peculiar nature of the Edison family. As a later child, he'd witnessed his siblings fight for independence. After assessing the mixed results, Theodore decided to contend with his mother. Mina was at her usual point of an emotional precipice, and she agreed to let him travel across the country with friends and their families. Mina wrote Theodore, often wondering why the family with whom he was traveling did not telegraph home regularly. Mina had been preconditioned for years during the Millers' various travels. Her family was overly sensitive and eager to get the news to other family members during their journeys. When Theodore reached Detroit and was able to stay a night at the Fords', she missed speaking with him. Having no one to complain to, Mina wrote to Clara Ford, thanking her for her hospitality and hoping to get news of Theodore's well-being.

Once Theodore returned, he planned to enter MIT, seeking to differentiate himself from the family. More creative than Charles and Madeleine, he soon became well-spoken and confident in his decisions. Moreover, while his siblings were in college, Theodore had spent much time around grown-ups, often acting as a bit of an adult. During that time, he realized his inquisitiveness, and at the same time, that his sensitive character did not connect well with the flow of the family. In his memoirs, Theodore recalled that his father never had the time nor the interest to question in what he was learning in school, whether it was at Montclair Academy or later as he entered MIT. As a child, Theodore even built a small laboratory in the basement at Glenmont, yet Theodore recalled his father had never come down to look at it or even inquire about his son's interests. Although Theodore entered MIT to continue his education, he studied physics and slowly deviated from his father's interests.

As the war raged on in Europe, Edison told a reporter for the *New York Times* that America needed to prepare its defenses. This helped to set in motion the creation of the Naval Consulting Board, with Edison as its chairman. In addition, the embargo on chemicals from Germany created a shortage for his manufacturing plants, as well as led him to build his own chemical plant and become a supplier for American industries and allies.

As Edison's wife, reporters also sought Mina's opinions. At the Panama Pacific Exposition, she was accosted by journalists shouting questions left and right. Mina understood her role in history, and believing the United States was at a cultural transition point for women and families, she advocated for the mores she had grown up with in Akron.

When asked about her social life and what she did in the evenings, she stated that her "Children are as much a business as inventions." She added that "it is a wife's job to attend to her husband, take care of his heath and attend to his clothes." Reporters pushed back and inquired about Edison's habit of missing critical social events. One commented about Edison's appearance: "Sometimes, you are called to remonstrate your husband; he spills acid and paints on his clothes." Mina was trained to pivot. She used her public-relations acumen and confidently declared, "I suppose all men are distracted; they must be if they give their minds wholly to business." Her patience and tolerant smile were always at the forefront.[16]

Women's Suffrage was another topic that troubled the traditional Mrs. Edison. Not only was it a widespread issue that yielded debate, but it sold newspapers. Mina unabashedly stated, "women in the aggregate, are not interested in political problems. . . . Wait and the privilege [will] come to us. Then, the American man will see that the American woman has what she asked for reasonably."[17]

Pressing further, the journalist boldly asked what was vital to her besides her husband and children. "I have no fads. I attend my church work and try to do my duty in my home community, charities, philanthropies."[18]

As America entered the war, community charities and philanthropies would have to be put on hold. Edison started conducting anti-submarine experiments for the U.S. Navy. He left for Washington, DC, and set up an office in the Navy Annex in a room once occupied by Admiral George Dewey. He remained there for several months.

After the New Year, when the weather turned colder, Edison and Mina left for Key West, where they stayed in a house at the U.S. Naval Station. Edison conducted research there for four more months. Mina was uncomfortable and very much out of her element, often grumbling that the other military wives did not like her.

Edison spent six weeks conducting experiments aboard a private yacht commissioned by the navy for military service. His unstructured way of doing research clashed with the bureaucratic methods of the navy. The men of the navy followed strict protocols and conduct. Yet, Edison refused to surrender his views on practices and procedures when he invented them. Even in wartime, Edison often debated research methodology, many discussions ending in rancor and bitterness.

Mina had a vague sense of what her husband was doing. She would have responded that he was conducting experiments for enhanced torpedo detection if pressed. He was also compiling data on ship sinkings and devising a plan for night shipping to avoid enemy submarines.

As much of a patriot as Mina was, fighting the enemy was not her genuine interest. Unlike other women at that time, she did not believe women were equal to men, and she did not want the same responsibilities on her shoulders. Instead, Mina's thoughts centered on her new grandsons and their health. Once satisfied with their progress, her mind turned to her beloved Charles. His love life occupied her daily thoughts, which were becoming more dampened with the invasion of the young lady from Cambridge and a broken home.

Charles was savvy enough to avoid the draft. He claimed he needed to take charge of his father's company and further asserted that his hearing was impaired, and deafness would be useless in combat. Theodore was quite the opposite. Wanting to do his part for the county, he enlisted. Although Mina could be with Edison during his research, she was lonely and missed her children. She wrote to Charles, "It grieves me to think you and Theodore are so far away from me, but I am hoping I am doing the right thing being here with Father." Appreciating all of Charles's help, she further ingratiated herself with her son by thanking him for "looking after matters at home." After hearing about Theodore's patriotic stance, she wanted Charles to help dissuade him and "dread[ed] the thought" of Theodore enlisting but realized he wanted "to do a big thing for his country." Mina further complained to Charles that she felt "so far away and helpless to do anything."[19]

While in Florida, Charles had been alluding more and more that Carolyn was his one true love. Freely admitting he had his pick of any girl because of his looks, wealth, and personality, he'd decided on Carolyn to be his wife. Mina was miserable when his decision was made clear. She knew not to talk to Madeleine about her unhappiness, nor did she pick at the slowly healing wound as she wrote to Theodore and her brother John. Instead, Mina would use this afront as an opportunity to gain sympathy from her younger son and brother.

Astute to his mother's moods and feelings, Theodore told his mother to "Cheer up . . . I'm still sticking by the pond." John took a more practical approach and informed Mina that Charles had recently had an emergency appendectomy. He was still frequently ill from overwork and exertion and would now be in the hands of a capable woman who worked for a doctor. His overall health would no longer be a concern. Even with this newfound optimism about the circumstances, however, Mina remained depressed.[20]

Unwisely, Mina wrote Charles directly about her concerns with Carolyn as his wife. She stressed that he was the future of the Edison Company, and he would need a spouse who understood the importance of her role. Edison would leave a crucial mark on the world, and Charles was expected to continue what he started. Charles's life would have a richness that an ordinary person's life would not. Ultimately, the story of Charles's life would be much larger than the value of a random individual. The Edison name had a lasting impact on people and places. Unfortunately, Mina did not think Carolyn was refined or trained enough to fill those shoes.

Mina, starved for her husband's attention, looked elsewhere for verbal declarations of love. She was overly generous with gifts and money, waiting patiently for return notes of praise. Unfortunately, she was never able to fill the void left by Edison. Moreover, this need transformed itself into peculiarly overly affectionate words of love to her boys. Her letters were often filled with queries of whether they missed her or was she the "best and only." Charles assured Mina that she would always be his "first love." Now that Charles would be marrying Carolyn, she would turn to Theodore as her devotee.[21]

Never good at keeping a poker face in front of her children, it was not difficult for Charles to realize Mina's feelings about Carolyn. But Charles was in love, and he was going to push back, determined to marry her anyway. While Mina was in Florida, Charles wrote his mother an epistle stating his genuine love for Carolyn. He cautioned his mother that he was concerned she would never get along with Carolyn after they married and that Mina would "remain a thorn in their side." He added that Carolyn "won't embarrass you with your friends or make you feel like you have to apologize for your son's choice." But Mina continued to tell her son that she did not think Carolyn would mix well.[22]

Despite their disagreement, Charles asked Mina if he and Carolyn could visit her in Florida. Mina was perturbed at that request and told Madeleine it was not proper for Carolyn to visit with Charles unchaperoned. But the couple came down regardless of Mina's feelings on the matter.

Once there, Charles and Carolyn enjoyed the atmosphere and much-needed respite. Carolyn worked assisting doctors and went overseas for the servicepeople in the war; she was exhausted from the winter months and exertion. The couple had known each other for six years and had been dating seriously for the last two. Charles knew it was time to settle down and asked "if she wanted a large wedding." Carolyn, sensible that it was wartime and not wanting the fuss, replied, "No." They both decided they would get married right away in Florida.[23]

When the couple approached Mina with the idea, her first inclination was to send a telegram to Edison for approval. However, Edison had no desire to leave his invention on the ship and wrote back, "If it's going to be, then the sooner, the better." Edison, still feeling the same way as he always did about the institution of marriage, wrote, "Anyway, it won't be worse than life in the front line trenches. You have my blessing."[24]

The next few days, they applied for the marriage license. The couple thought the grounds were beautiful and decided to get married outside. They rolled a little carpet to a small altar with two candles. Mina gave away Carolyn. The butler and the children's nanny, who became Mina's companion, were the witnesses. The war precluded a lengthy honeymoon, so the couple traveled to Key West for a short stay, then returned to New Jersey with little fanfare.

In the meantime, the hot-blooded Madeleine was only alerted to the wedding via telegram. This might have been sufficient for Edison and the cerebral Theodore, who preferred working on gasoline motors for trench warfare in Key West, but not for Madeleine.

While she and Mina responded to life differently, Madeleine could read her mother's actions or inactions. In her usual snarky manner, she told her mother, "The recent nuptials seem to have paralyzed my writing force, for I have not been able to put to pen to paper since hearing about it—I might add that it seems to have affected you in the same way—this news almost bowled me over, and I haven't yet recovered from the shock." Madeleine continued, "I am trying to swallow my feelings and not be hurt by anything. . . . Something a little more personal than a telegram would have been appreciated." Indeed, Madeleine realized that Charles and Carolyn had forced Mina to accept their wedding, but Mina had hardly finished chastising her for suffering when she wanted to marry John.[25]

The war affected all of the Edisons; however, living in Germany, Marion was damaged the most. Although Mina never placed Marion at the top of her priorities, her relationship became friendlier after the family trip to Europe. The family was pleased with Oscar and the way he conducted himself. Now, however, he was considered the enemy, making Marion's life more precarious than before.

Before the United States entered the war, Edison had attempted to write to Marion and inquire about her safety. Her infrequent letters back revealed a frightening view of the war and how the world would now deal with Germany. They sent her much-needed supplies because of the rations, yet once Americans declared war, Madeleine and others warned against it.

After America declared war on Germany, Marion was trapped behind enemy lines, and she fled to Switzerland. She had difficulty getting across the border and was required to leave her possessions in a villa in Germany. Marion traveled to Switzerland with other war refugees, only taking one suitcase. Once she arrived, she stayed in an overcrowded hotel. She spent the rest of the war terrified by world events and waiting for mail or funds from home.

After the war, Marion returned to a war-torn Germany. She reunited with her husband, but she discovered incriminating pictures of Oscar with a waitress from a local bierhaus, Clara Berger. Eventually, Oscar admitted to the affair. He said the darkness of war had caused him to find comfort when they were apart. Marion felt betrayed and wanted a divorce. Realizing that Marion's allowance would terminate if that took place, Oscar refused to divorce her.

Moreover, Oscar thought she would change her mind if he made up a rumor about her taking a lover for herself. As an Edison, Marion had had years of training in psychological warfare. Oscar would never be a challenge after she had endured what her father had inflicted upon her.

Once the divorce proceedings began, Oscar began to saunter through the streets with Clara. Marion's lawyers supported her ordeal and told her how lucky she was to have missed venereal disease like many other wives whose soldier husbands cheated on them.

As a soldier familiar with combat, Oscar used scare tactics to threaten Marion. Suffering from insomnia, her lack of sleep affected her decision-making. She felt out of control and outnumbered by the taunts from Oscar's friends. He burglarized her house and stole many of her possessions. He refused to vacate their home and used his force to live there with her. After months of torment, she went to a sanitarium for weeks to recover.[26]

After her departure, she was eventually able to sell the villa and prove to the court that Oscar was at fault. Finally, after two years and a drawn-out legal battle, Marion put her thirty years of life in Europe behind her. Before returning to the United States, she confessed to Mina, "I was living a life of illusions, and once the war came, it was like someone took the blindfold off my eyes."[27]

Marion was not the only Edison woman who lived a life of self-deception. Mina could never acknowledge that she was inflexible when interacting with others who were unlike herself. All her life, especially her married life, she had required an ideal home for her children. The food, conversations, and interactions at the Edison table set a particular mode. She wanted the next generation to emulate her methods. Unfortunately, Mina's prescribed environment was consumed with rules and regulations; punctuality, order, neatness, temperance, generosity, and hospitality. Edison did not surrender to her ways because Mina could never tame him. But the home was her laboratory, and she had wanted to invent three remarkable creations.

A letter to Theodore encapsulates her struggle within herself about her relationship with her children and their spouses. Yet again, the letter revealed the abnormal bond Mina had with her son, a mere first-year student in college: "There is a tense strain or some uncomfortableness that can't seem to get away from. . . . Carolyn feels it, and I feel it, which makes Charles unhappy . . . We get on all right, but there is just something lacking. There is the same strained condition but not as much with Madeleine and John. There again, it is a divergence of interests."[28]

Their father's fame exposed the children to so many different facets of life that they would never fit into the mold of Mina's childhood. The world of the 1920s was different from the world in 1870. Moreover, Mina became incompetent when she needed to be a mother. She told Theodore that "Madeleine thinks Carolyn is usurping her place, that she more is like stepdaughter." Edison would dismiss his wife's assessment, so she childishly asked her son, "What are we to do?" Finally, baring her soul, she admitted, "I feel more like a stepmother to Madeleine. I try to do everything that I know to do, and yet it does not move Madeleine. So, I am going to let her alone, and when she wants me, she can ask for me."[29]

Foolishly, Mina used all her repressed anger toward her husband to complain about her children's failures. Mina was oblivious to their need to individuate, and the more she criticized, the more they pulled away.

"You know, selfishness is at the root of all troubles. We must learn to give and take." So tragic were Mina's words, but she could not suppress her thoughts to Theodore: "Dearie, don't desert me yet I will have to give you up someday, but I can't bear to have it yet. I dread the day when you take unto yourself a wife. I know I should be unselfish, for it is right for you to have a companion, but I am so afraid that she will not fit; oh, I am afraid of it."[30]

16

Wrestling with the Remaining Years

CORAL IS BEAUTIFUL FROM AFAR. THE DECEPTION OF THE LIGHT IN THE ocean makes it look that way. But up close, it is just a big lump of rock on which one can unexpectedly slash one's feet. After thirty-five years of marriage with Edison, on their coral anniversary Mina chose to reveal to the world its beauty and suffer the lacerations in secret.

Mina's religious belief in the divine and adherence to Methodist theology was unwavering. This discipline helped her live through the vicissitudes of her marriage and life. Moreover, her total deference to the values espoused by the Methodist faith kept her focused on the work and duty she did for her husband, as she trusted it would benefit both the individual and society as a whole. To Mina, her diligence became a mark of grace. Hard work and personal prudence were necessary to ensure her soul would go to heaven.

Not all the Miller children's marriages were fraught with self-flagellation. Although there were plenty of bastions of women dedicated to their husbands' careers, they subsumed their self-determination. Whether planned or not, Mina's sisters Grace and Mame waited until their forties to marry. Having a similar upbringing as their sister Mina, they were blissfully married—socializing, dining, and traveling extensively. Both sisters continually tried to include Mina and Edison in their exciting plans. Unfortunately, Mina would never seize those opportunities. Regretfully she explained to them, "I am pretty much tied to Thomas; he does not want to do anything . . . his being so deaf pretty much keeps us alone and turns us back into our shell."[1]

Mina never felt she had control over her own choices in life. Her lack of ability played a critical role in her psychological health and well-being. It impacted her motivation. As a result, she had a manic response to her circumstances, either involving herself in every civic organization possible or sitting at home depressed, mulling over thoughts and poor decisions.

The tragedy is that she never learned from her experiences. This vicious cycle was the cornerstone of her life. Unfortunately, Mina was robbed of the moments in a marriage when partners are shouting at each other, moments when they are crying in each other's arms, or moments when they laugh out loud together. Her children Madeleine and Charles witnessed their mother's unhealthy marriage and unequivocally married for love.

Mina's youngest surviving brother, John, had recently found a wife named Florence after being overly selective. Mina adored her and wrote glowing letters about her seamlessly fitting into the family dynamic. She attended church with Mina and looked up to her as a wise, guiding force. The couple later had two children, whom Mina adored and showered with gifts.

Mina's oldest brother, Ed, surprised everyone and also decided to marry. In his mid-fifties, he wanted to keep his wedding low-profile. Even more embarrassing than his brother Lewis marrying his twenty-three-year-old secretary, Ed decided to marry his Welsh housekeeper, Elizabeth, who had been working for him for the last ten years. There was no correspondence about their wedding or a formal announcement in an Ohio paper as his siblings had done. They were married in Windsor, Ontario. However, the family considered her family and included Elizabeth in family functions.

Her last hope was Theodore, but Mina would soon learn that he would be pursuing the same route as his siblings. The most independent child would eventually make a decision that would forever affect the Edison name.[2]

Unlike Charles, Theodore's mind took advantage of MIT's education; he was more inclined to study science and engineering. He thoroughly enjoyed learning new things, pursuing new passions, and finding his place in the world.

Mina's three prized possessions no longer needed her daily counseling about life, culture, and religion. Alone with her brooding thoughts, she'd recently opened a small window to Tom Jr. and William, allowing them to reenter the Edison family. Yet this would only be on Mina's terms.

As much as Tom Jr. wanted to be part of the famous family again, he was now an adult in his forties, and he cognitively reflected on countless years of being emotionally abused. He realized Mina was as much to blame as his father. Throughout the years, Tom Jr. and Beatrice were kept afar from the glowing lights of Glenmont. With all Mina's religious adherences, she still saw Tom and Beatrice as lesser than herself. Beatrice tried her best to be part of Mina's inner circle and hoped news of her pregnancy would soften her mother-in-law's stance. Rather than embrace the possible next generation, however, Mina was devastated and responded to the information by "hoping and praying that Tom's baby, which they are expecting this month or next, will be a little girl . . . it would be awful to have Thomas A. Edison III, Poor papa and poor us." But the baby never came.[3]

Even after years in agriculture, William and his wife, Blanche, were still figuring out a profitable farming business, often living from paycheck to paycheck. More forceful than his emotional brother Tom Jr., William unabashedly wrote to his father via his secretary requesting loans to cover debts for farming machinery. Invariably, Edison refused.

Theodore was thrilled with life at that time. The intellectually stimulating environment suited him well. However, meeting a young woman named Ann Osterhout was more thrilling than being challenged at work. She was graduating from Vassar and was interested in continuing her studies at Johns Hopkins to become a doctor. Theodore took her out every week and reported to his mother how fond he was of Ann.

Once Mina heard that her "baby" was deeply interested in this woman, she complained to her sister Grace. She said that Theodore was the most sensitive and caring of her three children and that he needed "a compassionate and understanding partner." In Mina's mind, no such woman could exist, and she added that love and marriage "is such a lottery." She continued to badger Theodore about the importance of a good mate and told him, "You have a big place to fill in the world." Adding further pressure to his decision-making, Mina said, "Father is so concerned you get the right woman. He is anxious you get the right one. He has not been very fortunate in that line with the others. Poor dear!"[4]

Theodore was proud of his new girlfriend. She was intelligent and curious about the world. They shared a love of the environment and had the same temperament. Ann was a high achiever, as were many of his educated female peers of the time. She had no interest in staying home and being a housewife. After graduating from Vassar, she lived in Cambridge, where she met Theodore at dinner. Her father was a biochemist and a college professor. He was the cofounder and co-editor of the *Journal of General Physiology*, earning him membership in the National Academy of Sciences. Two years after Theodore married, her father left Ann's mother for a woman who worked for him at Harvard and moved to New York City.

Initially, Theodore was concerned that Ann did not return his affection and that she wanted to put her career first. But as luck would have it, "The romance caused her to change her plans." Ann visited Mina and Edison at Glenmont. Realizing how similar she was to Theodore, Mina forced herself to be happy for her youngest child. Attuned to Ann's overall persona, however, Mina lamented to her sister, "Ann will never wear an evening gown." Ultimately, after spending more time together, Mina said she did "feel a little happier now that I know Ann will be considerate to Theodore."[5]

Theodore and Ann were considered intellectuals. From MIT, Theodore earned a master's degree in physics. The jazz world was blossoming around them, as was the Art Deco movement. Although the Roaring Twenties were the backdrop of their courtship, the couple did not gravitate to the social and cultural trends that had come to New York and other large cities.

However, Ann abandoned the more restrictive wardrobes of the past for more comfortable clothing, and she smoked cigarettes. The couple opted for a simple church wedding at Harvard Chapel, with a house reception.

Theodore and Ann invited the entire family to their wedding, including Tom Jr. and Beatrice, William and Blanche, and Marion, who had recently returned from Europe. Mina had difficulty shaking off her despondency. She yearned for a life she never considered her own and told Grace that she "longed for people of culture and refinement." Sadly, not even her husband fell into either category.[6]

As Edison advanced in age, he swatted away any modicum of polish that Mina tried to foist on him. Yet, even with his declining health, he ignored the doctor's advice and continued an obsessive need to rely on a special Jersey cow milk diet.

Aware of the limitations of his age, Edison could have stopped working and enjoyed his twilight years with his wife, who had spent her life devoted to caring for him. Unfortunately, Edison refused to change his selfish habits. For example, Mina liked dancing, but Edison compared it to something monkeys enjoyed. As a result, she could not lure him anywhere; even the slightest suggestion received a rebuff. Ultimately, Mina stayed home as a nursemaid to a patient who hardly appreciated her services. Unhappily, she wrote to Theodore that when "her boys were home, she had love attention admiration with any effort on my part, but now my attractions are diminishing, which were mostly looks, and I find myself floundering."[7]

Edison was stingy with their daughter as well. Madeleine, who was on her third child and had recently moved to a new home, had trouble with her cash flow, and the doctor's bill from the third child put them into debt. John, who was not allowed to work at TAE, Inc., earned a meager salary. Madeleine begged Edison for help with their outstanding loan of $3,500 ($56,000 in today's money). Although disappointed with her daughter's choice of husband, Mina did not have the heart to let her daughter not have enough funds for her family. Edison did not want to help them out; John needed to pull his own weight. Essentially, he put them in a bind. Edison did not wish Madeleine to work because that was not acceptable, yet at the same time, John had no access to employment at TAE, Inc.

Mina was worried that Madeleine would never have ample funds to pay back the loan and put away for savings. Edison was aware of the predicament but not loving enough to write his daughter and help her. Finally, after considerable pleading, Mina convinced Edison to pay their daughter's loan. When Madeleine grumbled about the drawn-out ordeal, Mina defended her husband: "Madeleine, don't feel that he is not caring for you and looking out for you because he is." But in Madeleine's mind, her father was unkind. Edison watched John have great difficulty locating a job while there were countless jobs at TAE, Inc. Mina refused to see the stinginess in her husband.[8]

Madeleine watched as Charles and Theodore were both gainfully employed at the lab; neither of her brothers ever needed to borrow money from their father. Neither had children, and both spent money on items of their liking. As Charles rose in his father's business, he and Carolyn decided to build a home in Llewellyn Park, within walking distance of Glenmont. Built with limestone blocks from a quarry in Sussex County, the house, called Landmore, sat on six acres of land and had twenty-two rooms. The house was for Mina's benefit; it placated her, and she could tell her friends that Charles and Carolyn preferred to live near her.

The couple enjoyed the city nightlife and would often dance at the clubs and enjoy late dinners. Charles adored Carolyn and was a romantic husband throughout their life together. He would surprise her with poems accompanied by minks, gifts of cash to go shopping, and parties in her honor. Emotionally, Charles was nothing like his father. Like many children, he went out of his way to do the exact opposite of what he observed growing up.

Theodore was not like Charles. Charles wanted to be associated with the Goliaths of the world; however, Theodore was firmly on the side of David. Bookish and environmentally forward, he and Ann enjoyed traveling to what was, at the time, less-glamorous and undeveloped areas such as Yellowstone, Grand Teton, and Crater Lake. They did not enjoy going to clubs and dancing, which was all the rave in the 1920s. They instead stayed home and organized books in their many bookcases. Ann proved to be exceptionally intelligent, and she sometimes worked with Theodore on his experiments. With Ann's interest in science and her ultimate choice to become a pharmacist, raising children was of no interest. She and Theodore advocated for zero-population growth.

By the time Theodore joined the ranks at TAE, Inc., Charles had worked there for almost a decade. Having gotten his lively spirit and yen for travel out of his system, Theodore arrived at work motivated. Soon, he learned that many Edison employees had less zeal for Edison, and many were looking for better jobs. As the years waned, Charles climbed the ladder and took over much of the management portion of the industry. He was essentially in charge of the staff and attempted to drag Thomas Edison, Inc. into the modern age. Unfortunately, Edison was nearly but not entirely deaf and had difficulty hearing recording artists. However, he remained actively involved in the business side throughout the 1920s. But by the very end of that decade, the charge of the once-booming phonograph business had to pass down to Charles.

Edison was concerned about the financial woes that hit the country after the war. Needing to assert his authority over his company, he arbitrarily fired seven thousand of his ten thousand employees. The dismissing of personnel had devastating effects on the general morale of the company. Charles often had to put out administrative fires and was furious with the decision. People who had worked for Edison at that time said that Edison was "rotten, he was an SOB." Charles and Theodore faced significant conflict working for Edison. The disagreements were often heated, and these debates often led to Mina running interference. She was now in a complicated situation, caught between her ill-tempered husband, who refused to relinquish control, and her young, thoughtful sons, who were trying to steer TAE, Inc.'s future in the right direction.[9]

As all of Mina's life was marked and often interrupted by Edison's various inventions, her last married years with her husband would revolve around rubber research. Edison had no desire to retire, and he needed another innovation to focus his mind. His last major research campaign became finding another source of natural rubber. He, Ford, and Firestone were concerned about America's dependence on foreign rubber sources for its industrial enterprises. The three men formed the Edison Botanic Research Corporation and built a laboratory in Fort Myers. With Edison's leadership, he sought a source of rubber that could be grown and produced quickly in the event of a foreign supply shortage. He spent the rest of his working days testing more than seventeen thousand plant samples.

Before Mina and Edison returned to West Orange from their annual Fort Myers trip, she warned her sons of Edison's simmering rage: "Father is a little worried and upset over things, just know, So just let him get settled and realize that [it] is not your work that is annoying to him . . . but his experiments in rubber. It might make him irritable and critical so just understand and if anything does seem amiss, be and know it will pass." His mood would not lighten. Mina was fearful of what could transpire between her eighty-one-year-old husband and his sons. Their ideas and understanding of society's needs and the business were divergent. There were never open lines of communication about goals, nor were there clear boundaries between father and sons.[10]

The time had arrived when Charles could no longer tolerate a father who would not cede his reign. Charles decided to write a note threatening suicide if his father did not relinquish control. Charles's anxiety exceeded any prior experiences with his father, which caused him to write four drafts of the suicide note. One was in Charles's hand; one he had his friend and assistant, Charles Sumner Williams, write; and two of them he typed. The notes were heart-wrenching:

> *I hope sixteen years of service to you and your interests will grant me the privilege of speaking to you frankly. . . . Your son Charles is no longer a boy. Although not yet forty, he has worn himself gray in your service. His unswerving loyalty to you through the blackest of days has been a rare and admirable thing. . . . If you force him to obey you, he is through. He is in a condition of such despair that I am afraid of suicide. . . . You are too great of a man to fail him when he needs you most at this critical moment in his independent career. I urge you from my soul to let him fight out his battle if it means sweeping away all you have done.[11]*

Still fearful of his father, Charles signed it with his friend's name and added, "Charles does not know I am writing this." Dragging his mother down with his pain, he showed her all four letters. In turn, Mina showed them to her extraordinarily methodical and rational son and daughter-in-law, Theodore and Ann. Ann was wise beyond her years and did not venture into the hornet's nest. Theodore, who knew all the characters and had been planning his own exit plan, commented that it "was written like a man" and sounded "earnest." There is no proof that Edison read the letter or even knew it existed, but he eventually relinquished control of the company to Charles.[12]

The annual famed and highly publicized Edison, Ford, and Firestone camping trips did include the wives in 1920. The trip took on a more formal tone. Clara Ford brought along a cook, Mina a personal maid and chauffeur, and Idabelle Firestone brought a butler and a driver. Harvey Firestone Jr. also took along riding horses. Ford didn't like the change. All of the time Edison spent with Ford became grueling on Mina. She barely tolerated Henry Ford and found him ostentatious. They visited their home in Michigan, which Mina felt was an overly fancy and expensive home purchased just for excess.

Ford, however, knew of Mina's dislike and tried to appease her angry feelings toward him. The usual way he did this was by buying automobiles for those who did not like him. Ford was so wealthy the gifts meant practically nothing to his bottom line, yet they seemed overly magnanimous to the receivers. Ford had given Edison many cars, and he sent a blue to one Mina with every possible upgrade invented. Instead, in a passive-aggressive way, Mina claimed that the car he sent her made a terrible noise and that she did not ride in it because it rattled so much. Ford sent his mechanic to Glenmont to fix the noise, but he could not find anything wrong. Mina still claimed to hear the rattling after they looked at the car. His "engineers swore to him that every car rattled a little," but nothing was wrong with it. So, he sent the car back and promised to send her a new one if this one was unpleasant to drive in. Mina did not respond.[13]

The following year she complained to Ford that she wanted the car painted a particular shade of blue. A month after receiving the vehicle, Mina continued to badger the painters to mix the paint until the color suited her.

What did give Mina much pleasure was reviving her years as a princess of Chautauqua. Her civic involvement was one of the few areas where Mina felt confident and proved competent. Her community involvement in Fort Myers demonstrated leadership on her part. Mina successfully convinced the town's mayors, council members, and the county to work on civic reforms, including renovating local railroads, establishing parks, and fixing roadways.

Recently elected a board of trustee member at Chautauqua, she spent copious time creating a garden behind her father's cottage, and at Miller Park, another area named after her father at the institution. Mina had an intense love of birds and flora, and she wanted the surrounding atmosphere to have both. She invested time and money and, with a heavy hand, made sure her father's Chautauqua cottage and surrounding atmosphere would be preserved. Edison joined her in Chautauqua, commemorating the hundredth anniversary of her father's birth in July 1929. Mina was pleased with the success; she felt triumphant. Unfortunately, although Edison had acquiesced to being part of the fanfare, his poor health could not withstand the hype. Edison contracted pneumonia and was bedridden for three weeks upon returning to Glenmont.[14]

He needed to recover because he and Mina were off once again to other events. This time was Ford's tribute to Edison, which he called his Lights Golden Jubilee. The event began as a celebration organized by the General Electric Company with which Ford subsequently became connected, and he took over much of the planning, including moving the main celebration from General Electric headquarters in Schenectady to Dearborn. Against Mina's wishes, Henry Ford had Edison's Florida lab shipped to Greenfield Village, Michigan, where he was creating a museum, which opened during the fiftieth anniversary of the invention of Edison's electric light in 1929. Ford used his friendship with Edison as leverage to publicize his name and his business. Ford had unlimited money and loved showing it off; he made an elaborate celebration in honor of his hero and friend. The event received national media attention and was even attended by President Herbert Hoover. The guest list also included renowned scientists, inventors, business leaders, celebrities, politicians, and family and personal acquaintances of Edison. Among the guests were aviation pioneer Orville Wright and humorist Will Rogers.

Mina knew the big event would take a toll on Edison. Before the event, she confided in Grace, "it will be heavenly when everything becomes regular again." Mina had no desire to attend and relive one of her dark periods: "I am not the frame of mind to be with anyone right now; I should be a hermit."[15]

Along with President Hoover and Ford and their wives, Edison and Mina arrived by train with hundreds of fans awaiting them. Five hundred guests attended the sumptuous dinner, including politicians, celebrities, and business leaders such as Marie Curie; John Rockefeller; George Eastman; Charles Schwab; and William, Tom Jr., and their spouses. Marion did not attend. Edison's health, however, had declined to the point that he could not stay for the entire ceremony.

Edison thanked the audience with a short but scripted speech that Charles wrote for the occasion. Mina realized her husband's frail body was exhausted by the pomp and needed rest. They left the ceremony before hearing the president's address.

Back at Glenmont, Theodore became frustrated with his work at TAE, Inc. He was intelligent enough to work independently and did not need to take instruction from his flamboyant brother Charles. By 1929, the Great Depression had shut down the phonograph business, and his father was working on rubber experiments between bouts of what he claimed was indigestion, yet the countless doctors who examined him knew it was chronic diabetic gastroparesis.

In the Edison family manner, rather than confronting a person to their face, Theodore wrote a letter to Charles. He wanted to resign as a company director. Self-aware, he added, "I am so built that I can help bring a great deal of humanity into my business decisions." He further felt that it makes him "unfit to have an executive position . . . I feel strongly that it can be demonstrated that successful business and humanity are not compatible." He said he would want his own company and would name it Calibron, then added, "you need have no fear of any abuse of the name Edison."[16]

Mina was frightened to discuss the news with her husband. It harkened back to the days when his other sons were trying to break out on their own. Using Edison's name or not, Edison's imperviousness, especially at this age, was full of wrath. Mina could not see that Theodore marched to the beat of his own drum. Madeleine described him as "a square peg in the round hole." He never felt comfortable with his family's ways of being enmeshed in their world and goals when he was growing up. Naturally, he gravitated toward low-key and sensitive environments that his family could not provide, and he often connected with nature, animals, and the staff rather than the principals.[17]

Ann, ever supportive of her husband, formed a united front, telling Mina that "children with forceful and distinct personalities and abilities as your three must fulfill their ambitions each in their way." Mina lamented about the news and wrote Charles, "I am so sorry that you two could not be the team as dreamed."[18]

The local news got hold of the severing of Edison's ties. But for all Theodore's sensitivity, he was shrewd enough to have a prepared statement for the press when they descended: "My interest in the new company does not affect my connection with Edison Industries." Furthermore, after hearing his father's response, he enthusiastically wrote back to his mother, showing his new company's letterhead, and informed her of his first products. Theodore suffered no loss in ending his father's dream. Only Mina bought into Edison's guilt.[19]

All six Edison children were in an unusually relatively relaxed state. Edison bought Marion a trailer in Connecticut that even Mina visited once. Aging on her own, Marion had her bouts of physical maladies, yet she tried not to complain too much for fear of being jettisoned from the family.

Edison's advanced age softened him, and he hired Tom Jr. for small tasks at TAE, Inc., such as testing electric toasters for Edicraft, a subsidiary of TAE, Inc. The job was insignificant, and his chronic head troubles did not interfere with the work. William and his wife were infrequently in touch with Mina, often sending her fresh produce from their farm. Edison was not as attentive or interested in their personal needs.

Theodore, now on his own, was feeling vigorous and productive. Madeleine had her house loan paid off, and John was working for the stockbroking firm of Edward B. Smith & Co. in New York. They were beginning to live more comfortably. Charles, the prince, dutifully took the punches while climbing the ladder without falling off. He became chairman of the Board of Directors of Thomas A. Edison, Inc. in June 1916, vice president and general manager in January 1919, and president in August 1926. He was also a director and officer in numerous Edison-owned companies, including the Edison Storage Battery Co. and Edison Portland Cement Company.

Although there was relative calm among the children, they all knew their father could not survive much longer living on a milk diet and ignoring his doctor's instructions. In January 1931, Edison and Mina traveled to Fort Myers so he could work on his beloved rubber experiments, but they returned by June, and Edison had much of what he was working on shipped back north to New Jersey. He returned exhausted and was in bed for a few days. He finally got the strength to return to his lab and worked as long as possible.

In late July, Edison collapsed at home in his chair. Mina had his doctor arrive on a chartered plane from his vacation on Long Island, then escorted by police to Glenmont. Mina then telegrammed Madeleine that Edison was ill, but that the immediate danger had passed.

During the summer, Madeleine, Charles, and Theodore took turns visiting their father. By fall, Edison's body was giving in. The doctors brought in an oxygen mask, but Edison refused to use it.

Although Mina would not allow any newspapermen near the house, the Edison garage became the de-facto press room for journalists. Charles and his doctors gave daily bulletins about his progress. By October, President Hoover and other prominent men were sending their offers of prayers.

While the children took breaks walking around the estate's gardens, Mina never left his bedside. When the doctors and Mina noticed Edison's breathing turning shallow, she invited his first three children to Glenmont. The next day, after drifting in and out of consciousness, Edison died. The most famous and prolific inventor of all time was gone; Mina was now going to demonstrate what it meant to be a dutiful wife to the entire world.

A month before Edison's death, Mina sat down with Madeleine, Charles, and Theodore and discussed various matters about Edison's funeral. Detailed and copious notes were made, so nothing was left to chance. Assistants were assigned tasks and could not deviate from their assignments.

Edison would lie in state in the laboratory library for two days. Mina designated times for colleagues to view him one last time. Afterward, his adoring public would be allowed to pay their respects. Mina had specific rules about who was allowed to enter the lab. No one under the age of fourteen without an accompanying parent could attend, and no one could be intoxicated.

Mina was concerned with other various particulars. She wanted to choose the finest casket from three selected by the funeral director. Mina did not have Edison buried deeply; she wanted him close to the earth's surface.

When friends inquired, she wanted Mame, Grace, or Ann to review each visitor. The front door would be closed at all times. Friends would come in through the porch or around the conservatory and then enter the drawing room. The front hall was accessible only for the immediate family. Other assistants would be in charge of condolences and flowers sent to the home. The choice flowers would stay at home; the others would be sent to the laboratory.

Men from the laboratory, business friends, and those from engineering societies who wanted to pay their respects would only be allowed to do so at the laboratory. The library at the laboratory was decorated appropriately, and the American flag was kept at half-mast. President Hoover asked the citizens of the United States to remember Edison by dimming the lights at 10 p.m. across the nation.

Edison's body returned to Glenmont for a private service in which Mina selected the hymns, prayers, and music. The pastor from Mina's beloved Orange Methodist Church read a psalm. The most important aspect was the seating arrangement, which Mina altered after seeing Charles's first version. Mina organized three rows of seats for those she considered immediate family members. The first row included Mina, Madeleine, Theodore, Charles, and then Tom Jr. The second row included Marion, William, Blanche, Carolyn, and Beatrice. The last row included Ann, John Sloane, Florence, Mina's brother John, and Edison's cousin Edith.

After close to four hundred mourners left the funeral service, Mina permitted the Fords, the Firestones, and President Hoover to join the family as they proceeded to Rosedale Cemetery for the burial. As a final farewell, each person dropped a single white rose into Edison's grave.

Mina's meticulously orchestrated formality and sadness were now concluded. The tears and downcast faces would slowly transform into eager and impatient ones when the lawyers read the Edison will aloud to the children. Mina knew she was not mentioned in the will; Edison had made prior ample provisions for her through various stocks and real estate. Charles and Theodore, however, were made executors of the estate. They were privy to their father's opinions and judgments about his six children, but they were so wrapped up in their own importance that they did not expect the disaster that would ensue.

Eighty percent of Edison's $12 million estate ($219 million in today's money) was divided between Charles and Theodore. A few of Edison's trusted employees received cash gifts. The remaining sum was distributed equally between Madeleine, Marion, Tom Jr., and William.[20]

The shafted children were livid. William led the angry crowd and headed straight to the press to smear his father's name. Headlines read that the two branches of the Edison family were on the "Brink of Contest." William vowed to go to court to fight the will. He told every paper that would listen to him that his stepmother had unduly influenced his father.[21]

Furthermore, the papers wrote that Edison had made no bequests to science, charity, art, or education. Again, over thirty thousand newspapers picked up the story, spreading the scandal across the world. This time, however, Edison could no longer have the last word to defend himself.

William, forever reckless and headstrong, was ready to contest the will in court. He prepared to face an uphill battle against Charles to get what he believed was his rightful portion of the estate, and he did not care if the legal costs would outweigh his gain. Instead, he wanted to shout to the world that Mina and Charles were involved in coercion and had abused his father's diminished mental capacity.

Initially, Madeleine, Marion, and Tom Jr. planned to join in the suit, but they eventually decided to let William fight the battle against Charles and Mina alone. Within weeks, Marion told Mina that she believed she was no longer allowed to visit Glenmont once her father died, yet Mina surprised her and invited her at the last minute for Thanksgiving. Marion further said that she did not have the same nature as William and she did not intend to contest the will. Tom Jr., appreciating that he had recently been allowed back into the family fold, did not want to make waves. Still damaged from his mother's death and his father's abuse, he desperately craved Mina's droplets of affection more than the money.[22]

Madeleine, on the other hand, had a more formidable core. She had already fought her parents and won. Although she did not take the news well, Madeleine knew better than to air her grievance in public. On the back of a business envelope, however, she unloaded her thoughts. The memo was not addressed. The contents suggested that Madeleine had urgent questions that she wanted her mother to answer: "Why should Aunt Mame tell Marion 2 years ago that no one would get anything but Chas. and Theodore? Did Father discuss the will with Charles?" Madeleine did not comprehend why Charles was getting a salary from TAE, Inc., a fee for being an executor, other prior gifts, and was still receiving more than the others from the estate. Her father knew she needed money more than her brothers; her expenses far exceeded theirs. Madeleine had just given them their fourth and final grandchild that same year. Her reflections on her predicament were solidified and clarified, and she wrote down more of her ideas. Theodore had once told her he and Charles were "worth a million dollars"; Madeleine now understood her brothers had known all along what was coming to them. Madeleine now understood her mother had stood by, knowing that from beyond the grave, Edison would punish her again for marrying John. As an adult, Madeleine realized that her Methodist upbringing had indoctrinated Mina to be loyal to her man and never fail him. That was the measure of a good woman. It now was clear to Madeleine that she was and always would be secondary.[23]

The grief and mortification paralyzed Mina. Her Christian fortitude could not withstand the embarrassment. William was erasing all the hard work she had done in her life to perfect the Edison name. Utterly unable to cope with the situation, she remained in her home for days and refused to leave or show her face to anyone. She could not even grasp her own feelings. Edison had defined her entire being; she went from girlhood directly to becoming Mrs. Edison. For the first time in forty-four years, Mina had to make decisions on her own without consulting Edison.

In the wake of the chaos, Mina could not muster the strength to rise and confront the world. Despite all the women around her who had developed into solid, independent thinkers, Mina was still firmly planted in the past. Not knowing where to turn, Mina "wished she could go backward." In her suffering, she prayed for "wisdom" and what she deemed as "right thinking." Finally, feeling weak and unprotected, Mina, "always afraid of hurting the Edison name," abandoned her family for Christmas and sailed to Puerto Rico to be with her ever-trustworthy and steadfast supporter Louise.[24]

Epilogue
After Edison

UPON MINA'S RETURN TO NEW JERSEY, WILLIAM'S ENRAGED REMARKS were still fodder for journalist stories repeated in hundreds of papers. A hot-tempered lawsuit between the Edison children on the front pages of newspapers would push Mina toward a nervous breakdown. It had become vital that Charles control the negative publicity. He owed his mother as much. Smug and pretentious, Charles considered William as lesser than and treated him as such. Knowing he was far more worldly and educated than his impetuous half-brother, he manipulated him to drop the lawsuit.

Edison did not distribute his estate equally; he did not consider his children equal. William, Marion, Madeleine, and Tom Jr. were to receive money in trust from the Cement Company—$50,000 a year ($900,000 in today's money). This was considerably less than Charles and Theodore's share and not a direct cash distribution. Before the children received any actual cash, years of various business transactions had to occur. Charles had to explain this and various other legal matters to William, Tom Jr., and Marion. Charles had mastered a pretentious demeanor from his relations with past girlfriends and numerous business dealings. He now used it to cow his half-siblings, informing them he considered it "good judgment" to accept the conditions of the will. After much back and forth, William was finally placated, dropped the suit, and patiently waited for the money.[1]

Madeleine did not intend to sit tight and wait like her half-siblings were doing. She realized that stock meant cash once it could be liquidated. She continued to write Charles in the following years, often contentiously, about the best way to secure the money for her family. These disagreeable negotiations transformed Charles's relationship with Madeleine for the rest of their lives. For Mina's sake, they were civil and agreed to be in the same house on holidays, but the days of going out for dinner together and dancing were over.[2]

Charles, Madeleine, and Theodore knew the bickering over the will disturbed Mina. They tried their best to keep the arguing out of her purview. Although rich from his recent windfall, Theodore preferred not to quibble with siblings and allowed Charles to negotiate. He was so disgusted with the quarreling that he told Mina she should not leave him any money in her will. If she insisted, he would be giving it all to Edison employees whom he thought had been grossly underpaid by his father. In his own will, Theodore, a man of his word, later left the employees $1 million ($12 million in today's money).

During her time away with Louise, Mina felt shielded. Unlike Grace and Mame, Louise did not have the baggage of growing up in the Miller household. But as a sister-in-law, she knew the inner workings of Mina's upbringing and could respond to Mina's fears and lift her spirits. Louise was a strong, self-aware widow who was compassionate enough to understand Mina's insecurities.

Even with Louise's positive affirmations, Mina still said, "It is hard to carry on as I often feel what the use is. It is hard to make myself feel like I am of use to anyone." Forever needing to fill a void and understanding that her children did not need her or want intervention, Mina left New Jersey again, this time for Fort Myers.[3]

Fort Myers was a comfort zone for Mina. She had never shed her Methodist Midwestern roots. She was too timid to cavort in the larger neighboring realms of Palm Beach or Miami, whose affluence and recreational facilities, shops, restaurants, and social scene were more East Coast–centric. Nevertheless, Fort Myers remained small enough for a woman of Mina's sensibilities, and the townsfolk considered her essential there.[4]

Mina had been hesitant to go to Florida alone the winter after Edison died. Still dressed in black, she said, "I can't bear to cast a shadow upon them there." Mina did not understand that those small townspeople

278

viewed her as royalty. Being Mrs. Edison had subsumed her identity. She never believed she had any self-worth without Edison.[5]

Ultimately, Grace spent weeks coaxing her out of her hermit-like shell while in Florida. Once in the familiar milieu of Fort Myers, Mina slowly immersed herself in civic duties. In widowhood, her time was now her own. Mina was no longer yanked around by a cranky and unsociable older man who needed her attention or desired to be left alone to his thoughts. It was difficult for her to adjust to her new reality. Lacking her desire to feel needed, she soon filled her lonely dark period and adopted a grueling schedule. Throughout the next four years, Mina got involved in any civic or beautification program that benefited Fort Myers, Chautauqua, or West Orange.

After gaining her emotional footing, she took on a more relaxed state in her widowhood. She found Fort Myers a congenial society, telling her children that "many fine people are here, and everything seems prosperous and happy." Further, she revealed that an old friend had reentered her life. "Mr. Hughes has made us a visit … he loved it here and wants to come again." Edward Hughes had been a childhood playmate of Mina's. During the 1870s, their families had summer homes in Chautauqua; they had become reacquainted years later when their families began wintering in Florida. Edward Everett Hughes was an attorney and steel manufacturer. Born in Shippensville, Pennsylvania, he practiced law in Franklin, Pennsylvania, serving as city solicitor until 1900, when he turned to the steel business. He became head of the Franklin Steel Co. and was the founder and president of the Rail Steel Bar Association until his retirement in 1930. His first wife, Susan, died in November 1932. They had two adult sons, Charles and Henry.[6]

In the following five months, Mina experienced what it felt like to be courted and appreciated by a man for the first time in her life. She and Edward both loved Florida and had a solid connection to Chautauqua. They spent as much time together as their schedules and families allowed. He would write her letters addressed to "Dearest Sweetheart," and she would respond with "Precious Edward." His love gave her the happiness she'd always craved. She told Theodore, "I am running away and meeting a very, very dear friend of mine—Can you Guess? Well, I have decided that life is pretty sad without him, and he feels the same way about me."[7]

Unfortunately, Mina's blissful, new life was interrupted by another Edison scandal. That summer, Tom Jr. died under strange circumstances in a hotel in Springfield, Massachusetts. He was fifty-nine. Tom Jr. had traveled to East Orange, New Jersey, after visiting Charles's summer estate in New Hampshire. He stopped in Springfield with two companions, H. W. Hildebrand and J. J. Griffin. Tom registered under an assumed name— J. Byrne—ostensibly to avoid the press. Feeling ill upon his arrival, his friends called a doctor to examine him. Tom Jr. died only a few hours later. The death certificate listed the causes as "Coronary Thrombosis, Pulmonary Edema (terminal), Sudden death." He was leading an unhappy life, and recently, Marion had written Mina that his wife, Beatrice, had been cheating on him for more than a decade with his friend Wilson. Tom had demanded that she choose either him or Wilson. Lewis Jr. had the boldness to write his sister Mina that it was "good he could go as he did and not be a burden to you." Tom Jr. left the small remainder of his estate to Madeleine instead of his wife.[8]

Mina did not dwell on Tom Jr.'s death for long. Still glowing from the excitement of Edward entering her life, she announced to her children that they planned to marry in the fall, having found much "contentment" in each other. By that time, the children had met Edward, and they adored him. He provided their mother with a serenity and joy they had rarely witnessed.

On October 30, 1935, the wedding took place at Mina's father's cottage in Chautauqua. Edward then moved into Glenmont. After the ceremony in Chautauqua, the children called him "Daden," and his two sons called her "Mother Mina." She wrote her sister Mary that "Edward and I are happy together, enjoying it all. He is very gentle, thoughtful, understanding, and bright, which chases away all the gloom." Mina's years with Edward could not have been more pleasant. As she explained to her family, they "planned on taking many beautiful drives, reading, walking, golfing, and playing dominos. All are wonderful to us, and we are thanking God constantly for our loved ones and our many blessings."[9]

Mina and Edward spent much of their time at Glenmont in West Orange. Unlike her marriage with Edison, travel was one of their principal joys. In addition to visits to Chautauqua, they traveled widely through the United States and took one extensive trip through Europe, including England, Norway, Sweden, Finland, Russia, and Denmark. Mina kept a detailed diary of this trip abroad, starting the day before they sailed aboard the U.S. *Statendam* in the summer of 1937.

Much like Edison's diary written fifty-two years earlier, Mina's journal was meant for the public rather than having been written as a private document. The journal is a 164-page typed copy, which often reads more like a travel guidebook of the hotels and an epicurean review of the various restaurants in which they dined.

What is clear to its reader is what was essential to Mina on the trip. Regardless of the locale, she commented on the horticulture and often deemed a place worthwhile based on the sumptuousness and upkeep of the blooms. Mina found the English people "most attentive, kind and gracious," a stark contrast to her experience of the French during her trip to Paris with Edison in 1889.[10]

Mina turned seventy-two years old aboard the ship. It was an opportunity for Edward to express how much he loved her and valued the significance of the day. When Mina entered the dining room, Edward had arranged for the orchestra to play "Happy Birthday." In addition, there was a cake waiting at Mina's seat. Aboard the ship, "embarrassed beyond words," Mina stood up in front of everyone and acknowledged the compliment. It was an uncommon feeling for her. Her life with Edison had been filled with her always recognizing her famous husband's birthday, and him rarely, if ever, reciprocating the sentiment.[11]

The trip made Mina introspective. She enjoyed the opera and thought of Marion. She saw a busy mother with children and thought of Madeleine. At other times, she felt a void in her knowledge and wanted to "learn more about nature" when she returned home. At other moments, Mina poignantly realized that "time is short" but she wanted to make her "last years more interesting." She envisioned herself and Edward taking ample time in the future to delve into and study what they experienced on their travels and disregard the busy world around them.[12]

Her time in Norway, Denmark, and Sweden seemed not to elicit much serious contemplation; however, Mina thought they were being watched when she arrived in Russia. She believed there was "a considerable drunkenness" about the men of Russia. She said there was "no order of anything" and noted a "do as you please" lifestyle. Mina remarked about the overwhelming number of poor people waiting in line for stores to open and that there was virtually no middle class. While passing the railroad track, Mina saw women working as hard as men digging dirt. She commented on how devoted everyone was to Stalin. Although she and Edward had the luxury of touring parts of the Kremlin, Stalin himself did not appear to the public. At one point, an impoverished elderly woman approached them on the street for charity, but their guide warned them not to give her money because there was "much work for her." When Mina observed that perhaps she was too old to work, the guide replied, "There are plenty of old people homes for her."[13]

Mina's compassionate side left her with a distaste for Moscow, calling it an "unwholesome dirty city smelling and altogether an unpleasant place to be in." When they arrived by train in Leningrad, they both marveled at the architectural splendor of the czar's former palace. When they crossed the border to Finland a day later, Mina remarked that she felt like she had "escaped prison."[14]

However, most notable about the entire trip in the summer of 1937 was the absence of Mina's awareness of an impending war. It would have been difficult to avoid noticing that the Europeans were in a state of heightened anguish. Essentially everyone was concerned about the depraved arm of Germany eventually entering their country, taking over, and causing an imminent world war.

While on the trip, misfortune hit the Edison family again. After a six-week illness, William Edison died just shy of his sixtieth birthday. Madeleine and John made the day trip to Delaware for the funeral and ensured flowers would be sent. Theodore and Ann also felt obligated to attend. Marion attended the service but left before the burial. There was no record of Charles or Carolyn attending at all. Mina did not come home for the obsequies.

Madeleine notified the press of her mother's return to New Jersey. Having learned from her parents to decide what should be conveyed to the public meticulously, she had the headlines read that her mother found "Russia amazing."[15]

Unfortunately, Mina's bliss did not last long. Edward Hughes died in early 1940, after the couple had spent five happy years together. Mina stayed in touch with his children after he died. Mina, at seventy-four, would live another seven years.[16]

After Edward's death, Mina resumed using the name of Mrs. Thomas A. Edison. She returned to her dutiful days as Edison's wife and toiled hard for the next seven years to preserve her husband's name. She pushed herself so hard that it was as if she needed to make a personal apology to Edison for finding happiness with another man.

Mina ensured that Edison's name would be remembered as the most famous inventor in American history. She spoke of or memorialized his inventions and 1,093 patents in various fields from event to event. In addition, she safeguarded his public image as a homespun, natural genius.

Although Mina was blessed with four grandchildren and three great-grandchildren, she lamented that none had the Edison name. She was crestfallen that neither Charles nor Theodore would fulfill her dream to continue the legacy. Mina would have to build a shrine to her husband all by herself.

Robert Halgrim, a newspaperman and personal friend of Edison's, wanted to create a celebration and living memorial called the *Edison Pageant of Light*. His father owned and operated the Court Theater in Fort Myers. In 1926, when he was twenty-one, he began working for the Edisons. When Mina decided to turn over their Fort Myers home to the city as a museum, he became curator at her request. The irony is that Edison disliked formal and extravagant displays that had no natural substance. On the other hand, Mina needed this pomp to create a façade of happiness and festivities that the world could now link with her husband. It was the ideal repackaging to overlook any prior undesirable associations. The Fort Myers Women's Community Club and other groups enthusiastically helped him develop the mythical Kingdom-of-Edisonia concept. The organization enjoyed putting on a King and Queen's Ball, a Coronation Ball, the Thomas Alva Edison Birthday Party, and an Edison Festival of Light Parade Party. Mina fully embraced and extolled the day, celebrating the inspiring legacy of her husband.

Taking a cue from the enthusiasm of the Florida residents the following year, Mina conceived of building an Edison memorial library
and museum to honor her late husband's memory and provide a valuable resource to the town. By 1941, she had hired architect William E.
Frenaye Jr. of Howard & Frenaye to draw up specifications and selected
the contractors. The site would contain a library, art gallery, music rooms,
and cloisters, and it was built on the site of the Edison rubber laboratory
across the street from their home in Fort Myers. Unfortunately, the coming of World War II interrupted Mina's plans, and financial constraints
prevented Mina from carrying on the work after the war.[17]

The following year, Mina christened a destroyer, the *Edison*, at a ceremony in Brooklyn's Navy Yard. The following January, during Charles's
inauguration as governor in Trenton, she revisited the destroyer with him
for a photo opportunity.

In 1946, the Thomas Alva Edison Foundation was formed "to advance
education and scientific research," and Mina became its honorary chairman. In another move to help perpetuate the name and fame of Edison,
in 1947, she deeded Seminole Lodge, the Edison winter home for sixty-
one years, to the City of Fort Myers as a botanical garden and memorial
to her husband.[18]

Mina and Madeleine decided to also make Edison's birthplace a
memorial to the public. The museum became Madeleine and Mina's
joint project. She restored his birthplace in Milan, Ohio, into the Edison
Birthplace Museum, which opened on the centennial of the inventor's
birth in 1947.

What Mina lacked emotionally, she made up for in physical stamina.
All her siblings predeceased her save for her sister Grace. She attended
the funerals of all her siblings. Ira died in 1934, as did Edward while he
and his wife were on an extended vacation in 1936. In the following years,
Louise died in 1937. Then Lewis Jr. and John both died in 1940. Lastly, in
1946, her beloved sister Mame died.[19]

On July 16, 1947, Mina entered Columbia Presbyterian hospital with
a weakened heart. Time was running out for Mina. On Sunday, August
24, 1947, she died at the age of eighty-two at the Harkness Pavilion
of the Columbia-Presbyterian Medical Center in New York City after

an eight-day illness. At her bedside when she died were her children, Charles, Madeleine, and Theodore, and their spouses.

That was the last day of the Chautauqua season in 1947. Her beloved Chautauqua Amphitheater, where she'd grown up, prayed, sang, and even spoke from the pulpit, was filled with seven thousand devotees for the sacred song service that closed the session for the season. A tradition that Mina started had been to close the session with the song "Abide with Me."

Charles sent a telegram to Chautauqua the following day, and the personal grief was palpable as the news spread through the grounds of its residents. They knew that Mina Miller Edison not only cared about Chautauqua with her soul, but she also served it with her wallet, her actions, and her presence.

Throughout her lifetime, Mina gave unsparingly of her time, talents, and money to institutions and activities memorializing Edison. The four homes lived in by Mina are recognized for their historical importance: Oak Place in Akron and Miller Cottage in Chautauqua honor her father, Lewis Miller, and Seminole Lodge in Fort Myers honors Edison. "My faith and belief in the sincerity of the people of Fort Myers prompt me to make this sacred spot a gift to you and posterity . . . in the memory of my honored and revered husband," she said at its dedication. In addition, Mina deeded Glenmont to Thomas Alva Edison, Inc., understanding that the house would become a memorial to Edison after her death. A year after Mina died, Charles ensured that the West Orange laboratory was turned into a museum, and in 1955, Charles donated the mansion and the lab to the National Park Service.[20]

Mina was buried next to Edison in a large plot in Rosedale Cemetery. Sixteen years later, their remains were reburied at Glenmont as the one last scheme to exalt the couple together in perpetuity. The transfer was carried out with the blessing of the Edison children's families.

Mina was a performer. She portrayed an ideal image of Edison for so long that one could no longer distinguish the façade from reality. The veneer became her truth. Indeed, her identification with him was so complete that Mina said she never actually had a life of her own, but "it has been worth everything I could give—worth it a thousand times over."[21]

Postscript

The Children of Thomas Edison

After his father's death, Charles Edison unilaterally assumed the role of the patriarch. In 1937, he took an extended leave of absence from TAE, Inc. to serve as assistant secretary (and later secretary) of the navy in the administration of Franklin D. Roosevelt. After resigning from the cabinet in June 1940, he used his political savvy to run a successful campaign for governor of New Jersey. He promoted to revise the state's antiquated constitution during his single term, though this was not accomplished during his tenure. After leaving office in 1943, he returned to TAE, Inc. and served as its president until May 1950, then he became chairman of the Board of Directors. After the company merged with McGraw Electric Co. in 1957, Charles served as chairman of the McGraw-Edison Co. until his retirement in 1961. He lived at the Waldorf Towers in New York City during the last two decades of his life and became close friends with former President Herbert Hoover, a fellow resident at the hotel.

After her payout from her father's will and John's rise as an investment banker in New York, Madeleine eventually had enough money to move into a home in Llewellyn Park. As a result, her four sons grew up with all the advantages wealth provided. Her oldest son, Thomas Edison Sloane, attended Phillips Exeter Academy and then enrolled at Yale, graduating in 1938. On February 19, 1938, while still attending Yale, he secretly married Elaine Bernice Levy of New Haven. The wedding was not revealed until after he graduated, perhaps because the bride was Jewish. However, Mina had been more forgiving of the difficulty the intermarriage presented to the family and told her son Theodore to "try to see his point of view and be a true uncle to him, not critical." The couple had two children, Thomas Edison Sloane Jr., born in 1940, and David Edward Edison Sloane, born in 1943.[1]

Madeleine's second son, John Edison Sloane, affectionately called Jack, also attended Phillips Exeter Academy and Yale University and served during World War II with the 102nd Calvary in England, Africa, and Italy, attaining the rank of captain. After the war, he lived in Pittsburgh and worked for Westinghouse. He later got a job as head of public relations at TAE, Inc. He married Jule Day on May 27, 1942, just a few days after being commissioned as a second lieutenant in the U.S. Army. However, Jule's upbringing was more fitting for the family. She graduated from Holy Child and Rosemont College and was a member of the Junior League. They had three children: Madeleine E., called "Madalee," who was born in 1946; John Heywood, called "Heywood," born in 1948; and Christopher Barry, called "Barry," born in 1960.[2]

As a newborn, Madeleine's third son, Peter Edison Sloane, was called "Peter Rabbit" by his grandmother Mina. Peter attended Phillips Exeter Academy, graduated from Yale, and was a frequent Fort Myers visitor during the 1930s. During World War II, he served in the military. After the war, Peter became a professor of economics at Clark University in Worcester, Massachusetts. He married twice, first to Edith Staiger on May 13, 1949. Although quite attractive, Edith was a stenographer from the Bronx. The papers described the match as a "1949 Cinderella Eyes an Edison." He had one daughter by his first marriage, Lizabeth, in 1956, but the marriage did not last. He married Barbara Blais Milford on July 14, 1965, and had one son with her, Michael Blais, born in 1966.[3]

Madeleine's youngest son, Michael Nicholas Samuel Edison Sloane, was born the same year Edison died. Unfortunately, at the age of seventeen, he died from exposure and blood loss after a fall while mountain climbing in Austria. He had been vacationing in Europe with his parents and decided to remain there after Madeleine and John returned home. Michael had suffered from chronic depression, and some family members thought the fall might actually have been suicide.

Theodore and Ann happily enjoyed their life of intellectual and environmental pursuits. Theodore became an ardent environmentalist, helping to preserve Corkscrew Swamp Sanctuary, a National Audubon Society sanctuary located in southwest Florida. Ann earned a bachelor's degree from the New Jersey College of Pharmacy in 1937. Rewarded for her talents and hard work, she received the New Jersey Pharmaceutical Association Prize in practical pharmacy. She also earned a master's degree in public health at Columbia University during the 1950s. She eventually became a registered pharmacist and worked at the Merck Institute for Therapeutic Research in Rahway.

ACKNOWLEDGMENTS

WRITING A BOOK IS MORE REWARDING THAN I EVER IMAGINED. DOING so would have been possible only with the support of three brilliant men with whom I have had the privilege of working and learning from over the past seventeen years. First and foremost, I am thankful for the assistance and support of Dr. Paul Israel, the director and general editor of the Thomas A. Edison Papers Project at Rutgers University. I feel very grateful to have had the opportunity to work with Paul, who is the world's leading expert on Thomas Edison. He has been an ever-so-patient mentor to me as I thought through and asked him questions about the narrative of Mina and the family. He also gave my manuscript a full scholarly review. I truly appreciate all the valuable skills I have learned from him over the past years. I am also indebted to Dr. Louis Carlat, the associate editor of the Thomas Edison Papers Project, who helped me with my narrative and endnotes, and whom I forced to listen to all foibles of the Edison family as they unfolded in my research.

Additionally, I am forever indebted to Dan Weeks, the assistant editor of the Thomas Edison Papers Project, for the book's title, among other countless suggestions and edits. When I decided to write this book, I bombarded him with numerous questions, concerns, hopes, anger, and other emotions that come into an author's head when writing a book. I would also like to thank Thomas Jeffries, an emeritus editor of the Thomas Edison Papers Project, for his encyclopedic knowledge of the Edison and Miller families and for graciously answering all my questions while I was conducting research for the book. Last but not least, I want to thank Rachel Weissenburger, the former office manager of the Thomas Edison Papers Project, for her constant support throughout the entire writing process.

I also want to thank my literary agent, Jaqueline Flynn of Joelle Delbourgo Literary Associates, who made things happen and gave me her invaluable advice and assistance in writing this book.

Next, I want to thank Lyons Press for publishing this book. I would particularly like to thank Rick Reinhart and Brittany Stoner at Lyons Press, for their expertise and time on this book and their patience in bringing it to print.

I also have to thank my remarkable friend Belinda Ehrlich, who happens to be a crackerjack copy editor, for editing early drafts of this book. As I introduced her to stories of the Edison and Miller families, she not only elevated my early prose but kept me on track with what was essential and intriguing about the family. Moreover, she kept me sane throughout the long, arduous journey. Thank you so much.

I am also so grateful to Michelle Albion, who sent me her well-organized research from her previous books on the Edisons and spoke to me at length on several occasions, when we analyzed Mina and her relationship with Edison.

There are three essential archives where I accessed much correspondence and all the letters of Mina Miller Edison. First and foremost, the Thomas Edison Historical Park staff assisted me in my research. They helped me expand my knowledge of the Edison family: Thomas Ross (superintendent), Lenny DeGraff (archivist), Michelle Mihalkovitz (supervisory museum curator), and Beth Miller (curator of Glenmont). I am also grateful to Jon Schmitz, the archivist at the Oliver Archive at the Chautauqua Institution. Finally, Brent Newman (chief curator) and Matthew Andres (registrar and archivist) were so helpful in all my research at the Edison & Ford Winter Estates in Fort Myers. Finally, I am also very grateful to Rita DeMatteo, the archivist at the Llewellyn Park Historical Society.

I want to thank Lewis Smiler, a fantastic researcher in his own right, who aided in my research and organized my work in many valuable ways.

Also, I am deeply grateful to Ted and Nancy Arnn (Pittsburgh, Pennsylvania) for generous access to the Miller family correspondence before it was accessioned by the Chautauqua Institution and to David E. E. Sloane (New Haven, Connecticut) for generous access to other family correspondence and documents. Dr. David Sloane gave the Thomas Edison Papers Project access to his private collection. And a special shout-out to John

Keegan, chairman and president of the Charles Edison Fund, for giving me access to the collection in Newark.

Finally, thanks go to my family; my husband, David; and my children, Zach, Dalya, and Jacob. They were patient with me these past years when I said I had to work. In their unique ways, each encouraged me to continue during the most challenging times. However, they also knew to tell me to stop working, to pay attention to them, or to get outside for some fresh air. I love all of you very much; without you, this book would have been finished ten years earlier.

SOURCE NOTES

Frequent correspondents are abbreviated as follows:

Mina Miller Edison MME

Thomas Alva Edison TAE

Madeline Edison Sloane MES

Charles Edison CE

Theodore Miller Edison TME

Marion Edison Oeser MEO

Thomas Edison Jr. TEJ

William Leslie Edison WLE

Grace Miller Hitchcock GMH

Mary (Mame) Miller Nichols MMN

Lewis Miller LM

Mary Valinda Miller MVM

Jennie Miller Marvin JMM

Edward Miller EM

Ira Miller IM

Louise Igoe Miller LIM

Robert Miller RM

Lewis Alexander Miller LAM

Notes

Chapter 1: SECRETS AND COURTSHIPS

1. *The Boston Directory* (1885), 450; *Pond* (1930), 54–68, 112–29, 142, Chap. 12.

2. *GMO*, s.v. "Emery, Stephen Albert"; Paul Israel et al., eds., *The Papers of Thomas A. Edison* (book edition) (TAEB), 9 vols. (Baltimore, 1989–2021), 8:163; *Hendrick* (1925), 103–104.

3. *Hendrick* (1925), 103–104.

4. *TAEB* 8:164, 191–92; "Local Notes," *The Summit County Beacon*, 7 May 1884, 7; JMM to MME, 27 Jul. 1877; 28 Mar. 1878; 19 Apr. 1878; 6 Jul. 1878. CEF.

5. MVM to MME, 20 Nov. 1883; MME to GMH, 23 Mar. 1884, CEF.

6. *TAEB* 8:164, 182; *ANB*, s.v. "Vincent, George Edgar," 22.

7. *ANB*, s.v. "Vincent, George Edgar," 22; *TAEB* 8:164, 694; U.S. Dept. of State (n.d.), Roll 2405, George Edgar Vincent, Passport Certificates: 359850-360349, issued 21 Dec. 1923–24.

8. George Vincent to Elizabeth Vincent (undated, 1885); MVM to MME, 16 Apr. 1885, CEF.

9. MVM to MME, 16 Apr. 1884, CEF.

10. MVM to MME, 16 Apr. 1884, CEF.

11. JMM to MME, 27 Jul. 1877, 15 Sept. 1879, and n.d. JMM to MVM, 21 Nov. and 17 Dec. 1885. CEF.

12. *Hendrick* (1925), 83–85.

13. MVM to MME, 20 Jul. 1884, 10 Nov. 1884 CEF; 16 Apr. and 26 Apr. 1885, 25 Jul. 1886, CEF.

14. John Heyl Vincent to MME, n.d., and 22 Oct., 23 Jan., 23 Dec. 1881; 24 Jan. 1883, CEF.

15. *Tarbell* (1939), 64–88.

16. John Heyl Vincent to Elizabeth Vincent, 4 Sept. 1883, TxDaM-P.

17. MVM to MME, 10 Feb., 31 Oct., 30 Nov., 4 Dec. 1884; CEF.

18. MVM to MME, 25 Oct. 1884; 7 Jun. 1884, CEF; TAEB 8: xxv–xxvi; 20; *Israel* 1998, 28–35.

19. *Israel* (1998), 52, 118, 122–23; Lemelson Center, The Lemelson Center for the Study of Invention & Innovation, "Electric Pen," Thomas A. Edison Papers, http://edison.rutgers.edu/pen.htm; Emily Glynn-Farrell, "The Irish-American Who Invented the Modern Tattoo Machine," *Irish Times*, 16 Oct. 2018.

20. *TAEB* 8: 148; *TAEB* 7: 620; Marion Edison Oser (1956). "Early Recollections of Mrs. Marion Edison Oser." Typescript of oral history, Edison Biographical Collection, TENHP.

21. *TAEB* 7: 4, 21, 590, 660; LIM to MME, 13 Jan., 4 Apr. 1884; MME to GMH, 24 Jan. 1885; LIM to MME, 8 Feb. and 18 May 1885, MVM to MME, 1 Jul. 1885, EFWE.

22. *TAEB* 8: 165.

23. John Heyl Vincent to TAE, 25, 27 Feb., and 12 Dec. 1878, TENHP.

24. *TAEB* 8: 165, 308.

25. LIM to MME, 8 Feb. and 18 May 1885, MVM to MME, 1 Jul. 1885, EFWE; *TAEB* 8: 308.

26. Marion Edison Oser (1956). "Early Recollections of Mrs. Marion Edison Oser." Typescript of oral history, Box 16, Edison Biographical Collection, TENHP.

27. George Vincent to Elizabeth Vincent, n.d. and 6, 10 Sept. 1885; George Vincent to John Heyl Vincent, 15 Sept. 1885, TxDaM-P.

28. *Hendrick* (1925), 86, 108–13.

29. *Albion* (2008), 12–18, 23–26.

30. *TAEB* 8:148–50, 162–66, 169–98.

31. Ibid., 148.

32. *TAEB* 8:148–50, 162–66, 169–98.

33. Marion Edison Oser (1956). "Early Recollections of Mrs. Marion Edison Oser." Typescript of oral history, Box 16, Edison Biographical Collection, TENHP.

34. *TAEB* 8:162–66, 169–98.

35. Ibid.

36. Ibid.

37. Ibid.

38. Ibid., 235–37.

39. Ibid.

40. Ibid., 217–18, 235–37.

41. Ibid., 217–37; George Vincent to John Heyl Vincent, 28 Aug. and 10 Sept. 1885, TxDaM-P.

Chapter 2: COST OF CONSENT

1. "Personals," *Summit County Beacon* (Akron, Ohio), 16 Sept. 1885, 7.

2. *Baldwin* (1995), 161–62; *Hendrick* (1925), v.

3. *Israel* (1995), 5–8.

4. Ibid., 24; *Baldwin* (1995), 17–20.

5. Ibid., *Israel* (1995), 5–10.

6. Ibid., 24; *Baldwin* (1995), 17–20.

7. Ibid., 22, 40–41, 42–48; *Morris* (2019), 601.

8. Ibid., 118, 196, 200–201, 235–37.

9. *Baldwin* (1995), 72–73; *Hendrick* (1925), 13–14.

10. *Hendrick* (1925), 14–19, 34.

11. Ibid., 19–22.

12. Ibid., 39–46, 47–51.

13. Ibid., 51, 62–66, 82.

14. Ibid.

15. Ibid.

16. Ibid., 67–73.

17. Ibid.

18. Ibid., 82–84.

19. Ibid., 67–73.

20. Ibid.

21. Ibid., 102.

22. Ibid., 82–84.

23. Ibid., 155, 159, 162–64; *Morrison* (1975), 32–33; "Stark County S. S. Union, First Annual Convention, Special Correspondence of the Cleveland Leader, Delayed Letter, Carlton, O., September 13, 1865," *Cleveland Leader*, 19 Sept. 1865, 2.

24. Ibid.; *Hurlbut* (1921), 38–43.

25. Ibid.

26. Ibid., 130–31, 168, 184–86.

27. *Hurlbut* (1921), 14, 69; *Hendrick* (1925), 173.

28. Ibid.

29. Ibid., 67, 160–61, 168, 186; *Hurlbut* (1921), 122, 155, 196.

30. Chautauqua University. [Chautauqua University: The Chautauqua Literary and Scientific Circle, 1885–1886], pamphlet, 1885/1886, 3–7; University of North Texas Libraries, UNT Digital Library, https://digital.library.unt.edu; crediting UNT Libraries Special Collections; Theodore L. Flood, ed. *The Chautauquan* vol. 5, May 1885, no. 8; 1885–1886. Mina Miller Edison Accounts, Account Series Edison Family Accounts (1885–1886), TENHP; JMM to MME, 17 Dec. 1885, TENHP; *Rieser* (2003), chap. 1; *Vincent* (1886), 37–40, 44–53, 283.

31. TAE to LM, 30 Sept. 1885; TAEB 8, 246.

Chapter 3: *A GIRL BORN TO LUCK*

1. JMM to MME, 17 Dec. 1885, TENHP; *Israel* (1998), 247–48; *Baldwin* (1995), 162–63; "Mr. Edison's Wedding," *New York Times*, 25 Feb. 1886, 5: "Personals," *Akron Beacon Journal*, 20 Feb. 1886, 1.

2. JMM to MME, 17 Dec. 1885.

3. JMM to MME, 17 Dec. 1885, TENHP; *TAEB* 8:301–02; *Hendrick* (1925), 103–104, 108–13; *Vincent* (1899), 6–9.

4. Ibid.; "Fires Fury," *Summit County Beacon*, 4 Nov. 1874, 3; "Chautauqua Founder Honored In Centenary," *New York Times*, 21 Jul. 1929, 120; "Manufactures," *Summit County Beacon*, 28 Dec. 1867, 3; "The Miller Family," *Summit County Beacon*, 30 Sept. 1885, 5.

5. "Valuable Property Sold," *Summit County Beacon*, 12 May 1864, 3.

6. *Vincent* (1899), 6–9; *Henrick* (1925), 103–04; ANB, s.v. "Miller, Lewis"; DAB, s.v. "Miller, Lewis"; *Summit County Beacon*, 12 Mar. 1873, 3.

7. Ibid.; "Lewis Miller Dead," *Akron County Beacon*, 17 Feb. 1899, 1; Chautauqua MME Biographical Collection; *Jeffrey* (2008), 170–74.

8. MMH to MME, 19 Apr. 1885, CEF.

9. *Hendrick* (1925), 131–33, 144–53, 167; *Israel* (1998), 8–9, 246–47.

10. *TAEB* 8:301–303.

11. *TAEB* 8:305–306.

12. *TAEB* 8:313–15.

13. Ibid.; *Chattanooga Daily Times*, 30 Jan. 1886, 2.

14. LIM to MME, 8 Feb. 1886, CEF.

15. "Celebration of the Fourth," *Cleveland Daily Leader*, 6 Jul. 1865, 4.

16. "Income Tax Payers," *Summit County Beacon*, 7 Sept. 1865, 2; City of Akron, 207–208; 1880 United States Federal Census: Akron, Summit, Ohio; Roll: T9_1068; Family History Film: 1255068; Page: 60. 3000; Enumeration District: 162; Image: 0572.

17. RM to MME, 17 Apr. 1881, 2 Nov. 1883; EM to MME, 2 Jul. 1879, 2 Nov. 1883; 22 Feb. 1885, CEF; JMM to MME, 28 Sept. 1878; JMM to MME, 16 Jun 1884; MME to LM and MVM, 25 Jun. and 2 Jul. 1884, all CEF.

18. MME to MVM, 20 Jul.; 1, 5, 12, 20, and 31 Aug.; 14 Sept. 1884; all CEF. *Jeffrey* (2008), 171.

19. "Annual Meeting of the W.F.M.S.," *Summit County Beacon*, 16 Mar. 1881, 4: MVM to MME, 17 Feb. and 18 Jun. 1884, CEF; "1881 Well Begun," *Summit County Beacon* 5 Jan. 1881, 5. "The Knickerbocker Way," *Summit County Beacon*, 4 Jan. 1882, 3; "Personals," *Summit County Beacon*, 7 Sept. 1881, 5; " Social Events," *Summit County Beacon*, 22 Mar. 1882, 3; "Personals," *Summit County Beacon*, 23 Feb. 1881, 4.

20. https://ohiomemory.org/digital/collection; "High School Honors," *Summit County Beacon*, 20 Jun. 1883, 2; MVM to MME, 13 Jan.; 17, 24 Feb.; 27 Oct.; 6 Nov. 1884, CEF.

21. JMM to MME, 11 Jan. 1884; MME to GMH, 1, 9 Dec. 1883, 3 Feb 1884; MVM to MME, 20 Jan. 1884; GMH to MME, 10 Feb. 1884; MME to GMH, 23 Mar. 1884, CEF, TENHP.

22. MVM to MME, 25, 27 Oct. 1884, 6 and 16 Nov. 1884, TENHP.

23. MME to GMH, 23 Mar. 1884, CEF, TENHP.

24. MVM to MME, Oct. 1883, CEF.

25. Ibid.

Chapter 4: BECOMING MRS. EDISON

1. "Inventor Edison's Wife," *Aurora News-Register* (Aurora, NE), 23 Jan. 1886, 3; "Thomas A. Edison's Plans," *Boston Globe*, 27 Jan. 1886, 1; "New York Society," *Times* (Philadelphia, PA), 31 Jan. 1886, 2; "Saturday's News," *Record-Union* (Sacramento, CA), 1 Feb. 1886, 4; "Marriage of Thomas A. Edison," *New Haven Register*, 2 Feb. 1886, 3; "The News in Brief," *Daily Republic* (Springfield, OH), 2 Feb. 1886, 2; "Current Events," *Brooklyn Daily Eagle*, 3 Feb. 1886, 2; "Edison's Choice," *Galveston Daily News*, 3 Feb. 1886, 2.

2. *TAEB*, 8:257–58.

3. Morris (2019), 365.

4. Marion Edison Oser (1956). "Early Recollections of Mrs. Marion Edison Oser." Typescript of oral history, Box 16, Edison Biographical Collection, TENHP.

5. *TAEB*, 8:337, 339, 348. Vouchers unselected, 1885.

6. MVM to MME, n.d. 1884.

7. *TAEB* 8:337, 339, 348. Vouchers unselected, 1885.

8. "Edison-Miller," *St. Louis Post-Dispatch*, 23 Feb. 1886, 8; "Marriage of Thomas A. Edison," *New Haven Register*, 2 Feb. 1886, 3; "Under the Wish-Bone," *Akron Beacon Journal*, 25 Feb. 1886, 4.

9. "Under the Wish-Bone," *Akron Beacon Journal*, 25 Feb. 1886, 4; *Jeffrey* (2008), 171–74.

10. *Jeffrey* (2008); "Edison-Miller," *St. Louis Post-Dispatch*, 23 Feb. 1886, 8; "Mr. Edison's Wedding," *New York Times*, 25 Feb. 1886, 5; "The Bride and Bridegroom," *Detroit Free Press*, 27 Feb. 1886, 1.

11. "Edison Here," *Atlanta Constitution*, 27 Feb. 1886, 1; *Albion* (2008), 20–24; *TAEB* 8:342–44.

12. *TAEB* 8:342–44.

13. *TAEB* 8:342–44.

14. *TAEB* 8:342–44.

15. *TAEB* 8:342–44.

16. *Albion* (2008), 19–26; JMM to MME, 26 Mar. 1886, TENHP.

17. JMM to MME, 26 Mar. 1886, TENHP.

18. *Albion* (2008), 22–27.

19. Ibid.; *TAEB* 8:347–49.

20. *Albion* (2008), 22–27.

21. *Albion* (2008), 25–27; RM to MME, 16 May 1886, TENHP.

22. *TAEB* 8:347–49.

23. *TAEB* 8:363, 377. TAE to Samuel Edison, 29 Jan. 1877, HFMGV; *Albion* (2008), 24.

24. *Albion* (2008), 25–27.

25. *TAEB* 8:525–27.

Chapter 5: AN ARDUOUS ADJUSTMENT

1. *TAEB* 8:525–27; *Morris* (2019), 215, 460.

2. MVM to MME, 9 May 1886, TENHP; JMM to MME, 22, 23 Sept. 1886, TENHP; IM to MME, 6 Oct., and Oct. 1886, CEF; "Mr. and Mrs. Robert Miller's First Reception," *Summit County Beacon*, 30 Mar. 1887, 3.

3. MVM to MME, Jun. and Jul. 1886, CEF and TENHP; MVM to MME, Jun., Jul. 1886, CEF, TENHP; JM to MME, 12 Sept. 1886; EM to MME, Sept. 1886, CEF, N(ChaCI).

4. MVM to MME, 9 May 1886, TENHP; JMM to MME, 23 May and 21 Jul. 1886, TENHP and N(ChaCI).

5. "Driven Away by Strikes," *New York Times*, 24 Jun. 1886; *Baldwin* (1995), 177–78.

6. MVM to MME, May, Jun., Sept., and 12 Dec. 1886, CEF, TEHNP; JMM to MME, Sept. 1886; *TAEB* 8:525–26; Morris (2019), 489.

7. JMM to MME, 23 May and 21 Jul. 1886, TENHP.

8. MVM to MME, May and Jun. 1886, CEF and TENHP; *Jeffrey* (2008), 171–73; EM to MME, 14 Jun. and Sept., Oct. 1886; MMN to MME, May, Jun. 1886, CEF and TENHP.

9. LM to MME, 3 Dec. 1886, CEF.

10. MMN to MME, May, Jun. 1886, CEF and TENHP.
11. MMN to MME, May, Jun. 1886, CEF and TENHP.
12. MVM to MME, May and Jun. 1886, CEF and TENHP; JVM to MME, 23 May 1886, 14 Oct. 1886, TENHP.
13. LM to MME, 3 Dec. 1886; MVM to MME, 28 Dec. 1886, CEF.
14. JMM to MME, 19 Sept. and 18 Dec. 1886, 19 May 1887, TENHP; WLE to MME, 13 Jun. 1886, CEF; LM to MME, 22 Jun. 1886, CEF; JMM to MME, 21 Jul. 1886, TEHNP. *TAEB* 8: 559.
15. JMM to MME, 22 Sept. 1886, TENHP; "The Most Difficult Husband in America," *Collier's*, 18 Jul. 1925.
16. RM to TAE, 13, Dec. 1888, TENHP.
17. *TAEB* 8:559, 751–52.
18. "A Talk with a Wizard," *Akron Beacon Journal*, 23 Aug. 1886, 3.
19. MVM to MME, 1887–1888, TENHP.
20. JMM to MME, Sept., Oct., Dec. 1886, and Jan. 1887; MVM to MME, Mar. 1887, TENHP.
21. JMM to MME, Sept., Oct., Dec. 1886, and Jan. 1887; MVM to MME, Mar. 1887, TENHP.
22. "Miller-Wise Nuptials," *Akron Beacon Journal*, 19 Oct. 1886.
23. *TAEB* 8:667, 694; JMM to MME, Jan. 1887; MVM to MME, Feb. 1887, TENHP.
24. MVM to MME, Feb. 1887, TENHP.
25. MVM to MME, Feb. 1887, TENHP.
26. Louise Miller to MME, 22 Nov. 1886, CEF. *TAEB* 8:667, 672.

Chapter 6: INABILITY TO BOND
1. *TAEB* 8:672, 682–84.
2. MVM to MME, Jun. and Jul. 1887, TENHP.
3. *TAEB* 8:179.
4. *TAEB* 8:667–69.
5. "Wizard Edison in Florida," *Fort Myers Press*, 14 Apr. 1887; *Albion* (2008), 28–33.
6. MEO to TAE, 24 Apr. 1887, TENHP.
7. Ibid.; LM to MME, 26 Apr. 1887, TENHP.
8. MEO to TAE, 24 Apr. 1887, TENHP.
9. Ibid.; LM to MME, 26 Apr. 1887, TENHP.
10. Ibid.; *TAEB* 8.
11. LM to MME, 26 Apr. 1887, TENHP.
12. JMM to MME, 8 Mar. 1887, TENHP.
13. JMM to MME, 8 Mar. 1887, TENHP.
14. *TAEB* 8:735–37.
15. Ibid.
16. TAEB 8:737–39, 814; Cora Miller to MME, Jul. 1887, TENHP.
17. MEO to MME, May 1887 and undated 1887; MVM to MME, 19 Sept. 1887, 1888, TENHP.

18. MEO to TAE, 1887 and undated 1887; MVM to MME, 19 Sept. 1887, 1888, TENHP; Cash Book 1 Jan. 1887–30 Mar. 1888: 142, 144; Accts. John Randolph to TAE, 29 June 1887; Randolph to MEO, 20 Dec. 1887, TENHP.

19. *TAEB* 9:48–50.

20. Ibid.

21. *TAEB* 9:127, 165, 251, 332.

22. *TAEB* 9:360; MEO to MME, undated and Oct. 1888; Samuel Insull to Alfred Tate, 28 Nov. 1888, TENHP.

23. MEO to MME, undated and Oct. 1888, TENHP.

24. *TAEB* 9:127, 165, 251.

25. *TAEB* 9:360.

26. MVM to MME, Dec. 1888, TENHP; TAEB 9:387–88; MMN to MME, 14 Feb. 1889; GMH to MME, 25 Feb. 1889; JMM to MME, 24 Feb. 1889; LM to MME, 28 Feb. 1889, TENHP.

Chapter 7: *IF YOU WANT TO SUCCEED, GET SOME ENEMIES*

1. *TAEB* 9:501–502; MEO to MME, undated, Apr. and May 1889, TENHP.

2. TAEB 9:501–502; MEO to MME, undated, Apr. and May 1889, TENHP.

3. LM to MVM, undated 1889, TENHP; TAEB 9:207, 508–10, 523; *Morris* (2019), 290.

4. "A Warning from the Edison Light Co.," Feb. 1888, 31, TENHP.

5. Ibid.; *Morris* (2019), 93, 152, 406; *Stross* (2008), 53.

6. Morris (2019), 87.

7. Ibid., *TAEB* 9:316, 387.

8. Ibid.

9. *TAEB* 9:500, 598.

10. *TAEB* 9:500, 598, 830, 831.

11. *TAEB* 9:500, 598, 813–22, 831.

12. Ibid.

13. Ibid.

14. Ibid.

15. Ibid.

16. Ibid.

17. Ibid.

18. Ibid.

19. Ibid.

20. Ibid.

21. Ibid.

22. Ibid., *TAEB* 9:1006

23. Ibid.

24. TAEB 9:893–98; *Herron* (1998), 1:41.

25. Ibid.; *TAEB* 384, 441, 897, 923, 1008.

26. Ibid.

27. *TAEB* 9:897–98, 1007.

28. "Mr. Edison's Escape," *Morning Post* (Camden, NJ), 26 Nov. 1888, 1.
29. "Edison's Narrow Escape," *St. Louis Post-Dispatch*, 2 Mar. 1889, 1.
30. Ibid.
31. *TAEB* 9:386–87, 995; Alfred Tate to William Hibble, 20 Dec. 1889, TENHP.

Chapter 8: OUT OF SIGHT, OUT OF MIND

1. *TAEB* 9:598, Elizabeth Earl to MME, 13 Aug. 1889; MEO to MME, May, Oct., and Nov. 1889; MMN to MME, 17 Nov. 1889, TENHP.
2. MEO to MME, May, Oct., and Nov. 1889, TENHP.
3. Ibid.
4. Ibid.
5. *TAEB* 9:598; Elizabeth Earl to MME, 13 Aug. 1889; MEO to MME, May, Oct., and Nov. 1889; MMN to MME, 17 Nov. 1889, TENHP.
6. Ibid.; "European Notes by Cable," *New York Herald*, 19 Jan. 1890, 17; U.S. Census Bureau 1963? [1850], roll M432_732, p. 388A, image: 248 (Akron, Summit, Ohio); ibid., 1970 [1880], roll 840, p. 51D (enumeration district 003, Brooklyn, Kings, NY); marriage record of Elizabeth A. Ford, Ohio, County Marriage Records, 1774–1993, online database accessed through Ancestry.com, 26 Sept. 2019; Find A Grave memorial, no. 5414685, online database accessed through Ancestry.com, 26 Sept. 2019; MEO to MME, n.d., Apr., Jun., 6 Oct. 1889; S. Brigham to MME, 7 Apr. 1890; MMN to MME, Jun. 1889; TENHP; Elizabeth Earl to MME, 9 Jan. 1890; TAE to John Randolph, 10 Jan. 1890; S.W. Brigham to TAE, 3, 4, and 6 Jan. 1890, TENHP.
7. Ibid.; Friedrick Siemens to Henry Villard, 4 and 5 Jan. 1890; Henry Villard to TAE, 6 Jan. 1890; Brigham to TAE, 7, 8, and 9 Jan. 1890; "Supposed to Be Mr. Edison's Daughter," *Akron Daily Beacon*, 23 Jan. 1890, 2; Earl to TAE, 3 Mar. 1890; Alfred Tate to TAE, 3 Mar. 1890; MEO to MME, n.d. Mar., Nov. 1890; Henry Villard to TAE, 22 Jan. 1890; Elizabeth Earl to MME, 19 Apr., 6 May, 8 Oct. 1890; Josiah Reiff to TAE, 4 Jan. 1890, TENHP.
8. Ibid.
9. MVM to MME, undated 1890, TENHP.
10. WPE to TAE, undated 1890, TENHP; "Edison's Gratitude," *Buffalo Courier*, 15 Mar. 1890, 1; Elizabeth Earl to MME, 10 Mar. 1890; TAE to Drexel, Morgan & Co., 6 Apr., 29 Dec. 1890; Tate to Brigham, 6 Jan. 1890, TENHP; S. Brigham to TAE, 27 and 31 Jan. 1890; Elizabeth Earl to MME, 10 Mar. 1890, TENHP.
11. Ibid.
12. Ibid.
13. Elizabeth Earl to TAE, 3 Mar. 1890; Alfred Tate to TAE, 3 Mar. 1890; MEO to MME, n.d. Mar. 1890, TENHP; Elizabeth Earl to MME, 19 Apr. and 6 May 1890; MEO to MME, n.d. Nov. and 11 Nov. 1890; Elizabeth Earl to MME, 8 Oct. 1890, TENHP.
14. Ibid.
15. Ibid.
16. Ibid.
17. Ibid.

18. TAE to Drexel, Morgan & Co., 6 Apr., 6 Aug. 1890; TAE to Drexel, Morgan & Co., 29 Dec. 1890; MEO to MME, n.d. Mar., Apr. 1890, TENHP; S. Brigham to MME, 7 Apr. 1890, TENHP.

19. Ibid.

20. Ibid.; MEO to MME, 11 Nov. 1890, TENHP.

21. Vouchers (Household). Box 1-2; WLE to MME, undated, 1890 CEF; *Herron* (1998), 19–21.

22. *Whittmore* (1896), 232, 325, 331; *Herron* 1998, 37.

23. *Herron* 1998, 37.

24. *Herron* 1998, 40–45.

25. Ibid., 66–67; MEO to MME, Nov. 1890; MEO to TAE, 28 Dec. 1890; TEJ to MME, 20 Aug., 1 Oct., 16 Dec. 1890; and c. 1891, TENHP.

26. *Israel* (1998), 258, 385–86; Morris (2019), 279; WLE to MME, 3, 18, 31, Oct. 1890, TENHP.

27. Ibid., WLE to MME, undated 1890.

28. Ibid.

29. TAE to Drexel Morgan, 29 Dec. 1890, TENHP; MVM to MME, 6 Jul. 1890, CEF.

30. WLE to MME, undated 1890–1893, CEF; MEO to MME, Aug. 1890, TENHP.

31. "Where the Great American Wizard Lives and Works," *Boston Record*, 1890.

32. MVM to MME, 21, 28 Sept. and Oct. 1890, CEF and TENHP; *Jeffrey* (2008), 158; *Venerable* (1978), 1.

33. MMH to MME, 28 Nov. and Dec. 1890, CEF; Israel (1998), 289–90, 344–48.

34. Ibid., WLE to MME, 23 Sept. 3 and 31 Oct. 1890, TENHP.

35. WLE to MME, 23 Sept. 3 and 31 Oct. 1890, TENHP.

36. Ibid.

37. MEO to MME, 28 Dec. 1890, TENHP.

38. WLE to MME, 22 Nov. 1890, TENHP; MVM to MME, 23 Nov. and 5 Dec. 1890; MEO to MME, 28 Dec.1890, TENHP.

Chapter 9: DISTURBANCES

1. *Israel* (1998), 64; *Jeffrey* (2008), 163; James Symington to TAE, 12 Feb. 1891, TENHP.

2. Ibid.

3. *Heron* (1996), 2; "Unknown Wives of Well-Known Men," *Ladies' Home Journal*, Jan. 1891, 3.

4. *Israel* (1998), 349–52.

5. Vouchers Household, 1890–1900, TENHP; *Israel* (1998), 233; *Morris* (2019), 462.

6. TAE to Improvement Society of Menlo Park, 11 Jun. 1891; Alfred Tate to Margaret Stilwell, 8 Jun. 1891, TENHP.

7. Lynn Given Interview, 20 Mar. 1990, TENHP.

8. Israel (1998), 274; Morris (2019), 241, 314.

9. Ibid.

10. Ibid.

11. Ibid.

12. Ibid.

13. *Morris* (2019), 311. TEJ to MME, Apr. and May 1892, TENHP.

14. TEJ to MME, Apr. 1892, TENHP.

15. TJE to John Randolf, Aug.–Dec. 1891, TENHP; WLE to MME, 1890–1893, n.d., TENHP.

16. TJE to MME, 15 Jan. 1892; TJE to TAE, 16 Jan. 1892, TENHP.

17. Henry Augustus Coit to TAE, MME, 1892, CEF.

18. Elizabeth Earl to MME, 1891, Sloane; Vouchers Household, 1 Jun. 1891, TENHP; "At Long Beach Hotel," *Evening World New York*, 21 Jul. 1891, 2; TEJ to TAE, 14 Aug. 1891; TEJ to MME, 24 Aug. 1891, CEF.

19. MEO to MME, 1891 undated, and 13 Jul. 1891, TENHP.

20. Ibid.

21. Ibid.

22. Ibid.

23. Ibid.

24. MVM to MME, 14 Aug. 1893; MVM to MME, 6 Sept. 1893, CEF; MVM to MMN, n.d. 1892; TEJ to MME, 30 Mar. 1892; MEO to MME, 5 May 1892, CEF; MEO to MME, Aug. 1893, TENHP; "In Silken Bonds," *Akron Beacon Journal*, 21 Apr. 1892, 1.

25. Ibid.

26. "In Silken Bonds," *Akron Beacon Journal*, 21 Apr. 1892, 1.

27. "The Life and Inventions of Edison," *Cassier's*, Nov., Vol 3., 1892.–Vol. 5, 26 Dec. 1893.

28. Ibid.

29. Ibid.

30. Ibid.

31. Ibid.

32. Ibid.

33. TJE to MME, 7 Mar. 1893; WLE to MME, undated 1893, CEF.

34. Ibid.

35. *Farm Implement News*, 1891–1893.

36. "Elected Officers," *Akron Beacon Journal*, 5 Jan. 1893, 1; "A Sudden Attack," *Akron Beacon Journal*, 3 Apr. 1893, 3; "Receiver," *Akron Beacon Journal*, 11 Dec. 1893, 1; IM to TAE, 7 Jun. 1893, CEF.

37. JM to MME, 1 Feb. 1893, CEF; TM to MVM, Apr. 1893, EFWE; MVM to MME, 12 Jan. 1893; MVM to MME, 11 Jun. 1893; MVM to MME, 27 Aug. 1893.

38. MEO to MME, Mar. 1894, TENHP.

39. Ibid.

Chapter 10: ISOLATION

    1. LAM to MME, 21 Dec. 1893, CEF; LIM to MME, 17 Dec. 1894, EFWE; *Steeples* (1998), 170.

    2. *Israel* (1998), 336; *Morris* (2019), 296, 281.

    3. *Israel* (1998), 347, 351, 356; *Morris* (2019), 280–81; *Josephson* (1959), 367–79.

    4. Ibid.; *Israel* (1998), 347, 351, 356; *Morris* (2019), 280–81, 351–53; *Josephson* (1959), 367–79.

    5. TEJ to MME, 28 Apr., 16 Jul., 27 Aug. 1894, 1894–1897, n.d., CEF.

    6. Ibid.

    7. Ibid.

    8. Ibid.

    9. WLE to MME, n.d. 1894, CEF; John Hawkins to MME, 2 Mar. 1894, Dec. 1895, Feb., Aug., Sept. 1896, CEF.

    10. Ibid.

    11. TEJ to MME, Feb., May, Jun., Aug., Sept. 1894, CEF.

    12. TEJ to MME, Feb., May, Jun., Aug., Sept. 1894, CEF.

    13. TEJ to TAE, 14 Jan. 1894, TENHP.

    14. TAE to MME, 1894, n.d., Swann Galleries

    15. Ibid.

    16. Ibid.

    17. Ibid.

    18. Ibid.; Reminiscences of Madeleine Edison Sloane: oral history, 1973, Columbia Center for Oral History, Thomas Edison Project, Columbia University.

    19. Ibid.

    20. TAE to MME, 1894, n.d., Swann Galleries.

    21. Ibid.

    22. Ibid.; TAE to Bowker, 6 Aug. 1897, TENHP; *Nerney* (1934), 153.

    23. *Nerney* (1934), 153.

    24. TM to MME, Jan. 1895; JM to MME, Feb. 1895; TENHP.

    25. Ibid.

    26. JM to GMH, 5 Feb. 1896, N(ChaCI).

    27. Alfred Ord Tate to IM, 23 Apr. 1890; TAE to George Washington Crouse, 6 Feb. 1894, TENHP; Walter Seeley Mallory to Ira Miller, 29 Jan. 1898, TENHP.

    28. TAE to MME, 1896 and Aug. 1896, 1897, Swann Galleries; *Morris* (2019), 310, 354.

    29. Ibid.

    30. *Morris* (2019), 323; Conot (1986), 357; MEO to TAE, 24 Jul., 24 Aug., 17 Sept. 1894, CEF.

    31. Ibid.

    32. Ibid.

    33. Ibid.

    34. MEO to TAE, 24 Jul., 24 Aug., 17 Sept. 1894, CEF.

    35. Louise Juechzer to TAE, 23 Jul. 1894, TENHP.

    36. Oscar Oeser to TAE, Jul. 1894, TENHP.

37. MEO to TAE, 24 Jul., 24 Aug., 17 Sept. 1894, CEF.

38. Ibid.

39. Ibid.

40. Ibid.

41. Op.cit; Simeon Ogden Edison to TAE, 10 Oct. 1894; MEO to TAE, 24 Nov. 1894, Jul. 1895, Sept. and Oct. 1895, CEF.

42. TAE to J. P. Morgan, 12 and 13 Sept. 1895, TENHP.

43. Ibid.

44. Marion Wallace Edison to MME, 25 Jul. 1895 and 7 Aug. 1896, CEF.

45. "Inventor Edison's Father Dead," *Columbus Republican*, 28 Feb. 1896, 1; Interview, Thomas Alva Edison, February 1896, Unbound Clippings, TENHP.

46. *Baldwin* (1995), 251.

Chapter 11: BURY THY SORROW

1. MMV to MME, 23 Jan. 1898, TENHP.

2. "John H. Vincent: The Founder of the Chautauqua Movement," 26 Sept. 1896; John H. Vincent to George Vincent, 28 Apr. 1896; Baldwin (1996), 263.

3. Ibid.

4. WLE to TAE and MME, 1897, undated, TENHP.

5. WLE to MME, 7 Sept. 1897, 2, 1898, CEF; TM to LM, 15 Apr. 1898, Sloane.

6. Ibid.; TAJ to TAE, 3 Feb. 1898, TENHP.

7. Ibid.

8. TEJ to MME, 14 Mar. 1899; *Morris* (2019), 347.

9. TEJ to MME, 14 Mar. 1899; *Morris* (2019), 347.

10. *Morris* (2019), 348; *Israel* (1998), 388–89.

11. *Morris* (2019), 354; WLE to MME, TAE 1896–1897, undated, TENHP.

12. Ibid.

13. WLE to MME, TAE 1896–1897, undated.

14. Ibid.

15. Ibid.

16. Ibid.

17. Ibid.

18. "Young Edison's Eyes Affected," *New Haven Register*, 12 Mar. 1898, Clippings; WLE to MES and CE, Jun. 1898, CEF.

19. WLE to MES and CE, Jun. 1898.

20. Ibid.

21. Op.cit., "Educational," *Montclair Times*, 5 Oct. 1878, 3.

22. George E. Vincent, Theodore W. Miller, *Rough Rider*, 1899.

23. Ibid.

24. Ibid.

25. Ibid.; MMN to MME, 11 Jul. 1898, CEF.

26. Ibid.; TAE to LM, 11 Jul. 1898, N(ChaCI); LIM to MME, 23 Jul. 1898, CEF; *Jeffrey* (2008), 172–73.

27. MMH to MME, 16 Jul. 1898, N(ChaCI).

28. TAE to MME, 1898, TENHP.

29. RM to MME, 12 Jul. 1898, TENHP.

30. George E. Vincent, Theodore W. Miller, *Rough Rider*, 1899; *Jeffrey* (2008).

31. Ibid.

32. MMN to MME, 11 Sept., 16 Oct. 1898, CEF.

33. Ibid.

34. MVM to MME, 30 Oct. 1898; Jeffrey (2018), 171; "Grim Reaper, Edison's Sister-in-Law, Special Dispatch to the Enquirer," *Cincinnati Enquirer*, 30 Nov. 1898, 3; "Mrs. Jane Marvin," *Pittsburgh Daily Post*, 30 Nov. 1898, 4.

35. TAE to MME, 1 and 5 Dec. 1898, Swann Galleries.

36. WLE to TAJ, Dec. 1898, CEF.

37. "Young Edison Takes a Bride," *World* (New York, NY), 8 Nov. 1899, 6; "Gossip of New York," *Inter Ocean* (Chicago, IL), 12 Nov. 1899, 17; TEJ to MME, 19 Oct. 1898, CEF.

38. Ibid.

39. Ibid.

40. Ibid.

41. Jeffrey (2018), 173; "The Postmaster of Ponce: Robert A. Miller, of Canton, Will Sail December," *Canton Repository*, 28 Dec. 1898; "Ponce: The Future Home of a Well-Known Canton Citizen: Robert A. Miller Chosen," *Canton News-Democrat*, 17 Dec. 1898, Clippings.

42. RM to MME, 16 and Feb. 1999, CEF; "Lewis Miller Is Dead. One of God's Noblemen Has Been Called to His Reward," *Akron Daily Beacon*, 17 Feb. 1899, 1.

Chapter 12: HIDING FROM THE PRESS

1. "Lewis Miller Is Dead. One of God's Noblemen Has Been Called to His Reward," *Akron Daily Beacon*, 17 Feb. 1899, 1.

2. WLE to MME, 2 Mar. and 25 May 1899, CEF; WLE to Mallory, 4 Sept. 1900; Blanche Travers to TAE, undated, CEF.

3. MEO to MME, 18 Mar. 1899, TENHP.

4. Op.cit.; "Edison's Estranged: Father Now at Outs with Three Children," *St Louis Star*, WLE to MME, 1899; WLE to TAE, 21 Jan. 1899, TENHP; "Edison's Son Has Stormy Season of Love," *New York Times*; "Thomas A. Edison's Son Weds: Married to Miss Blanche F. Travers at Elizabeth," *Newark News Journal*, Clippings.

5. Ibid.

6. WLE to MME, 1899; WLE to TAE, 21 Jan. 1899, TENHP.

7. Blanche Travers Edison to TAE, 1900, undated; WLE to TAE, 6 Feb. 1900, CEF.

8. Morris (2019), 216, 228; "Young Edison Wife Leaves Him," *Boston Globe*, 6 Aug. 1900, 3; "One More Chance," *Akron Beacon Journal*, 20 Sept. 1900, 3; "Thomas Jr. Seeks Divorce," *Muscatine Semi Weekly Tribune Iowa*, 30 Nov. 1900.

9. Ibid.

10. *Israel* (1998), 389–92; Morris (2019), 244; Charles Stilwell to Randolph, 18 Dec. 1903, TENHP; "Edison and His Children," *Inter Ocean Chicago*, 12 Nov. 1899, 17.

11. Israel (1998), 389–92; Morris (2019), 252; John Randolph Memorandum, 27 Mar. 1900; TEJ to John Randolph, 10 Apr. 1900; Randolph to TEJ, 9 May and Dec. 1900, TENHP; Charles Stilwell to John Randolph, 18 Dec. 1903; John Randolph to TEJ, 3 Mar. 1904; John Randolph to Welshman, 4 Mar. 1904, TENHP.

12. Ibid.

13. Ibid.

14. Ibid.

15. Ibid.

16. *Israel* (1998), 389–92.

17. *Israel* (1998), 392–95; WEJ to TAE, 12 Aug. 1903; WEJ to TAE, 13 Oct. 1903, TENHP.

18. Ibid.

19. *Israel* (1998), 389–92; Morris (2019), 252; John Randolph Memorandum, 27 Mar. 1900; TEJ to John Randolph, 10 Apr. 1900; Randolph to TEJ, 9 May and Dec. 1900, TENHP; Charles Stilwell to John Randolph, 18 Dec. 1903; John Randolph to TEJ, 3 Mar. 1904; John Randolph to Welshman, 4 Mar. 1904, TENHP.

20. Ibid.; *Israel* (1998), 392–95; WEJ to TAE, 12 Aug. 1903; WEJ to TAE, 13 Oct. 1903, TENHP.

21. Ibid.

22. MME to MMN, 8 Oct. 1903, EFWE; MME to MVM, 19 Jan. 1900, EFWE; "Edison Not Dangerously Ill," *New York Tribune*, 7 Feb. 1900, 7.

23. MME to MVM, 4 Jun. 1900, TENHP; MME to MVM, 20 Nov. 1900, EFWE.

24. Reminiscences of Madeleine Edison Sloane: oral history, 1973 Columbia Center for Oral History, Thomas Edison Project, Columbia University.

25. *Albion* (2008), 47–50.

26. Ibid., 51–61.

27. Ibid.

28. "West Orange Items," *Advertiser* (Newark, NJ), 8 Apr. 1901; "A Portrait of Mr. Edison," *Republic* (St. Louis, MO), 14 Apr. 1901; "Marconi Visits Edison," *Newark Evening News*, 16 Apr. 1901; "Marconi the Guest of Edison," *New York Times*, 17 Apr. 1901, 9.

29. "Edison Admits He Got a Letter," *Advertiser* (Newark, NJ), 25 May 1901; "Edison Daughter's Kidnapping a Joke," *Hoboken Observer*, 25 May 1901; "Kidnaping Story Denied," *Brooklyn Daily Eagle*, 25 May 1901, 20.

30. Ibid.

31. *Israel* (1998), 403–404.

32. COL Columbia Center for Oral History, Thomas Edison Project Columbia University, NY; Reminiscences of Charles Edison, 1953, 39–40; "Kidnapping Threat," *Jersey City News*, 25 May 1901, 1.

33. *Albion* (2008), 60–63.

Chapter 13: BETWEEN TWO FIRES

1. "Kaiser's Phonograph Talks," *St. Louis Dispatch*, 17 Feb. 1906, 3.

2. MME and TAE, Biographical Collection (1910–1912), TENHP.

3. *Venable* (1978), 4; Reminiscences of Madeleine Edison Sloane: oral history, 1973 Columbia Center for Oral History, Thomas Edison Project, Columbia University.

4. Vouchers (1912–1914), TENHP.

5. Ibid.

6. *Israel* (1998), 10; *Venerable* (1978), 7–8.

7. Ibid.

8. *Venerable* (1978), 8–11.

9. Ibid.

10. Ibid.

11. Ibid.; Vouchers (1910–1913), TENHP; Reminiscences of Madeleine Edison Sloane: oral history, 1973 Columbia Center for Oral History, Thomas Edison Project, Columbia University; MME to MES, 20 Apr. 1906, Sloane; *Atlantic Monthly*, 1900, 20; CE to MME, Sept. 1907, Sloane; MME to CE, 21 Sept. 1907, CEF.

12. Ibid.

13. Reminiscences of Madeleine Edison Sloane: oral history, 1973 Columbia Center for Oral History, Thomas Edison Project, Columbia University; MME to MES, 20 Apr. 1906, Sloane.

14. *Atlantic Monthly*, 1900, 20; CE to MME, Sept. 1907, Sloane.

15. MME to CE, 21 Sept. 1907, CEF.

16. Ibid.

17. *Jeffrey* (2008), 171; "Brother Go to Law over Money," *Akron Beacon Journal*, 1 Jul. 1905, 4.

18. Ibid.

19. MES to MME, Aug. 1909, Sloane; Vouchers, 1908–1912, TENHP.

20. CE to MME, 1909, CEF.

21. Vouchers, 1908–1912, TENHP.

22. Ibid.

23. MME to JM, undated, 1908, TENHP; Clippings, 17 Feb. 1908; MME to CE, 17 Feb. 1908, CEF.

24. CE to MES, 27 Oct. 1907; MME to CEF, 11 May, 3 Oct. 1908, CEF.

25. Reminiscences of Madeleine Edison Sloane: Oral history, 1973 Columbia Center for Oral History, Thomas Edison Project, Columbia University, Oct. 7, 1905; John A. Boehme Memoranda, 7 Oct. 1905; John Randolph to Arthur Laning, 2 Nov. 1905, TENHP.

26. Ibid.

27. Ibid.

28. TEJ to TAE, 3 Oct. 1905, 9 Feb. 1906, TENHP.

29. Ibid.

30. Ibid.

31. Morris (2019), 272.

32. MME to TME, Jun. and Jul. 1909, CEF.

33. Morris (2019), 256.

34. CE to MES, Dec. 1907, 8 Jan. 1908, CEF.

35. MES to MME, Oct. and Dec.1906; 1906–1908; Bryn Mawr College Reports and Statements; MES to MME, Apr. and May 1907, Sloane.

36. Ibid.

37. MES to MME, Aug. 1909, CEF; Edison, Madeleine–Reminiscences Sloane; MME to MES, 28 Mar. 1908, Sloane; MME to CE, 20 Sept. 1910, CEF.

38. Ibid.

39. Ibid.

40. Ibid.

41. RM to MVM, 15 Feb. 1910, TENHP.

42. Cora Miller to MME, Oct. 1909; MMN to MME, Dec. 1909, 27 Dec. 1909, EFWE.

43. Ibid.

44. MMN to MME, Dec. 1909, 27 Dec. 1909, EFWE.

45. Ibid.

46. MMN to MME, 1 Nov. 1909, CEF.

47. "Thinks Chances Are Pretty Good," *Pittsburgh Headlight*, 8 Dec. 1910, 10.

48. MME to CE, 20 Nov. 1910, CEF.

49. MES to John Eyre Sloane, 30 Nov. 1910; CE to MME, 28 Aug. 1910; MME to CE, Nov. 1910, Sloane; MME to MVM, 1909, TENHP.

Chapter 14: CONCEALING THE TRUTH

1. CE to MME, undated, 1909; CE to MME, 15 May 1909, Sloane.

2. Ibid.

3. MME to CE, Oct. 1909; CE to TAE and MME, 11 May 1910, CEF.

4. *Morris* (2019), 111; *Israel* (1998), 427, 433–34.

5. MME to CE, 8 Mar. 1911, CEF.

6. MES to John Sloane, 1911–1994, DSP.

7. *The Guardian* (London, Greater London, England), 19 Sep. 1911, 5; "Edison Starts Abroad Today," *Chicago Tribune*, 2 Aug. 1911, 1

8. MES to John Sloane, 1911–1994, DSP; MES to Julia Thompson, Jul. 1914, CEF.

9. Ibid.

10. Ibid.

11. Ibid.

12. GMH to MME, Aug. 1911, CEF.

13. "Last Sad Rites at the Miller Home," *Akron Beacon Journal*, 29 Jul. 1911, 5; MVM to TME, 11 Aug. 1911, CEF; GMH to MME, Aug. 1911; MME to MVM, 10 Aug. 1911; LIM to MME, 28 Apr. 1911, CEF.

14. LIM to MME, 28 Apr. 1911, CEF.

15. MEO to TAE, 11 Jun. 1911, CEF.

16. CE to MME, 2 Oct. 1911, CEF; *Venerable* (1978), 14–16; Reminiscences of Madeleine Edison Sloane: oral history, 1973 Columbia Center for Oral History, Thomas Edison Project, Columbia University; Reminiscences of Charles Edison, COL Columbia Center for Oral History, Thomas Edison Project, Columbia University.

17. Ibid.

18. Ibid.

19. "Elaborate Wedding Among Akron Fashionable Society," *Akron Beacon Journal*, 26 Jun. 1912, 6.

20. MVM to MME, Sept. 1912, CEF.

21. MES to John Sloane, 1911–1912, Sloane.

22. Ibid.

23. Ibid.

24. Ibid.

25. *Venerable* (1978), 38–44.

26. Ibid.

27. *Morris* (2019), 148.

28. MES to John Sloane, 1911–1912, Sloane.

29. "Speaker Clark's Daughter," *Cincinnati Enquirer*, 3 Nov. 1913, 7.

30. MME to MEN, 25 Mar. 1914, TENHP.

31. "Madeleine Edison, Inventor's Daughter, Weds John E. Sloane," *Hartford Courant*, 18 Jun. 1914; "Miss Edison Married to John Eyre Sloane," *New York Sun*, 18 Jun. 1914; "Miss Madeleine Edison Bride of Mr. J. E. Sloane," *New York Herald*, 18 Jun. 1914; "Miss Edison Weds John Eyre Sloane," *Newark News*, 18 Jun. 1914, Clippings; *Jeffrey* (2018), 177–78.

32. MME to GMH, Jun. 1912, CEF.

33. *Guinn* 2019, 151–54. *Albion* 2008, 76–77.

34. MME to GMH, June 1912, CEF

35. Ibid.

36. Ibid.

37. "Madeleine Edison, Inventor's Daughter, Weds John E. Sloane," *Hartford Courant*, 18 Jun. 1914; "Miss Edison Married to John Eyre Sloane," *New York Sun*, 18 Jun. 1914; "Miss Madeleine Edison Bride of Mr. J. E. Sloane," *New York Herald*, 18 Jun. 1914; "Miss Edison Weds John Eyre Sloane," *Newark News*, 18 Jun. 1914, Clippings; *Jeffrey* (2018), 177–78.

38. Ibid.; Reminiscences of Madeleine Edison Sloane: Oral History, 1973 Columbia Center for Oral History.

39. Op.cit.

Chapter 15: DOMESTIC LIFE IN THE TRENCHES

1. Reminiscences of Madeleine Edison Sloane: oral history, 1973 Columbia Center for Oral History, Thomas Edison Project, Columbia University; COL Columbia Center for Oral History, Thomas Edison Project, Columbia University; Reminiscences of Charles Edison, 1953.

2. Ibid.

3. Ibid.

4. Ibid.

5. *Venerable* (1978), 60–64.

6. Thomas Edison Project, Columbia University Center for Oral History; Reminiscences of Charles Edison, 1953.

7. Ibid.

8. Ibid.

9. MES to MME, 17 Feb. 1916; MES to John Eyre Sloane, 21 Mar. 1918; TAE to MME, 1916.

10. GMH to MME, undated, 1916, CEF; Halbert Hitchcock to MME, 31 Jan., 14 Feb. 1916, CEF; TAE, MME Invitations and Announcements, CEF; MES to MME, Mar., Feb. 1918, CEF; MES to John Eyre Sloane, 21 Mar. 1918, CEF.

11. Ibid.

12. MME to GMH, 1916, CEF.

13. LAM to MME, 13, 24 Nov., 9 Dec. 1916 and 9 Mar., Apr. 1917, CEF.

14. MES to MME, Mar., Feb. 1918, CEF; MES to John Eyre Sloane, 21 Mar. 1918, CEF.

15. MME to CE, 17, 23 Nov. 1917, CEF.

16. "Wife Task Is to Care for Her Husband," *San Fransisco Examiner*, 20 Oct. 1915, 14.

17. Ibid.

18. Ibid.

19. MME to CE, 17, 23 Nov. 1917, CEF.

20. TME to MME, 3, 20, 26 Mar. 1918, CEF.

21. Ibid.; MME to CE, Nov. 1917, CEF.

22. COL Columbia Center for Oral History, Thomas Edison Project, Columbia University; Reminiscences of Charles Edison, 1953.

23. Ibid.

24. Ibid.; TAE to CE, 1917, CEF.

25. MES to MME, 18 Feb. 1918, CEF.

26. MEO to MME, Mar., Apr., May, Jun. 1920, CEF.

27. Ibid.

28. MME to TME, Mar. 1918. CEF.

29. Ibid.

30. Ibid.

Chapter 16: WRESTLING WITH THE REMAINING YEARS

1. MME to GMH, 4 Mar. 1925, CEF.

2. Ibid.

3. MME to TME, 13 Mar. 1925, N(ChaCI).

4. MME to GMH, 21 Mar. 1925, N(ChaCI).

5. Ibid.; MME to GMH, 4 Mar. 1925, N(ChaCI).

6. *Jeffrey* (2008), 1901, 12 Jul. 1924, Clippings, N(ChaCI); MME to GMH, 4 Mar. 1925, N(ChaCI).

7. MME to TME, Mar. 1925, N(ChaCI).

8. MES to TAE, 4 Apr. 1923, CEF; MME to MES, 23 Apr. 1923, CEF.

9. *Morris* (2019), 77–79; *Guinn* (2019), 140.

10. Ibid.

11. Ibid.

12. Ibid.

13. Guinn (2019), 145–53.

14. Ibid.

15. MME to GMH, 1929, N(ChaCl).

16. TME to MME, 5 Apr. 1931; MME to TME, 10 Apr. 1931; TME to CE, 1 Apr. 1931; TME to TAE, 5 Apr. 1931, CEF.

17. MES to MME, undated, Sloane; Reminiscences of Madeleine Edison Sloane: oral history, 1973 Columbia Center for Oral History, Thomas Edison Project, Columbia University.

18. Ann Edison to MME, 15 May 1931; MME to CE, 10 May 1931, CEF.

19. "Edison's Son Files Incorporation Papers," *Bristol News Bulletin*, 10 Mar. 1931, 10; "Edison Son Starts Firm for Research," *Central Jersey Home News*, 10 Mar. 1931, 3.

20. "Nation To Be Dark One Minute Tonight After Edison Burial," *New York Times*, 21 Oct. 1931, 1. TAE, Wills and Estate Records, 30 Jul. 1931.

21. "Split in Edison Family Widens," *Indianapolis Star*, 1 Nov. 1931, 9.

22. Ibid.

23. William Wallace Nichols to MME, 7 Nov. 1931; GMH to MME, 12 Nov. 1931; MEE to MME, 23 Nov. 1931; Memorandum MES, Jan. 1932; MME to TME, 6 Apr. 1932; MME to GMH, 9 Jul. 1933, CEF.

24. Ibid., "Mrs. Edison Leaves for Puerto Rico," *Newark Evening News*, 18 Dec. 1931, 6.

EPILOGUE: AFTER EDISON

1. CE to MES, 8 Sept. 1934, Sloane.

2. TAE, Wills and Estates Records, 30 Jul. 1931, Swann Galleries.

3. MME to GMH, 9 Jul. 1933, N(ChaCI).

4. Reminiscences of Theodore Edison: Oral history, 1970 Columbia Center for Oral History, Thomas Edison Project, Columbia University; "Edison's Youngest Son May Give $1,260,000 for Worker Aid Plan," *New York Herald Tribune*, 8 Apr. 1947, 24.

5. MME to Sidney Davis, 14 Dec. 1931, EFWE; MME to GMH, 9 Jul. 1933; MME to TM, Jul. 1933, N(ChaCI).

6. Ibid.; MME to GMH, 9 Jul. 1933; MME to TM, Jul. 1933, N(ChaCI).

7. MME to TME, Feb., Mar., Jul., Sept. 1935, N(ChaCI).

8. MME to TME, Feb., Mar., Jul., Sept. 1935, N(ChaCI); MEO to MME, 17 Aug. 1937, N(ChaCI); MES to MME, 6 Aug. 1937, CEF; Central Hanover Bank and Trust to MES, 8 Jul. 1937, Sloane; LAM to MME, 25 Aug. 1935, CEF.

9. MME and Edward Everett Hughes, Invitations and Announcements; MME Diaries and Journals, 1937, N(ChaCI).

10. MME Diaries and Journals, 1937, N(ChaCI).

11. Ibid.

12. Ibid.

13. Ibid.

14. Ibid.

15. Ibid.; MEO to MME, 17 Aug. 1937, N(ChaCI); MES to MME, 6 Aug. 1937, CEF.

16. "Edward Hughes Dies at 77; Was Popular Visitor Here," *Fort Myers Press*, 20 Jan. 1940, 1.

17. *Albion* (2008), 178–81; Edison Centennial, 1847–1947; Pageant of Light, n.d., 1947.

18. Smoot (2004), 292–93. "DESTROYER EDISON COMMISSIONED HERE; Ceremony in Brooklyn Yard Attended by Woodward," *New York Times*, 1 Feb. 1941, 7.

19. *Morris* (2019), 48; *Jeffrey* (2008), 170–73; *Albion* (2008), 187.

20. *Albion* (2008), 187.

21. "The Most Difficult Man in America," *Collier's*, 18 Jul. 1925.

POSTSCRIPT: THE CHILDREN OF THOMAS EDISON

1. MME to TME, 9 Jul. 1938, N(ChaCI).

2. *Jeffrey* (2008).

3. "1949 Cinderella Eyes An Edison," *Pittsburgh Sun Telegraph*, 2 Jan. 1949, 1.

Bibliography

The primary documents I collected for *Seduced by the Light* came from the following archives, oral histories, and libraries.

Manuscript and Archival Sources

Accts.	Accounts, NjWOE
COL	Columbia Center for Oral History, Thomas Edison Project Columbia University, NY
DSP	David E. E. Sloane Papers, Hamden CT (private collection)
EFWE	Edison-Ford Winter Estates, Fort Myers, FL
ENHS	Edison National Historic Site, West Orange, New Jersey
HFMGV	Henry Ford Museum and Greenfield Village Museum, Dearborn, MI
N(ChaCI)	Oliver Archives Center, Chautauqua Institution, Chautauqua, NY
TAEP	The Papers of Thomas A. Edison (online edition)
GMO	Grove Music Online (oxford musiconline.com)
TxDaM-P	Bridwell Library, Perkins School of Theology, Southern Methodist University, Dallas, Texas

Books

Albion, Michele W. *The Florida Life of Thomas Edison*. Gainesville: University Press of Florida, 2008.

Appleton's Handbook of Winter Resorts. New York: D. Appleton & Co. 1884.

Baldwin, Neil. *Edison: Inventing the Century*. New York: Hyperion, 1995.

DeGraff, Leonard. *Edison and the Rise of Innovation*. New York: Union Square & Co., 2013.

Edison, Thomas Alva. *The Diary and Sundry Observations of Thomas Alva Edison*. New York: Philosophical Library, Inc., 1948.

Fancher, Pauline. *Chautauqua: Its Architecture and Its People*. Miami: Banyan Books Inc., 1978.

Guinn, Jeff. *The Vagabonds*. New York: Simon & Schuster, 2019.

Hendrick, Ellwood. *Lewis Miller: A Biographical Essay*. New York: G. P. Putnam's Sons, Knickerbocker Press, 1925.

Herron, Kristin S. *The House at Glenmont*: Edison National Historic Site, West Orange, New Jersey. 2 vols. West Orange, NJ: National Park Service, 1998.

Israel, Paul. *Edison: A Life of Invention*. New York: Wiley, 1998.

Israel Paul et al., eds., *The Papers of Thomas A. Edison* (book edition) (TAEB), 9 vols. (Baltimore, 1989–2021).

Jeffrey, Thomas E. *From Phonographs to U-Boats: Edison and his "Insomnia Squad" in Peace and War, 1911–1919.* Bethesda: Lexis Nexis, 2008.

Josephson, Mathew. *Edison: A Biography*, 1959. New York: McGraw Hill, 2003.

Kellogg, John Harvey. *The Battle Creek Sanitarium System: History, Organization, Methods.* Michigan: Gage Printing Co., 1908.

Lane, Samuel A. *Fifty Years and Over of Akron and Summit County.* Ohio: Beacon Job Dept., 1892.

Meadowcroft, William H. *Boys' Life of Edison.* New York: Harper & Brothers, 1921.

National Park Service. Historic Furnishings Report: Edison Laboratory. Harpers Ferry: 1995.

Nerney, Mary Childs. *Thomas A. Edison, A Modern Olympian.* New York: Harrison Smith & Robert Haas, 1934.

Newton, James, *Uncommon Friends: Life with Thomas Edison, Henry Ford, Harvey Firestone, Alexis Carrel, and Charles Lindbergh.* New York: 1913.

Oeser, Marion Edison. *"The Wizard of Menlo Park, by His Daughter."* West Orange: TENHP, 1956.

Rieser, Andrew C. *The Chautauqua Moment: Protestants, Progressives, and the Culture of Modern Liberalism.* New York: Columbia University Press, 2003.

Smoot, Tom. *The Edisons of Fort Myers.* Sarasota: Pineapple Press, 2004.

Steeples, Douglas O., and David O. Whitten. *Democracy in Desperation: The Depression of 1893.* Westport: Greenwood Press, 1998.

Stross, Randall. *The Wizard of Menlo Park: How Thomas Alva Edison Invented the Modern World.* New York: Crown Publishers, 2007.

Venable, John D. *Out of the Shadow: The Story of Charles Edison.* East Orange: The Charles Edison Fund, 1978.

Vincent, George E. *Theodore W. Miller, Rough Rider.* Akron: Privately printed, 1899.

Williams, Samuel Crane. *Historical Sketch of the Growth and Development of West Orange, NJ, 1862–1937.* West Orange: Chronicle Press, 1937.

Yocum, Barbara A. *The House at Glenmont: Edison National Historic Site, West Orange, New Jersey. 2 vols.* Lowell, MA: National Park Service, 1998.

Whittmore, Henry. *The Founders and Builders of the Oranges.* Newark: L. J. Hardham, 1896.

Articles

Battle Creek Moon-Journal. "Reluctance to Change Diet Robbed Edison of 15 Years, Believed Dr. J. H. Kellogg," 20 Oct. 1931.

Cassier's magazine, vol. 3, Nov. 1892–Apr. 1893. 1891. https://library.si.edu/digital-library/book/cassiersmagazi318921newy.

Coman, Martha, and Weir Hugh. "The Most Difficult Husband in America." *Collier's, The National Weekly*, July 1925.

Connell, Louis. "Feeding Your Husband." *Charm*, Feb. 1924.

Crowell, James. "What It Means to Be Married to a Genius." *American Magazine*, 109, Feb. 1930.

Douglas, Marjory Stoneman. "Mrs. Thomas A. Edison, as Home." *McCall's*, Oct. 1929.

Lanigan, Alice Graham. "Unknown Wives of Well-Known Men." *Ladies' Home Journal*, Jan. 8 1891.

Lathrop, George P. "Talks with Edison." *Harper's Magazine*, 8 Feb. 1890.

Ludwig, Emil. "Edison: The Greatest American of the Century." *American Magazine*, Dec. 1931.

Tyrrell, Henry. "Edison." *Frank Leslie's Popular Monthly*. Oct. 1895.

"Tables Set for Special Occasions." *Ladies' Home Journal*, Oct. 1899.

"The Anecdotal Side of Edison." *Ladies' Home Journal*, 15 (1898): 7–8.

"Wives of Well-Known Men," *Ladies' Home Journal*, Jan. 1891.

Newspapers

Akron Beacon Journal
Akron City Times
Atlanta Constitution
Aurora News-Register
Boston Daily Globe
Boston Record
Brooklyn Citizen
Brooklyn Eagle
Buffalo Commercial
Buffalo Evening News
Camden Courier-Post
Charlotte News
Chattanooga Commercial
Chicago Tribune
Cleveland Leader
Fort Myers News-Press
Galveston Daily News
Hartford Courant
Indianapolis Journal
Kansas City Chapman Star
Milwaukee Sentinel
Montreal Gazette
Montclair (NJ) *Times*
New Haven Register
Newark Evening News
Newark Star-Ledger
New York Times
New York Tribune
Ohio Tiffin Tribune
Orange (NJ) *Journal*
Orlando Sentinel
Oshkosh Northwestern
Paterson Evening News

Philadelphia Inquirer
Philadelphia Times
Piqua Miami Helmet
Salt Lake Herald
Springfield Daily Republic
Springville (NY) *Journal*
Summit County Beacon
Stark County Democrat
St. Louis Globe-Democrat
St. Louis Post-Dispatch
Wichita Daily Eagle
Wilkes-Barre News
Wilmington News Journal
Wisconsin State Register
Yonkers Statesman

Index